THE
POPES
AND
WORLD
GOVERNMENT

THE
POPES
AND
WORLD
GOVERNMENT

by

EMILE GUERRY, *abp., 1891–*

Archbishop of Cambrai

Foreword by Paul Emile Cardinal Léger

translated by Gregory J. Roettger, O.S.B.

HELICON   Baltimore — Dublin

Helicon Press, Inc.
1120 N. Calvert St.
Baltimore, Maryland 21202

Helicon Limited
53 Capel Street
Dublin 1, Ireland

Nihil Obstat: Carroll E. Satterfield
Censor Librorum

Imprimatur: ✠ Lawrence J. Shehan, D.D.
Archbishop of Baltimore
October 22, 1963

The *Nihil Obstat* and *Imprimatur* are official declarations that a book or pamphlet is free of doctrinal or moral error. No implication is contained therein that those who have granted the *Nihil Obstat* and *Imprimatur* agree with the opinions expressed.

PRINTED IN THE UNITED STATES OF AMERICA BY
GARAMOND/PRIDEMARK PRESS, INC., BALTIMORE, MARYLAND

*F*OREWORD

AT THE time of his death, in 1958, Pius XII was unanimously hailed as the Pope of Peace. This title was given to him by all peoples because of his numerous and constant efforts to remove the causes of war and to foster friendship between nations; but his greatest claim to the title came from the untiring doctrinal guidance that he dispensed, during the twenty years of his pontificate, on the conditions and requirements of true international peace.

To become acquainted with this teaching of Pius XII no better guide could be found than His Grace Archbishop Guerry of Cambrai, author of *The Popes and World Government*. Rarely has the thought of Pius XII been so faithfully understood, so finely analyzed and so fully presented in a coherent synthesis. The underlying theme which inspired this great pope in his teaching on international questions is clearly brought out by the author, namely, that all peoples of the earth, whatever their color, race, religion or culture, form one large community, and that the moment has come to organize for the common good of all.

To organize the world community on a solid basis, to endow it with real authority and a juridical system capable of protecting the rights and facilitating the fulfillment of the duties of all, be it states or individuals—this, said Pius XII on many an occasion, is one of the great tasks of our times.

This obligation is incumbent particularly upon states, especially the most powerful. These states must understand that the era of absolute sovereignty has come to an end and that the era of solidarity and co-operation between peoples has definitively begun. The most apparent and striking sign of this new era is the United Nations Organization. Pius XII had ardently desired its

v

existence and, on many occasions, he assured it of the prayers and co-operation of the Church.

The teaching of this great pope is still timely, and it is the foundation upon which John XXIII built his great encyclical *Pacem in Terris* of April 11, 1963. The central idea of *Pacem in Terris*—that international peace depends on the establishment of order in the world: order in the individual human person, in the various social organisms and, finally, in the great community of nations—is an idea which was already contained in the teachings of Pius XII. The publication of the encyclical, and especially its clear and unequivocal support of the United Nations, was possible only because Pius XII had previously prepared the ground in doctrine and in fact.

To understand the full import of the encyclical of John XXIII, it is necessary to have a profound knowledge of the previous teaching dispensed by Pius XII during his twenty-year pontificate and so ably presented here by Archbishop Guerry.

I believe we can also go one step farther and state that the teachings of Pius XII are also largely responsible for the sympathetic attitude manifested towards the United Nations by Paul VI at the very inception of his pontificate. Having been very close to Pius XII as a collaborator of many years, the present Holy Father remains faithful to his inspiration in international matters. Last July 11th, when he received Mr. U Thant, the Secretary General of the United Nations, Pope Paul VI declared:

> The Holy See . . . has the highest esteem for this international organization. It considers it as the fruit of a civilization to which the Catholic religion . . . has given its essential principles. It looks upon it as an instrument of brotherhood among nations— a brotherhood which the Holy See has always desired and fostered, and consequently, a brotherhood understood as one which favors peace and progress among men. It considers the United Nations as the developing and constantly improving form of humanity in the historical and terrestrial order.

What more could be added to this statement of the present Holy Father? The time has come for all Christians to lay aside narrow and dangerous ideologies of absolutism, totalitarianism or state nationalism, to open wide their minds and hearts to international responsibility. The world is forming itself, organizing and unifying itself. Christians must co-operate fully, with intelligence and in as enlightened a manner as possible, with all that is being done in the gigantic and difficult work of creating world unity. The peace of mankind and the very work of the Church depend on it.

Christian co-operation in this all important work will be enlightened and intelligent in the measure in which it is penetrated by the pontifical teaching so competently presented by Archbishop Guerry.

I am happy to recommend *The Popes and World Government* not only to Catholic readers but to all who are anxious to devote themselves to the cause of world peace.

† PAUL EMILE CARDINAL LÉGER
Archbishop of Montreal

PREFACE

"Too many Christians still remain deaf to the admonitions of the Papacy, despite the terrible lesson of events. For example, how many continue to live within the narrow confines of a chauvinistic nationalism which is incompatible with the courageous effort required to embrace the idea of a world community, as demanded by recent Popes? More numerous, no doubt, are those who have done nothing to rid themselves of their strange apathy, despite repeated summons by the Holy Father 'to action against all inaction and every desertion in the tremendous spiritual battle, whose outcome will determine the character or, rather, the very soul of the society of the future' (Christmas Message, 1942). While we rejoice at the wonderful generosity of the many Catholics who are laboring for world peace, at the same time the thought keeps recurring that for half a century we have witnessed another matter of equal seriousness, a similar contrast between the far-seeing firmness of a great Pontiff and the fears, doubts, and pettiness of far too many. . . . In the face of the dramatic breakup of the world, the call of the common Father becomes all the more urgent. 'Have faith in the Church,' he says to all his children, 'when she asks you to labor for the community of nations.' "[1]

To this pressing and very impressive appeal of the common Father, this book is designed above all to be a faithful response.

This is the reply of a bishop who is conscious of the heavy responsibility he has of transmitting to his people, in all their purity and integrity, the doctrines of the Church and the teachings of the Popes on the problems of the present time. In fact we

1. Letter, dated July 5, 1953, from Msgr. Montini (then Prosecretary of Pius XII, now Pope Paul VI) to Charles Flory, for the Social Week of Pau (1953).

ix

recently published *The Social Doctrine of the Church* in order to fulfill this very mission. We showed how this doctrine, by clarifying the study of social problems and guiding the action of men resolved to find positive solutions of them, contributes a concept of man, a concept of social economy, a concept of human society—the community of nations. The earlier book presented the first two concepts. The third part, concentrating on the problems of international life, forms the burden of this present work.

It should not be necessary to emphasize the importance, the urgency and the extent of international problems. At the present time, as for many years past, they continue to threaten the fate of mankind. It is no longer possible for Christians to remain aloof and idle, ignorant of or indifferent toward this drama which men and nations live under the threat of a third war, which might very well, by reason of the advances in techniques turned from their true purpose, result in the destruction of a good part of humanity.

The Popes have spoken. The Church stands before this modern world, which feels its perilous way among multifold errors of thought and conduct. As in the case of social doctrine, so also in international problems, the Church offers a teaching that is clear, daring, of great sweep, a teaching both positive and realistic. All true Catholics have a duty, an obligation, particularly pressing at this time, to know it, to study it, and to spread it. This book has been written to aid them in that task. We shall invoke only the teaching of the Papacy. To tell the story of the charitable activity undertaken by the Popes in favor of the victims of two wars would demand another volume.

In every chapter where Popes prior to Pius XII have been inspired to make pronouncements, we have cited their words, in order to demonstrate the continuity of the papal teaching. But naturally the texts of the late Pope Pius XII are the most numerous. To them we constantly refer our readers so that they may have direct, personal, and frequent contact with them, and strengthen themselves by their light. The Pope's thought alone counts here. The brief commentary serves merely to make it more intelligible.

The reason for this emphasis is easy to see: Pope Pius XII had to face problems both numerous and unprecedented, problems of exceptional extent, of extraordinary gravity, first while war was raging and later when it was necessary to reorganize the world for peace and to re-establish relations between nations that were war-ravaged and exhausted, as well as mutually distrustful after four years of hostilities.

But divine Providence watched over the Church and over mankind. At the head of the Church it placed a pontiff destined to dominate this troubled period of history. By the lucidity and penetration of his spirit, the vigor and firmness of his thought, his long practice of law and diplomacy, his deep knowledge of languages and of peoples, the courage and fearlessness of his faith, the optimism radiating from hope in the Lord even in the darkest hours of the tempest, his great charity exercised with delicate feeling for man and his needs, Pope Pius XII gave not only to Christians, but to all men of good will, a teaching that is an application of the natural law, of the eternal verities and of the Gospel to the international problems of our days, with a comprehensiveness that embraces time and space, the world and history.

Pope Pius XII pointed out to heads of states and to nations the path to pursue by tracing the bold outlines and the foundations of a new international order (Chapter 2). This order is designed to help them rediscover the sovereignity of a universal moral law and of a natural law in their relations for the purpose of facilitating a knowledge of their rights and accomplishing their duties, as well as for the establishment of a true community of nations (Chapter 3). He has shown that the foundation of this community and of its juridical unity must be sought in the basic unity of human nature and of the entire human family. At the same time he has pointed out God's formal design for the community that all nations must form for the common welfare of mankind (Chapter 1).

Thereupon he denounced one by one, in the field of doctrine (notably the doctrine of the absolute sovereignty of the State), in the diversity of civilizations and the growth of armaments, all the obstacles standing in the way of the establishment of the world community (Chapter 4). As we shall see, an energetic struggle against the armament race has marked the constant tradition of the Papacy for three quarters of a century. Arguing from the grand design of peace willed by God, the Pope condemned in the most severe terms the upheaval produced by wars of aggression and the false concepts that posit war as inevitable or necessary or even beneficial. On the other hand, he also circumscribed the limited cases in which war is permitted as a legitimate means of defense (Chapter 5).

Furthermore, while war was still raging, Pius XII was the first to call for the creation of international instructions (see Chapter 6). He showed their need; once established, he encouraged them. He respected and supported the United Nations and its services in their proper sphere. He favored strengthening the authority of the international assembly. He asked Christians to co-operate actively in the peaceful undertakings of this vast community. He addressed himself to all, whatever their beliefs, who have confidence in reason and in man, to work unitedly for the establishment of a better society on the basis of an absolute respect of the order of beings and of ends, in accordance with the natural law and God's loving design for mankind.

Finally, together with this temporal community of nations, Pius XII also determined the relations fostered by the Church for the welfare of nations: in their regard the Church exercises its actions not to dominate, but to serve. And he enumerated all the benefits that the Church procures for the community of nations by her message of unity and of truth, by her efforts to educate consciences, by the atmosphere of mutual understanding and universal brotherhood she creates about herself, finally by her very existence as a universal society, one and supranational (see Chapter 6).

Over this entire vast program, on which the peace and well-being of mankind depends, Pope Pius XII breathed an ardent spirit of generosity, of humaneness and of grandeur, an appeal for an enlargement of horizons, for markedly wide views of the solidarity of nations in all fields—juridical, economic, social—in order to alleviate the misery of human kind, to free men from sickness, from ignorance, to understand and favor the progressive evolution of young nations toward autonomy, to co-operate sincerely in the establishment of a lasting peace throughout the entire world, a peace based on truth and liberty, justice and charity.

We know from personal contact with outstanding experts in the field of international public law, that they meditate and comment on the teachings of Pope Pius XII. Heads of State studied his annual messages and visited him in Rome. The moral authority of the Roman Pontiff has never been so strong, so respected, so venerated, as in our day. After 1941, Pope Pius XII in his Christmas messages addressed all mankind, not only believers. In the most disturbing circumstances, when force was triumphing and international law seemed to be foundering, the Pope made himself the mouthpiece and the conscience of the whole of mankind. For that reason his words found such wide echo.

Finally, among all the reasons that should convince Catholics of their obligations in the international sphere, there is the one stressed in the text cited from former Msgr. Montini. The Prosecretary of Pius XII recalled the mistake (and the fault) of far too many Catholics for far too long a time in the field of social questions. Pope Leo XIII had clearly pointed out the basic importance of the social problem toward the end of the nineteenth century and foretold that this problem would grow more and more pressing. In 1891 he published the encyclical *Rerum Novarum*. Forty years later Pius XI had to confess sadly that Leo XIII's appeal had not yet been heard or understood by very many Catholics. We know now what this grave lack of attention to the admonitions of the Pope and disobedience, conscious and unconscious, to his directives have cost the Church. It behooves us not to renew this mistake and this error in another field. Nowadays international problems (with which social problems are intimately connected) must occupy the first place in the concern, study, research and action of Catholics. The Popes bid them engage in a mighty crusade for the peace of the world and for the formation of a community of nations in accordance with God's design for the welfare of mankind.

We may hope that this collection of pontifical teachings will inspire Christians to become witnesses and apostles of this liberating and constructive doctrine in a world that is waiting for it in order to rediscover its balance and its peace!

CONTENTS

THE
POPES
AND
WORLD
GOVERNMENT

1

*T*HE FOUNDATION OF THE COMMUNITY
OF NATIONS

> [*According to the divine will, the nations
> together form a community having one goal
> and common obligations.*
> —Pius XII, Christmas Message, 1948]

WHY IS it that, in the first half of the twentieth century, states
and nations have become ever more aware of the necessity of
forming a union, since before that time a contrary tendency
prevailed?

Pius XII posed the question on a number of occasions, and
enumerated the principal reasons usually given for this historical
phenomenon. But he soon discarded them in order to delve more
deeply and to expose the profound reason for the tendency
toward the formation of a community of nations.

THE FORMATION OF A COMMUNITY OF NATIONS

In his discourse of December 6, 1953, addressed to the members of the Fifth Assembly of the Union of Italian Catholic
Jurists, Pius XII noted first of all that world history, which presents an uninterrupted series of struggles for power, might make
the establishment of a juridical community of free states appear
utopian. Only too frequently these conflicts were provoked by
the desire of one state to subjugate other nations and to extend
its own field of influence, or by the necessity of defending its
own liberty and independence. The Holy Father added:

1

This time, however, it is precisely the desire to forestall threatening conflicts which urges the formation of a supranational juridical community. Utilitarian considerations, which certainly play a notable role, are directed toward the works of peace. Finally, technical progress itself has perhaps awakened the belief, latent in the spirit and heart of individuals, in a superior community of men, desired by the Creator and having its roots in the unity of their origin, their nature and their destiny.

By way of commentary on this very concentrated statement we shall first recall briefly the historical facts that clearly show forth the problem and then present the doctrine of Pope Pius XII on the true foundation of the community of nations.

The Pope begins by mentioning three facts that explain the rapprochement among the nations and their desire to collaborate among themselves.

First fact: "The desire to forestall threatening conflicts." The history of the efforts undertaken by men since the beginning of the twentieth century to maintain, preserve and organize peace presents a moving document. Unfortunately, this history often deceives by the poverty of its results and the frailty of its organizations; furthermore, it brings to light the passions and the faults of men and of nations. At the same time it must command the respect of all those who understand the magnitude of the enterprise, the complexity of a difficult task that is only at its beginning. In any event it ought to silence the skepticism and the derision of those who still believe in the doctrine of force and in the moral value of war.

Three steps can be distinguished:[1]

First Step: The Hague, 1899–1907. The first peace conference opened on May 18, 1899, at The Hague, homeland of Grotius, the father of international law. It was without precedent in history. Twenty-six nations were represented by about a hundred political figures, diplomats, jurists, and military experts.[2]

1. See the well-documented work of Albert de la Pradelle, *La Paix moderne* (Paris, 1947), on these three steps.
2. All the states of Europe, the United States, Mexico, Russia, Persia, China, Japan; Africa was excluded, because of the England–Transvaal affair.

The principal result was that henceforth a permanent bond for international meetings existed.

Eight years later, in 1907 (May 15 to October 18), a new conference was held with forty-four nations represented, among which the Latin American countries were conspicuous.

The goal of this first effort was to forestall conflicts by facing the two problems of disarmament and arbitration. As far as the first problem is concerned, nothing came of the discussions except some platonic expressions that regarded limitation of armaments as "greatly" desirable in 1899 and "highly" desirable in 1907. Meanwhile the armament race went on.

As for arbitration, a decision at first caused great hope to spring up—the creation of a permanent court of arbitration. But in the face of the opposition of certain states, nothing remained but a list of arbiters, among whom the states could freely choose the persons who were to decide the individual controversies.

The weakness of the system set up at The Hague consisted in the fact that it remained merely facultative. Since it was not made obligatory, the states could not be forced to have recourse to it, and they remained jealously attached to their sovereignty.

While the effort undertaken at The Hague was powerless in the face of war, it nevertheless sought to humanize war once it was declared. The laws promulgated at The Hague obliged the belligerents mutually to respect the dignity of man, honor and loyalty, as well as the liberty of neutral nations.

Second Step: Geneva, 1920–1940—The League of Nations—After the war of 1914–18, the nations ardently looked for peace. Considerable progress was achieved by the creation in 1919 of the League of Nations, which associated the nations in a co-operative enterprise and in a common will to attain the goals specified in the pact: to eliminate war, to guarantee peace and security, to herald the day of international relations based on justice and honor, to observe strictly the rules of international law and the obligations of treaties in the relations of organized nations. For the first time the principle of the solidarity of states with regard to the danger of war was affirmed in a treaty: the pact of the League of Nations. For the first time fifty-six states united to form a League of Nations. Of these fifty-six, more than half did not exist at the beginning of the past century. An entire program for the elimination of war was envisaged: "reduction" of armaments, not only their limitation; the principle of obligatory arbitration, already decided by the protocol of Geneva (October 20, 1924), but later disputed; security with all its implications studied for the first time, namely, interdiction of at least all war of aggression and application of sanctions in order to discourage the aggressor.

Regarding the problem of applying sanctions in the case of Italy's attack on Ethiopia (1935–36), the League of Nations showed vacillation and disagreement. Then, after October 1933, the peace of the world was threatened. Germany withdrew from the disarmament conference and from the League. Other countries, like Belgium and Switzerland, reasserted their liberty or neutrality. Woodrow Wilson, the president of the United States, had played a decisive role in the preparation and the formation of the League of Nations; but at the last moment the United States failed to ratify the Treaty of Versailles. When Hitler attacked Poland at the end of August 1939 there was not even an immediate recourse to Geneva. The totalitarian states and the fact that the states which had united did not renounce their sovereignty corroded the foundation and consequently the second effort to ensure peace. And the League of Nations had no military force at its disposal.

Third Step: San Francisco—Organization of the United Nations. On August 14, 1941, two great heads of state, President F. D. Roosevelt, whose country was still neutral, and Winston Churchill, whose country was deeply involved in war, drew up the Atlantic Charter, in which they laid down the principles on which a new international society was to be organized.

Even before the end of World War II, between August 21 and October 7, 1944, a sketch for the establishment of an international organization was prepared at Dumbarton Oaks by representatives of Great Britain, the United States, Soviet Russia, and China.

This project was later incorporated into the Charter of San Francisco, where the new Organization of the United Nations was established. This is an association of national states formed with a view to outlaw war. Here again the essential purposes are the maintenance of peace among states and the protection of the fundamental rights of man and of nations. The Charter begins with the words: "Resolved to preserve future generations from the scourge of war, which twice in a generation has inflicted unspeakable suffering on mankind. . . ."

To achieve this end the United Nations undertakes to abstain from recourse to threat and force, whether it is against the territorial integrity or political independence of any state, or is in any other manner incompatible with the aims of the United Nations. Further, member nations bind themselves to the use of peaceful procedures to adjust and settle their differences. Finally, they oblige themselves to mutual aid and full support of any action undertaken by the United Nations, as well as to further social progress and to create better living conditions in an atmosphere of the greatest freedom.

The Organization has these divisions: 1. the Security Council, the central organ, which has eleven members, five of which are permanent (United States, Soviet Russia, Great Britain, France, China) and six non-permanent, chosen by the Assembly; 2. the General Assembly, which includes all the members of the Organization on an equal basis and which proposes recommendations; 3. the General Secretariate.

It must be emphasized that the UN makes the maintenance or the restoration of world peace depend on the agreement of the great powers; it gives them decisive power by means of the Security Council. Unfortunately, the system is vitiated by a measure capable of preventing effective action on the part of the Security Council, namely, the veto, which one of the permanent members can always invoke.[3]

The General Assembly has adopted some important resolutions.

3. As of September, 1959, Soviet Russia had employed the veto eighty-seven times. The UN suffers from other serious defects. Above all, it lacks a "universalist" conception, alone capable of bringing about a true community of nations. Some countries still have not been admitted as members. The admission of new members, as well as their exclusion, depends on the good will of the great powers and their unanimous decision. Besides, the UN is not obligatory for all international questions; it cannot intervene in matters that rest essentially on the national competence of a state.

It will suffice here to call attention to that of December 1, 1949 (twenty-sixth plenary session), on the fundamental principles of a lasting peace. We shall have occasion to refer to it later, in order to show its agreement on essential points with the teaching of Pope Pius XII.

This brief outline demonstrates the great acts by which the states have, during the first half of the twentieth century, shown their willingness to forestall threatening conflicts and to organize for peace.

Second fact: "Utilitarian considerations . . . are directed toward the works of peace." The Holy Father points out, as a second manifestation of the desire of the nations, the notable influence exercised by the works of peace organized by the nations to respond to a "common utility." They have become conscious of the needs of their peoples, of the common interests that unite them, of their solidarity and of their interdependence in the search for common solutions capable of answering their common needs. They have become aware, the Pope said in his Christmas message of 1942, "of their close and reciprocal dependence for good as well as for evil," and, in his discourse of October 13, 1955, "of the growing mutual interdependence of nations."

At Geneva the League of Nations had organized some public services in order to satisfy the common interests of states or their citizens: the Permanent Court of International Justice, the Commissions of Conciliation, an entire array of technical organisms in the field of economic and financial interests, of international communications; in the social field (the excellent work accomplished by the International Labor Office merits special mention); in the moral and intellectual sphere, in that of hygiene; further, works of peace, both necessary and beneficial, as the campaign waged by international organizations against opium and drugs, traffic in women and children, against disease.

The UN likewise sponsors a large number of specialized institutions to take care of the common interests of nations in their commercial, economic and financial relations. Some of these institutions already fulfill a very fruitful mission: the Universal Postal Union, the International Telecommunication Union (telegraph, telephone, radio), the International Labor Organization, the Food and Agriculture Organization, the International Trade Organization, the International Civil Aviation Organization, the Intergovernmental Maritime Consultative Organization, the International Bank for Reconstruction and Development, the International Monetary Fund. The United Nations Educational, Scientific and Cultural Organization plays a very important part in the field of international instruction and education and in a general manner in the cultural order.[4]

Third Fact: "Technical progress." Pope Pius XII has praised the benefits and the innumerable services that technical advances bring to mankind, on condition, however, that they always remain subject to a higher law.

We shall merely mention the contribution of technical progress to the growth of a sense and consciousness of the oneness of the human family. Space and time, which tend to separate men, are being progressively conquered, thus bringing the farthest reaches of the earth more closely together. We need but refer to the fantastic advances in aviation and communication, which have practically annihilated space. Consider the speed with which a news event is relayed to or from any corner of the globe. Thanks to radio, television, newspapers and cinema, everyone is brought into contact with other parts of the world. Thus men are induced to shed their isolation and their egotism. They behold entirely new and vast horizons. They get to know, and generally very graphically, the great catastrophes that strike a people till yesterday unknown, distant, and exotic (floods, fires, earthquakes, revolutions, and the like). In this way they can share in the misfortunes of those who become for them brethren of the same

4. We may cite the ten international organisms of a scientific, artistic or assistential character in which the Holy See has permanent or special representatives: the International Conference on the Peaceful Uses of Atomic Energy; the Food and Agriculture Organization of the United Nations; the United Nations Educational, Scientific and Cultural Organization; the International Institute for the Unification of Private Law; the International Committee on the History of Art; the International Union of Anthropological and Ethnological Sciences; the International Committee on Historical Sciences.

human family, as they likewise can participate in the most varied social and cultural manifestations of mankind. Thus men are brought in contact with one another; as Pope Pius pointed out in a letter to the Italian episcopate, they learn "to know and understand themselves better and to promote a more cordial union and greater reciprocal collaboration" (January 1, 1954).

A text of Pope Pius XII, one among many, sees in radio and television instruments for creating better understanding among the nations and for bringing them more closely together:

> While men were prisoners of space for so many centuries, they can now make their voices heard by their brethren wherever these may be—on the other side of oceans or continents, in the midst of the sea or in the heights of the heavens. They speak to one another and they see one another everywhere on earth, and therefore the globe appears as if it were the one house of all men, resounding with their voices. As a result, it is inevitable, but at the same time comforting, that, knowing each other better, and speaking directly with one another, they should be more profoundly penetrated by the great law of solidarity, which unites all men in a brotherly fashion, no matter what their race, culture or interests. In like manner rapid communications help to clear up the fundamental problem of a harmonious coexistence and of a common life among nations, to smooth out differences, to generate the consciousness of the moral responsibility of those to whom it belongs, in the international organisms, to bring about effective collaboration among the nations (Radio message to the Third International Congress of Communications, October 11, 1955).

Finally, besides the techniques of publicity and the means of communication, attention may likewise be directed to the socialization of contemporary life, produced by the advent of modern techniques, notably in the division of labor and the interlocking tasks in the economic life. These presuppose a high degree of collaboration in the relations between men and nations. An economist cites the striking example of the lead pencil everyone uses. "Its genealogy is without number," writes P. Bigo. "You think of the personnel engaged in preparing, assembling, varnishing and finishing pencils in a factory. But you forget the part played by California in supplying juniper wood or by Florida in furnishing the red cedar of America; you forget the graphite mine

of Ceylon or of Korea, the kaolin deposits of Limousin or Pied-
mont, since kaolin has to be mixed with the graphites, the
Egyptian fellahs who picked the cotton for the nitrocellulose
factories that supply the varnish. And you do not consider the
workmen who built the machines, the sailors on the ships that
transported the raw materials, the miners of all the pits who
delivered the coal without which the pencil could not have been
produced" (*Semaine sociale de Paris*, 1947, p. 63).

It would be premature still to itemize the effects of the atomic
age and of automation on relations between nations. It is certain
that they will be weighty.

DOCTRINE OF POPE PIUS XII

In a discourse of March 19, 1958, *To the Youth of Catholic
Action*, Pope Pius XII made an observation that illuminates the
basis of the problem:

> For the first time men take cognizance not only of their growing
> interdependence, but also of their marvelous unity.

In this discovery of passing from the idea of their growing
interdependence to an idea of their marvelous unity, the doctrinal teaching of the Pope played a decisive role; he helped the
nations take note of this unity and to discover its profound reality
as well as its sublime meaning. But this teaching on the foundation of the community of nations forms a complete whole; it is
an entire doctrinal synthesis no aspect of which may be over-
looked.[5]

First of all, the Pope mentions a *fact:* he analyses an ontological, psychological, and historical reality: the unity and identity
of human nature over the face of the earth.

Then in this fact he discovers the existence of *a law of nature,*
common to all. In the presence of human nature, two contrary

5. This synthesis is presented in numerous discourses. With regard to
the problem that occupies us here, it is necessary to consult three great
discourses: 1) that of October 3, 1953, to the Sixth International Congress
of Penal Law; 2) that of December 6, 1953, to the Fifth National Congress
of the Union of Italian Catholic Jurists; 3) that of October 13, 1955, to
the Italian Center of Studies for International Reconciliation.

currents of ideas manifest themselves. On the one hand are those that present an abstract and static concept of human nature; because the philosophers of the eighteenth century represented it under this aspect, the jurists of the nineteenth century rejected the natural law in the name of history and of the progress of the psychological sciences. On the other hand, some see only the evolutionary character of human nature and thence deduce the possibility of gradual change in the precepts of the natural law.

The Holy Father's teaching made clear that two complementary aspects must be strongly maintained. On the one side: a kind of immutability of human nature exists among the different races and at various epochs, since human nature is essentially the same, and this, as we shall see directly, is the foundation of the natural law, which contains strictly immutable precepts regarding everything that touches the substance of human nature.

On the other side: an immanent law of development exists within human nature; it is a constitutive element of that nature. This evolution, this dynamic aspect upholds its substantial identity, but manifests new exigencies as they occur. We shall see how this applies to the international organization. To the degree that some nations have experienced more pressing needs than others, the profound tendency existing in human nature has shown itself: a social rapprochement not only on the level of the nations, but on the level of humanity as a whole.

Pius XII discovers in the law of nature, with its character of immutability, this immanent law of development, an "inner impulse," which moves peoples to seek the society of other peoples for their own welfare and that of all mankind.

Deepening his teaching, Pius reveals, in the exigencies of this human nature, and above the very divergent laws of peoples, *a natural law*, which expresses these fundamental needs of nature; furthermore, *an international natural law*, which must regulate the relations between peoples in the human community.

Finally, given these presuppositions, through the natural law the Pope arrives at the existence of *an order established by God:* a natural order and a supernatural order, according to which a new united world must be constructed, more conformable to God's design for mankind than that under which we now live.

Thus, at a time when, amidst painful convulsions and through laborious research, mankind was truly becoming conscious of its unity, the Pope, who is the visible head of the Church, the guardian of the moral law, the defender of the eternal principles governing mankind, of justice, of charity, the teacher of the faith and of the message of truth, exposed to men and to nations the grand design of God's love for the community of nations, which they must construct and organize for the peace and well-being of all mankind.

These are the four points of the outline we must now study.

1. *An ontological, psychological and historical reality: the unity and the identity of human nature.* Over the face of the earth, in all climates, at all times, among all races and colors, there exists "a human nature substantially identical," as Pius XII observed in his *Discourse to the Members of the Sixth International Congress of Penal Law,* October 3, 1953. Men are everywhere men.

Some might be tempted to see here nothing more than an opinion—noble, no doubt—of a moralist and a philosopher, but of one who contemplates from afar human nature in the abstract, as it exists in itself. But besides being a moralist, a philosopher and a theologian, Pius XII was also head of the Church, who saw into the heart of mankind and attentively observed the movement of history, the progress of the sciences and the actions of men.

The teachings he proposed in a discourse of October 13, 1955, to the Italian Center of Studies for International Reconciliation, on the law of nature and the doctrine of Christ, take as their point of departure an historical event of recent date—the Conference of Geneva, which brought together the "Big Four" (United States, England, France, and Russia) to discuss the question of peace, from July 18 to 24, 1955. After an initial observation,

> The Geneva Conference of last July, which had aroused such great hope before its opening, has brought to light the deep disagreements that exist among the nations and how difficult it often is to settle them,

he immediately showed the necessity of appealing to two modern sciences, psychology and history, in order to resolve the problems affecting peace.

> It is necessary, then, to study the increasingly broad and deep aspects of the psychology and the nature of peoples, as well as the secret and opposite movements they reveal, and at the same time to foresee the conflicts that these movements can produce and only too often actually do produce.

> The preliminary study of these problems is of fundamental importance for the work of peace, no less than for the changes in thought and sentiment that disturb the nations.

We are far from static concepts and an abstract nature!

The Pope then points out, in the same discourse, that we are witnessing a rapid and profound transformation of the world.

> It is certain that, in the course of the first half of this century, the face of the world has been profoundly changed in the national, economic, social, cultural and ideological spheres.

In order to understand the psychology of peoples and to know how they will act, it is necessary to study history.

> For this purpose it is very useful to study and to understand, by means of documents and texts of the law, the thought of past centuries—we might even say, of past millennia. They show how the exigencies of the relations of peoples, in their fundamental lines, have always been the same, since human nature remains substantially unchanged.

Throughout all the evolutions and catastrophes of history one always perceives the repetition of the same acts of justice and injustice in the life of individuals and of peoples as well as in the relations between states. The imperatives of a law of nature, common to all, reveal themselves under the course of events. In short, it is necessary to recognize

> the fact of the identity of man's nature in all latitudes and in all climates. Everywhere there exists an innate sense of law, invariable and indestructible in itself, but susceptible of being altered by the passions. (Pius XII, Allocution to the delegates to the Thirty-Seventh Conference of the Parliamentary Union, September 9, 1948.)

2. *A natural law common to all.* This natural law has been inscribed by the Creator in the very being of man, in his animal and rational nature, and his intellect takes cognizance of it. It is the expression of the demands of our reason; it informs our conscience of what our free actions must be like in order to conform to our reasonable nature, so that they may not contradict what is good in man, what is most profound, most noble in him. This law tells us: "Do good and avoid evil"—the good, namely, that which is beneficial to our reasonable nature and conformable to it; the evil, namely, that which stands in the way of its true development.

Pope Pius XII demonstrated the existence of a law of nature common to all men and to all peoples, as well as its necessity for the community of nations:

> The first requisite for all peaceful action is the recognition of the existence of a law of nature common to all men and to all peoples, a law which is the source of all the norms of being, of activity, and of obligation, whose observance facilitates and assures peaceful cohabitation and mutual collaboration. . . . In the light of this principle everyone possesses the ability to distinguish, at least in their general outlines, justice from injustice, right from wrong; to point out the principles for settling conflicts; to understand the true teaching of history in the relations between nations; to perceive the formation and obligatory character of international law. In a word, the natural law is the common and solid basis of all rights and duties, the indispensible language for all agreements. This is the supreme tribunal of appeal to which humanity has always looked as a means of putting an end to the repetition of conflicts (Discourse of October 13, 1955, to the Italian Center of Studies for International Reconciliation).

Let us consider the thought of the Pope on this point in treating three successive ideas of this discourse:

There exist in human nature qualities and forces which are indicative of its needs and which reveal the grand directive lines of the plan of the order established by the Creator, the Author of human nature.

Pius XII explains that there are, in human nature, qualities and forces, endowments and tendencies, which indicate to men the course to pursue, the goal to attain, the direction they must take to fulfill the needs of reasonable human nature.

It must be understood that human nature does not possess innately any precision with regard to the concrete conditions to be realized. At what moment, in what place, under what form must these demands be met? Of all the means of the practical order, which will be most efficacious, which one must be preferred to another? For all these applications, human nature has recourse to the free determination of individuals and of groups.

A decisive role is played by the free and conscious will of peoples. Over against an animal society (for example, a hive of bees), where instinct determines everything, it is the free and conscious will of peoples which must finally intervene to interpret the demands of nature with a view to the organization of society.

But, then, under what conditions will this free will of nations choose means, take direction and arrive at a decision?

It is faced with two contrary influences: that of reason and of calm judgment on the one hand; that of blind instincts and undisciplined passions on the other.

If *reason* retains the upper hand, then the forces and tendencies of nature, properly channeled, disciplined and oriented, can become powerful means in the service of the goal being pursued. "The activity of the nations will know how to draw from the natural law the means of smoothing out difficulties" and how to transform into a source of collaboration and harmony what might have been an obstacle: as, for example, the diversity of natural dispositions, external circumstances, and even interests, which by themselves are often the inevitable causes of conflict. The Pope has further shown, in the encyclical *Summi Pontificatus*, how the nations, even though differing from each other according to their conditions of life and culture, their history and unique qualities, "are not destined to disintegrate the unity of the human race, but rather to enrich and embellish it by the communication of their special qualities and by the reciprocal exchange of goods."

If, on the other hand, the *passions* gain control, they tend to magnify and exaggerate difficulties and "to produce intolerable tensions, whose solution is settled by recourse to arms." In the play of the passions is found the origin and the reason of conflicts; and this explains how such great opposition can exist between nations, despite the fact that there is a natural law common to all and accessible to all.

3. *An immanent law of development.* Among the fundamental tendencies of human nature, there is one that urges nations, like individuals, to unite.

There exists, in the tendencies and qualities of human nature, an "inner impulse" that drives nations to seek the society of other nations, just as it urges individuals to find in others, in society, the means of remedying their personal deficiencies.

This is the action "of an immanent law of development" which is the expression of a natural tendency toward sociability (Discourse of December 6, 1953, to the Fifth National Assembly of the Union of Italian Catholic Jurists), since man is a social being, responsible for his social as well as for his individual goals. Very early in life he becomes conscious of the help of others in procuring for himself the necessities of his material, moral, and intellectual life and of his perfection as a man. In isolation, he cannot nourish himself, clothe himself, find lodging or care for himself properly; all the more is he powerless to develop his faculties of intellect, of heart, to enrich and to expand his human personality.

This law has been inscribed in man's human nature; he is made up of body and soul, an incarnate spirit; he is an intelligent, free, responsible being. Above all things and before all things he needs the family. But families in their turn, have to rely on society; they have a right to appeal for assistance to the state in order to procure the common good of civil society and of the nation.

Now, at the present time it is becoming increasingly true that the states themselves cannot remain isolated and separated from one another. The same immanent law of development impels them to seek mutual collaboration with other states, if they want to be in a position to fulfill their own mission with regard to their subjects and to procure for them what St. Thomas calls "the complete good of human life," that is to say, the fullness of human goods suitable to human persons.

Thus, under the will of the states, which tend to a community of nations to satisfy the interests that are proper to themselves and those common to all, it is necessary to discover an action more profound, more penetrating, that of an immanent law of development, that of nature itself, of a law of nature common to all men and to all nations. Over and above all differences that give them their characteristic physiognomy, one discovers a substantially identical human nature. Despite all the evolutions and catastrophes of history, one discerns the permanence of the imperatives of the natural law, one finds the same demands for the cohabitation of peoples in their fundamental outlines.

Speaking of the effort at rapprochement and collaboration which is making itself felt in the most diverse fields, Pope Pius XII declared that it proceeded from the profound transformation of all relations, adding that:

> Its ultimate cause must be sought in the very nature of man. It is the consequence of a natural law which proceeds from the unity of men's origin and urges toward a realization of a common task, to which all who live on the face of the earth are obligated. As the years pass, it becomes ever less possible for the nations to be self-contained, though occasionally a systematic and passionate tendency to the former isolation manifests itself. Everything that actually happens in one country calls forth a reaction among the others, thus forcing some sort of acknowledgement that the community of nations and of humanity resembles an organism, whose circulatory and lymphatic systems keep the different parties in constant communication. The same holds true of international currents, which must necessarily be recognized and taken into account (Radio message of September 11, 1956, to the Seventh International Congress of Catholic Physicians, held at Scheveningen, Netherlands).

The natural law forms the solid foundation of the system of natural right. The exigencies flowing from human nature are the ultimate norms of law. In his encyclical on Nazism of March 14, 1937, Pius XI defined this system, portraying it as

> inscribed by the hand of the Creator on the tables of the human heart, which right reason can read there if it has not been blinded by sin and passion. According to the precepts of this law of nature every positive law, of whatever legislator, can be judged with regard to its moral content and by the same token with regard to its obligation in conscience. Human laws which show an in-

soluble contradiction to the natural law are so basically vitiated that no constraint, no external application of force can heal them.

This text of Pius XI amply demonstrates that one must distinguish between natural law and the positive law of nations.

4. *A Positive Law.* Positive law is the sum total of external rules that govern social life; it is established by the legislative power of a nation. These laws, however, express merely the will of a majority in a country at a determined time. They do not necessarily express justice. There are unjust laws. Legality is not the same as justice; in order to be respected, the laws must conform to justice.

Pius XII frequently denounced the error of juridical positivism, at least that form which proclaims that the law is binding in a country at any given moment for the simple reason that it is the law. He remarked that with such a theory one arrives at recognizing as right what may be the fruit of unleashed passion, of caprice, of the brutal violence of a tyrant. History—including that of recent dictators like Hitler, Mussolini, and Stalin—offers plenty of examples of men who imposed their arbitrary will as law.

For this reason law must in the last analysis be based on an ontological order, that of nature. It must express the exigencies that derive from human nature. Not the Church but nature creates the natural law. The Church is merely its interpreter and custodian.

As for positive law, the Pope taught that

> it is likewise indispensable in the community of states. It has for its task to define more exactly the exigencies of nature, to apply them to concrete circumstances and, further, as a result of an agreement freely contracted that has become obligatory, to make additional dispositions, always in accord with the purpose of the community (Discourse to the Italian Catholic Jurists, December 6, 1953).

Whence, then, do the precepts of the natural law derive their power? In the last analysis its principles find their ultimate source in the very Creator of human nature.

If there were question of principles elaborated by the sole will of man, then their obligation would not have more binding force than that of men; they might be applied today and be considered outdated tomorrow. One country might accept them, another reject them. The matter is quite different if everything rests on the authority of the Creator (Allocution of October 19, 1953, to members of the Sixteenth International Congress of Military Medicine).

The Pope suggested an enlightening comparison, that of the pendulum. The exigencies deriving from human nature are, he put it,

like the dead center of a pendulum. Positive law goes beyond the dead center, both on this side and that, but the pendulum always returns, willy-nilly, to the dead center fixed by nature. It makes little difference whether these exigencies of nature are called "law" or "ethical norms" or "postulates of nature." But the fact of their existence must be recognized; namely, that they have been established not by the caprice of man, that they are rooted ontologically in human nature, that man has not fashioned them himself, that consequently they must be found everywhere and that finally all public law and all international law find in a common human nature a clear, solid and lasting foundation (Discourse to the members of the Fourth International Congress of Penal Law, October 3, 1953).

INTERNATIONAL NATURAL LAW

Now to extend the natural law to the field of international relations. Here, in a striking manner, arises the danger of juridical positivism which the Pope earlier denounced in the state. Consider a positive law voted or imposed by a state. If this represents right, then it puts the stability of international relations at the mercy of the absolute will of rulers of a country. It precludes all possibility of collaboration with a view to the institution of a community of nations.

Pius XII made this point in his first encyclical, *Summi Pontificatus.* After forcefully denouncing the danger of the absolute autonomy of the state in international relations, he proclaimed the existence and the imperatives of international natural law.

In order that harmonious and lasting contracts and fruitful relations may exist, it is indispensable that the nations recognize and observe the principles of international natural law, which regulate their normal development and functioning.

At that time—it was October, 1939—international natural law seemed to be a thing of the past. But he who did so much to preserve it fixed its essential object in a very important document of 1932, while still Secretary of State under Pius XI.

The text first of all enumerates certain capital truths that must make up the spiritual arsenal of a sane international economy: the closer unity of the great human family; the obligation of taking into account the legitimate interests of other countries and of practicing justice and charity among the nations. Then, it continues,

> It is especially the duty of all states to promote and to serve the common good, just as the citizens and the rulers of each of them have the obligation to promote and to serve a common good that is closer at hand and less extended. By the same token all peoples must be conscious of their interdependence and adapt to the different forms of their solidarity the corresponding ways of collaboration (Letter of Cardinal Pacelli, dated June 28, 1932, to M. Eugene Duthoit, for the Social Week of Lille).

This text connects the common good of a state and the common international good that all states together must promote and serve. The common good of a state he defined as the lasting realization "of those external conditions necessary for the ensemble of the citizens, so that they may develop their qualities, their functions, their material, intellectual, and religious life" (Christmas message of 1942).

Now, by reason of this interdependence and strict solidarity, of which the letter of the Holy See asks the states to take cognizance, every state, in order to fulfill its mission toward the common good of its own people, is obliged to weigh, to consider, and to pursue this common good in relation to the common good of the entire community of nations, to the unity of the human race. Let us study the following trenchant statement of Pius XII. Of the various societies (family, state, society of states), which each have the common good for their essential purpose, the Pope has this to say:

The common good, the essential purpose of each of them, cannot exist and cannot be conceived without their intrinsic relation to the unity of the human race. From this viewpoint the indissoluble unity of states is a postulate of nature; this fact imposes itself upon them (Christmas Message of 1951).

In other terms, in order to be able to fulfill its mission regarding its own citizens within the framework of the nation and in the economic, intellectual, and moral order, the state nowadays is obliged to extend that mission, in these various fields, to the totality of international relations. Each state must participate in the life of the community of nations, collaborate actively and loyally with the other states, co-operate in the organization of the international community.

In his Christmas message of 1956, Pope Pius XII called attention to the extremely serious consequences following upon the states' rejection of this law of international solidarity and their neglect of the common good.

It would be a fatal error to repeat what happened in similar circumstances in the years preceding the Second World War, when each of the threatened nations, and not only the smallest ones, sought to save itself at the expense of others, to use them as shields, and even to draw rather questionable economic and political advantages from others' difficulties. The upshot was that all saw themselves involved in the conflagration.

Now the entire force of the Pope's doctrinal teaching becomes clear: it rests on an internal need, that of the nature and unity of the human race.

From this point of view the indissoluble union of states is a natural postulate. It is a fact which forces itself upon them and to which they submit as to the voice of nature; further, it urges them to give to their union an external stable regulation, an organization.

Then, adds the Holy Father,

The state and the society of states with its organization—by their very nature, according to man's social character and despite all the failures to which history attests—are the forms of unity and of order among men, necessary for human life and co-operating for its perfection.

There is one final discovery in the same vein to be made: the discovery of an order established by God—a natural and supernatural order—for the welfare of men and the community of nations.

NATURAL ORDER

The natural order reflects the true human nature constituted by God as the foundation of a common life in space and in time. It conforms to the needs of true human nature and is based on respect for the natural law, which, as we have seen, has its source in God the Creator.

In his first encyclical, *Summi Pontificatus,* Pope Pius XII declared that the rejection of and insensibility to the natural law established by God were the basic and ultimate root of the evils from which modern society suffers. A judgment so serious and so absolute on the part of the head of the Church merits prolonged study in the face of those—among them philosophers, jurists, politicians—who have abandoned the natural law, and frequently have done so very lightly under the influence of the German philosophical and historical schools of the nineteenth century, of sociological doctrines or of existentialist theories.

> The profound and ultimate root of the evils which We must deplore in modern society is the negation and the rejection of a rule of universal morality, be it in individual life, be it in social life and international relations; that is to say, the modern widespread rejection of and the insensibility to the natural law itself, which has its basis in God, the almighty Creator and Father of all, the supreme and absolute Legislator, the omniscient and just Avenger of human actions. When God is denied, every foundation of morality is shattered at the same time; the voice of nature, which teaches even the ignorant and the still uncivilized tribes what is good and what is evil, what licit and what illicit, and makes everyone conscious of the responsibility for his actions before a supreme Judge, becomes completely stifled or at least is very much weakened.

We must stress here the very important place the natural order holds in this teaching. This comes as a surprise to those who are ignorant of the doctrine of the Church. Such people imagine that according to this doctrine only evil exists in human nature and that for this reason Christianity took a hostile position in the face of history, seeing in nature a manifestation of evil and of sin. Pope Pius XII refuted these errors; he affirmed that on the contrary the Church had always come out strongly in favor of human nature.

> From the days of Christian antiquity, from the Patristic era, but particularly since the spiritual conflict with Protestantism and Jansenism, she has taken a strong position in favor of nature. She affirms that sin has not corrupted it, that it remained interiorly intact, even in fallen man, that man before the advent of Christianity and those who are not Christians could and can perform good and honest actions, even abstracting from the fact that humanity, including that which existed before Christianity was established, is under the influence of Christ's grace. The Church recognizes good and great realities, even if they existed before her, even outside her domain (Discourse of September 7, 1955, to members of the Tenth International Congress of Historical Sciences).

Besides, this natural order bears strongly on the economy of salvation.

> "In this [natural] order, which is also destined for the salvation of the creature, God does not overthrow or withdraw anything, but He inserts a new element, destined to perfect and surpass it—grace" (Christmas Message, 1952).

The Church cannot be disinterested in the organization of this natural order, whether it be economic, social, political, whether national or international. It is in this order that men live their family, professional, social, and civic life and either work out their salvation or fail to do so. There are certain structures of the economic, social, and political order which constitute an obstacle to the temporal and eternal destiny of men, whereas the construction of an order that is more just and more human must put itself at the service of the human person so that he may accomplish his destiny.

In the same way it is necessary that a stable natural order exist in the international sphere. The state of peace or the state of war, the respect for or the violation of the rights of states, the safeguarding of natural morality in relations between nations as between men, a state of security, of liberty, of truth, of justice, of charity, of peace—all these things, all the actions of nations, have profound repercussions on the destiny of men. The moral evil caused by war—and even by preparation for war—in the life of individuals, of families, of nations, is terrible, not to mention the material destruction and the loss of human lives involved.

As Pius XII tells us in the following statement,

> The human race, despite the fact that it is, by reason of the natural order established by God, divided into social groups, nations or states, independent from one another as far as the manner of organizing and conducting their internal life is concerned, nevertheless is united by mutual bonds of a moral and juridical character into one great community, directed to the welfare of all the nations and governed by special laws which protect its unity and promote its prosperity (Encyclical *Summi Pontificatus*).

This text reveals that the natural order established by God contains two essential elements:

1. the existence and the diversity of nations or states, living their own life, autonomous, independent of others in the internal organization of the national community;

2. the existence also of a great international community, "directed to the welfare of all the nations," and governed by special laws. It consists of more than a mere juxtaposition of nations having only occasional relations with one another but without any organic bond. It forms a whole, a "unity"; its special laws, says the Pope, "protect its unity and promote its prosperity."

Furthermore, the same passage posits the necessity of an international natural law that commands recognition and observance on the part of the nations.

Thus Pope Pius XII unveils to men and to peoples the design of God contained in the natural order established by Him.

> According to the divine will the nations together form a community that has one goal and common obligations (Christmas message, 1942).

This community of nations willed by God rests ultimately on a unity of origin, of nature and of purpose, as was noted in the introduction to this chapter:

. . . the belief, latent in the spirit and heart of individuals, in a superior community of men, desired by the Creator and having its roots in the unity of their origin, their nature, and their destiny.

Let us consider once again this unity of the human race, so wonderfully described in the *Summi Pontificatus:*

A marvelous vision, which makes us contemplate the human race in the unity of its origin in God: one only God, the Father of all, who is above all and through all and in us all (Eph 4:6); in the unity of its nature, composed equally among all of a material body and a spiritual and immortal soul; in the unity of its immediate purpose and of its mission in the world; in the unity of its habitation, the earth, whose goods all men, by a right derived from nature, may use to sustain and to develop their life; in the unity of the supernatural goal, God Himself, to whom all men must tend, in the unity of the means that serve to attain this goal.

SUPERNATURAL ORDER

However beautiful and strong the unity of the human race on the level of the natural order may be, we find it reinforced and elevated in the supernatural order by an entirely freely given design of the infinite love of the heavenly Father. For God has called all men, whatever their race, by a completely freely given love, to a life of intimacy and communion with him. Because he is goodness itself, God has desired to give himself to man.

The sin of man disorganized this plan of love, but God reestablished it "in a far more admirable manner" (Offertory of the Mass). He sent his Son in the likeness of sinful flesh to save all men by his message of unity, by the gift of his life and his redeeming sacrifice, to enable them to become the children of the same Father. He has called them henceforth to be true brothers one to another by uniting them with his divine Son, so that they might form the great human family and that he might unite all of them on a superior plane in the Church, the community of salvation, his mystical and social body, the new people of God, "the family of God."

Salvation will not come to the world unless humanity, following the teachings and the example of Christ, comes to recognize that all men are children of the one Father who is in heaven, called to be true brethren through His divine Son whom He has sent as the Redeemer of all (Pius XII, Letter to President Truman, December 20, 1949).

Five texts of Pope Pius XII will serve to sum up this first chapter. The first text, while denouncing a harmful error, recalls the truth concerning the twofold foundation, natural and supernatural, of the community of nations.

> The first of these pernicious errors, very widespread today, is the rejection of this law of human solidarity and of charity, dictated and imposed both by common origin and by equality of a reasonable nature in all men, no matter to what nation they may belong, as well as by the sacrifice of the redemption offered by Jesus Christ on the altar of the Cross to His heavenly Father for sinful mankind (Encyclical *Summi Pontificatus*).

A second text asserts that international society must return to the great design of God if it wants to save the peace. The Pope demands

> . . . the return of international society to God's designs, according to which all nations, in peace and not in war, in collaboration and not in isolation, in justice and not in national egotism, are destined to form the great human family, directed toward common perfection by reciprocal help and by the equitable division of the goods which God has confided to mankind (Christmas Message, 1949).

Thus Pope Pius XII, following the absolute order of beings and of ends, presents an entire vision of the world. We have already considered this vision with regard to the social doctrine of the Church. It extends likewise to the whole international order:

> The absolute order of beings and of ends . . . implies also, as a moral postulate and as the climax of social development, the unity of the human race and of the family of nations. On the recognition of this principle the future of the peace depends (Christmas message, 1944).

Throughout this first chapter we have attempted to analyze, in accordance with papal teaching, the tendency toward the formation of a community of nations and to discover its basic purposes; ultimately it is destined to manifest and to serve God's design for humanity. A fourth and a very beautiful statement will sum up all this Pope's teaching on the essential foundation of the community of nations.

> One cannot, in the last analysis, derive its origin from the enormous progress of the means of communication and exchange, but rather from a deep-seated impulse flowing from the unity of origin, of nature and of purpose, which is manifestly intended for the full development, desired by the Creator, of various individuals, nations, of the entire human family, by means of an ever-growing collaboration which at the same time respects the cultural and moral heritage of each of the groups (Allocution to the Italian Center of Studies for International Reconciliation, October 13, 1955).

Finally, in April 1958, Pius XII unfolded the immediate effects of the organic development of the unity of humanity when each of the parties of this immense body would pass from the status of alliance to that of a true community:

> Our century witnesses a progressively greater and organic development of the idea of "one" humanity, in which each of the parties should look forward to a transition, in the near future, from the status of alliance to that of a community in the strict sense of the word, a living and working community (Discourse to the Marian Congregations of Italy, April 26, 1958).

In the same allocution Pius XII showed how much the Church, with her doctrine of the mystical body of Christ, contributes to the needs of the present hour: ". . . this doctrine which considers humanity as a single body, as it were, and which invites men to become one single heart and soul."

So it is that humanity will be more and more disposed to become the mystical body of Christ. Thus, too, the design of God vis-à-vis the progress of mankind, the community of nations, the genuine meaning of history, the mission of the Church, is made clear in all its aspects.

2

A PUBLIC INTERNATIONAL ORDER

> *An international order, which, assuring to all peoples a just and lasting peace, may be fruitful in well-being and prosperity . . .*
> —PIUS XII, Christmas Message, 1941

THE COMMUNITY of nations, whose place in God's design was outlined in the first chapter, must be protected and sustained, guaranteed and animated by an international order. Pius XII has characterized this order as an order of truth, of security, of justice, of charity, and of peace.

In grouping them in a synthesis that reflects the papal teaching, we find all the essential elements of the common international good as mentioned in the first chapter. First, the conditions of the international order: an order of truth respecting the understanding; an order of liberty respecting responsible wills and the solidarity of nations; an order of security respecting both persons as well as existing and independent nations.

These are the necessary conditions, but they are still external. The substance of the international order must also be taken into account—namely, the fundamental rule that directs, specifies, and animates the relations of the nations among themselves. This is an order of justice and of right. But that does not suffice. An order of justice, taken by itself, would not assure peace and the relations of the community among the nations.

The supreme law is also required, one that vivifies all things and must become the soul of the international community. This is the order of charity, an order to be constructed gradually and laboriously as the higher ideal to be pursued without cease.

Then, and then only, will there be peace, an habitual, stable, permanent order of peace, the ripened fruit of all these essential values forming the synthesis of the entire international order.

This is the program that should inspire the United Nations. Pius XII himself said of this existing form of the international community (still in its beginnings) that it proposes "to protect the absolute values of life which the nations have in common" (Christmas message, 1954). This order is not a static, external, coercive, administrative one; rather it is at the service of absolute values, for the purpose of defending, protecting, preserving them, and making them respected; it is an order endlessly inspiring and vivifying to the spirit, the soul.

THE CONDITIONS OF THE INTERNATIONAL ORDER

1. *An Order of Truth.* Already in his Christmas message of 1940 Pius XII called attention to the danger of lying propaganda:

> At the present time, in certain countries, an unbridled propaganda, which does not hesitate to pervert the truth openly, day by day and almost hour by hour presents the nations in the opposite camp to public opinion in a false and outrageous light.

Since that time the evil has only worsened. Calculated and intentional distortions of the truth have multiplied, and all according to a plan made still more effective and dangerous by the rapid development of the techniques of communication. Lying has become a habit and a system, in the face of which a drugged public opinion no longer reacts.

Likewise, in his Christmas message of 1947, the Pope forcibly spoke of this now very urgent problem; he denounced the evil, pointed out the purpose of the system, showed its consequences on the international level, and indicated the remedy.

> The sign which our time carries on its forehead, which causes division and decadence, is the growing tendency toward "insincerity"—a want of veracity, resorted to not only as an occasional expedient, as a means of freeing one's self from embarrassment in moments of sudden difficulty or in the face of unforeseen

obstacles. No, at the present time this "insincerity" appears erected into a system, elevated to the dignity of a strategy, in which lies, travesties of words and deeds, and deceptions have become the classic offensive weapons, which some handle in a masterly fashion, proud of their ability (Christmas Message, 1947).

It would be extremely easy to multiply examples of this "insincerity."[1] We shall choose but one, first because it touches precisely the points made by the Pope, and secondly because the fact of the lie is proved by the very authors of the campaign.

For many years Soviet Russia, the Communist parties, and the movements inspired by them have pursued a campaign of odious calumnies against the Pope, accusing him of desiring and favoring war. The Holy Father himself had to make an indignant public protestation against what he called "so violent an outrage." "Scrutinize the twelve troubled years of Our pontificate . . . study all the words that fell from Our lips, all the documents We have written. You will find there only exhortations to peace," he wrote in his Christmas message of 1950.

1. E.g., in 1958 Soviet Russia spectacularly announced that it would demobilize its troops and invited the other nations to do the same. At the same time, however, it failed to state that on the day after the Liberation the other nations had begun to demobilize and that Russia alone kept a strong army, ready to attack.

Through its propaganda Soviet Russia tries to give the impression that it alone seriously seeks disarmament and that the others are preparing for war. At the same time it conveniently ignores the fact that its delegate has constantly opposed inspection, the only efficacious way of bringing about the disarmament that all so ardently desire.

The Communist campaign incessantly attacks all the colonial powers and supports the armies that fight against them. Admittedly, colonialism is a thing of the past. But soon the countries of Central Europe, hitherto free, will all be dominated by Soviet Russia and they will remain subjected to the most dictatorial and oppressive of colonial systems. Here is a list of the territories that have lost their independence: East Poland (1919); Lithuania, Lettonia, Bessarabia, Bukovina (1940); Finnish provinces (1941); East Prussia (1944); East Czechoslovakia (1945). To them may be added the seven European countries practically put into the status of colonies: Albania, Bulgaria, Czechoslovakia, East Germany, Hungary, Poland, Roumania—a total of 103 million inhabitants subjected to Soviet colonialism.

On January 26, 1951, M. Joliot-Curie, president of the Second World Congress of Peace held at Warsaw in November, 1950—a congress whose relations to Communism are well known—wrote a letter to the Holy Father after the meeting, asking him to use his influence in favor of peace and to support with his great authority the resolutions of the congress with regard to the prohibition of weapons of massive destruction and the progressive and controlled reduction of armaments.

The author of the letter then cited, together with a text of Benedict XV, three documents of Pius XII: the Christmas messages of 1939 and 1941, expressing a condemnation of war and calling for simultaneous and progressive disarmament, and a passage from the encyclical of July 19, 1950, concerning murderous, inhuman, destructive weapons, whether atomic, bacteriological, chemical, poisonous, or radioactive. In recalling the Pope's constant action in favor of peace, M. Joliot-Curie gave irrefutable public proof of the calumnies of the Communist campaign.

The reply of the Vatican, dated February 16, 1951, takes note of these assertions: "One can only rejoice that thus recognition is given to the fact that the Sovereign Pontiff has always pronounced himself in favor of peace, of a true and just peace." The letter of Monsignor Montini (now Paul VI) declares that the Holy Father will always continue his action in favor of peace, an action independent of all outside influence, an action entirely personal, "in virtue of the very principles which guide his action and which have their source in the doctrine taught by Our Lord Jesus Christ."

In the paragraph just preceding the one quoted, the letter gives a masterly reply, direct and decisive, to the lying campaign.

> This is a point [namely, the overtures of the Holy Father in favor of peace] which has been denied or disregarded often and by many in these last years. The words and the actions of the Holy Father have even been travestied to the point that powerful organizations, which nevertheless profess to work for peace, have gone so far as to spread abroad among the masses the absurd calumny that the Pope desired and favored war.

It may indeed be observed that at the present moment no country is entirely free of the temptation of using propaganda in its favor, even though not always resorting to such gross and complete fabrication as in the case cited. The Holy Father, it is true, is considering lies only in the proper sense of the word. On the other hand, he also refers to "travesties of words and deeds, deceptions," tendentious ways of representing events.

The characteristic mark of today's propaganda is that its insincerity has become a "system," as the Holy Father points out, "elevated to the dignity of a strategy." On this score it may be put into the category of "classical offensive weapons." There are chemical weapons which, while not always fatal, poison human bodies and at the same time the international atmosphere (we may recall the hyperite and toxic gases of World War I). Now there are weapons designed to poison the intellect, to asphyxiate it, to bring it into bondage. These are indeed weapons of war, more dangerous and more perfidious than certain others whose harmfulness public opinion perceives far more rapidly. They are weapons of war, because, in modern war, public opinion plays a very prominent role. It has always to be directed, softened, without scruple, with a profound disregard not only for truth, but for the human person, a disregard of the people's intellect and spirit. The Goebbelses of yesterday and the propagandists in the totalitarian regime of today consider the great masses capable of accepting anything, of "swallowing" anything, without reaction, uncritically. This is a grave offense committed against a people by its rulers; it betrays a lack of respect and of love for them. They treat them like minors. Above all, there is a complete lack of moral sense, as Pope Pius points out in the same Christmas message of 1947:

> Such a want of all moral sense in their eyes [that is, of the leaders] becomes an integral part of the modern technique of forming public opinion, in directing it, in bending it to the service of their politics, resolved as they are of triumphing at any price in the struggle of interest and opinion, of doctrine and leadership.

Too many people do not perceive the evil consequences of such propaganda. Let them weigh these words of Pius XII . . .

> The inevitable consequence of such a state of affairs is the splitting of humanity into powerful and opposing groups, whose

supreme law of life and of action is a fundamental and invincible defiance, which at the same time is the tragic paradox and the curse of our age. Each of the opposing parties believes itself obliged to this defiance as a necessity of elementary prudence. As a result a gigantic wall is reared which renders futile any attempt to give back to the human family the benefits of true peace (Christmas Message, 1947).

As a result, too, of this "fundamental and invincible defiance," nations are forced to look to themselves alone, to put themselves on guard against every action of other nations, to suspect their intentions, to mistrust everything that might lead to a *rapprochement*. Later on, in the study of the order of security, we shall speak of this defiance under another aspect. Here, as the Pope emphasizes, what complicates and aggravates everything is the fact that in the eyes of the governments in the context of insecurity this defiance appears as a virtue, a duty, "a necessity of elementary prudence." In order not to be "taken in," the parties harden themselves in systematic opposition. And all the time peace recedes farther away. This is one aspect of the "cold" war, a truly new form of modern war.

Finally—and this is an important point that escapes many— what causes the extreme gravity and continuing danger of the situation is its identification with a *doctrine*, that of the totalitarian states. For them objective truth does not exist. A thing is true if it conforms to the interests of the party. As a case in point, when some event takes place, propaganda will not judge it on its own merits, but will seek solely the use to which it can be put for the advantage of the party, in order to extend its influence in the world. Hence follows that complete sense of insecurity. Propaganda's power of invention knows no limits.

Pius XII pointed out the remedy very clearly: a return to the spirit and practice of complete truthfulness.

To escape from the difficulties into which the cult of "insincerity" has plunged the world, only one road remains possible: a return to the spirit and practice of complete veracity. Nowadays no one, no matter to what social or political party he belongs, if he wants his convictions and actions to influence the destiny of people for the present and for the future, has the right to dissemble his intentions, to wish to appear different from what he is, to have recourse to the strategy of the lie, to force, to threat, in order to restrain among decent citizens of every land the exercise of their just liberty and their civil rights (Christmas Message, 1947).

The studies on war and peace—those of historians, diplomats, political scientists, and sociologists—generally pass over in silence the problem of insincerity. Even the best resolutions of the General Assembly of the United Nations, which propose means of fostering peace, apparently have not dared to face this question. And yet how many at the United Nations are personally convinced that this evil is very dangerous to peace! But they appear resigned beforehand to undergo in their meetings the ritual conflicts of the representatives of the totalitarian states, who attack the other nations in violent and damaging terms which, not long ago, would have sufficed by themselves to constitute *casus belli*. But now they are given a hearing. People say, "That is part of their propaganda." No one believes that the accusations have any foundation, not even those who use the rostrum of the Assembly to feed or to repeat their campaign of vituperation. It is high time that the peoples reassert themselves, protest, proofs in hand, against such lying accusations, and at last come to realize that such proceedings are a perpetual menace to peace.

In this entire context the message of Pius rendered the cause of peace an untold service. He was the only one who had the courage to face the problem, the clear-sighted lucidity to diagnose the cause of the evil and to indicate the remedy, and he did so with that love and respect for truth in all domains whose inestimable power as the instrument of reconciliation, agreement, union, reciprocal understanding, and collaboration among men and peoples he has demonstrated.

This devotion to truth, promoted by the Church with her tremendous apostolate of teaching, contributes a service of inestimable value for the reconciliation and the mutual understanding of men and nations, and for the exchange of ideas and collaboration of man with man, of nation with nation. If all nations really and sincerely wish and seek, welcome and acknowledge only the truth, then they are truly on the road that leads by its very nature to mutual understanding and union. Since truth is only one (whatever meaning it may have in each individual case), the universal desire for truth can only be one. On the other hand, error, since it is opposed to truth and reality, by its very nature divides (Address to the Italian Study Center for International Reconciliation, October 13, 1955).

Similarly, when he addressed the Diplomatic Corps on February 25, 1946, after recalling some of the elevated duties of diplomats, he drew their attention to propaganda: "This propaganda must make truth and objectivity its holy and sacred law."

2. *An Order of Liberty.* In his allocution of June 2, 1947, the feast of his patron, St. Eugene, Pope Pius XII called for "a beneficent organization of liberty." He then laid down its conditions. [Liberty] ". . . can flourish only where right and law govern and efficaciously assure respect for the dignity of individuals as well as of nations."

At Christmas, 1951, he stated a new and very important clarification of the Christian order of liberty.

> The Christian order, as well as the organization for peace, is essentially an order of liberty. It is the united effort of free men and nations for the progressive realization, in all domains of life, of the goals assigned by God to humanity. Nevertheless, it is a sad fact that nowadays true liberty is neither esteemed nor possessed. In these conditions the life of men in general, as well as the organization for peace, is internally weakened and anemic, externally exposed to constant dangers.

In this text he warns against the dangers to be avoided; he defines the order of liberty; he points out the goal to be attained and indicates the extent of the Christian order as well as of the organization for peace.

The time is December, 1940. Hitler is victorious. In the totalitarian states there is talk of a new order. Pope Pius, too, in his Christmas message speaks of the indispensable conditions for a new order. But first he cautions that

> . . . only by observing these conditions will it be possible to avoid the danger of conceiving and forming this new order as a purely external mechanism, imposed by force, an order without sincerity, without full consent, without joy, without peace, without dignity, without value.

Several times he warned the nations of the danger of a mechanical and tyrannical order, where there is no longer room for personal liberty or where the common life is paralyzed by excessive centralization.

> Society is nothing but an enormous machine, whose order is only apparent, because it is no longer the order of life, of spirit, of liberty, of peace. As in a machine, activity is purely material, destructive of human dignity and of liberty (Christmas Message, 1951).

The Pope was speaking here of the totalitarian states.

Already in his Christmas message of 1941 he had described the consequences of the fact that the mutual relations of social life had taken on a purely physical and mechanical character.

> The power of external constraint, the simple fact of the possession of power superseded the rules of the order which must govern the life of men in general, rules which, promulgated by God, specify what are the natural and supernatural relations which exist between law and charity, between individuals and society.

What constitutes the order of liberty?—"The united effort of free men and of free nations."

United effort. St. Thomas has asserted that "Every society is a group of men united to produce a common work." This common work for which they co-operate in a united effort must be the result of the free and voluntary action of men and of nations. This concept is opposed to the mechanistic concept of the sociological school of Durkheim, which enjoyed its hour of popularity in France and elsewhere. According to this theory, the social fact has its own nature, its special laws; it does not proceed from the free and voluntary action of human persons, but is independent of them.

The Thomistic concept is likewise completely opposed to that of the totalitarian states.

Whom did the Pope address when he called for a united effort of free wills?

First, rulers and all who bear the heavy responsibility of leadership in their country and in international institutions. Next, all the directors and members of movements and organizations who can contribute to the constitution of a true international community, whether in their own nation, or on the international level. For Pius insisted that bonds exist between the national and the international orders.

> International relations and internal order are intimately connected. The equilibrium and the harmony between nations depend on the equilibrium and the internal achievements of each state in the material, social, and intellectual fields. As a matter of fact, it will never be possible to establish a solid and safe front of peace toward the outside unless a front of internal peace inspires confidence. Only then the tendency toward an integral peace in these two orders [internal and external] will succeed in freeing nations from the horrible nightmare of war, by progressively weakening or uprooting the material and psychological causes of new disturbances and of new upheavals (Christmas Message, 1942).

Finally, the Pope spoke directly to the citizens of the nations, of the true democracies. For in a democracy worthy of the name —whether its internal structure or organization be monarchical or republican, the Church will not utter a judgment regarding it, but goes directly to man himself. As pointed out in the 1944 Christmas message, citizens have two essential rights: that of expressing their personal opinions about the duties and sacrifices that are imposed on them, and that of not being forced to obey without being heard. Moreover,

> In a nation worthy of the name, the citizen is aware of his own personality, of his duties and of his rights; this awareness of his own liberty is joined to respect for the liberty and dignity of others.

To all free men, to all free nations joined together in a united effort, the Pope proposed, beyond the particular and legitimate purposes they pursue by their action and by their alliances and movements, a superior and a very noble goal: a united effort, he says, "for the progressive realization, in all the fields of life, of the goals assigned by God to humanity." We know now what these goals are: the common good of every nation for the full development of human persons and the attainment of their destiny, but also the international common good, the order willed by God for the community of nations, the sovereignty of the moral and the natural law, the safeguarding of absolute values, true peace.

This order embraces all the domains of life, says the Pope; hence a united effort to realize the plan of God in personal, family, professional, economic, and social life, in national and international life.

On the national level, Pope Pius has shown what may be expected from the true liberty of men who are solidly bound together for the achievement of a concrete objective:

> True and healthy liberty can be nothing but the liberty of men who, conscious of being solidly bound together with a view to an objective goal of social economy, are in a position to demand that economics, far from affecting their liberty in the choice of the means adapted for this goal, should rather guarantee and protect it (Allocution to members of the Congress of International Exchanges, March 7, 1948).

On the international level, the liberty of rulers and peoples plays a considerable role in providing the form given the community of nations, the creation of organs and services of this community, the construction of the mechanism by which authority is exercised, the analysis of historical and geographical, economic and social, moral and religious conditions, intelligent research into the obstacles connected with the psychology and the diversity of civilizations, with the interests of nations and their tendencies, with their customs and deep-rooted prejudices, with their changing circumstances, and finally the discovery of the means of solidly establishing the community of nations, the elaboration of agreements, pacts and treaties, the constitution of regional unions as the point of departure for gradually extending to others the benefits of the community. In short, this international community is really a construction freely and unitedly raised up by men and nations themselves.

Here again, by emerging as a defender of liberty, by calling for an order of liberty, the Pope rendered the community of nations a new and signal service. Further, he enlightened them in another way, by teaching them the meaning of true liberty. Although there is much talk of liberty, of the "free world," as he observed in his 1951 Christmas message, at the same time there are enslavements of which people are ignorant; they do not know what authentic liberty is.

This free world suffers from illusions and does not understand itself. Its power does not reside in true liberty. This fact constitutes a new danger which threatens peace and which must be exposed in the light of the Christian social order.

Of those who are nothing more than cogs in the various social organisms, the Pope said, "These are no longer free men, capable of assuming or of accepting a share of responsibility in public affairs."

The free man, created in the image of God, knows that he is responsible for his acts and for his destiny, capable of governing himself, of being his own master, of controlling his instincts, his passions, his faculties, and of deciding his actions and omissions on the basis of a loving, faithful, and willing submission to a superior order of the moral law and to the transcendent will of a Master who acts in history and who is also a Father. For, as Pope Pius expressed it in his Christmas message of 1956,

> reality and human society are not founded on the results of mechanical necessity, but on the free and always benevolent action of God and on the free action of men, action composed of love and fidelity wherever they observe the order established by God.

The order of liberty as a condition of the international community he has admirably defined:

> It is the temple of the moral order built on harmonious lines; it is the sum total of the rights and duties of individuals and families, certain of which rights are inalienable, even when the common good apparently might be opposed to them, of the rights and duties of one nation or one state and the family of nations and states. These rights and duties are carefully secured and balanced by the demands of the dignity of the human person and of the family on the one side and by the common good on the other (Allocution to the representative of Great Britain at the Holy See, June 23, 1951).

3. *An Order of Security.* We pointed out in the first chapter that collective security was the original objective of the League of Nations. What was understood by this term was cessation of the uncertainty, the insecurity and tension that threatened to bring about violations of treaties, provocations, the possibility of aggression against the political independence and the terri-

torial integrity of a state. The small states in particular constantly lived under this threat and this fear. A general distrust resulted from this, and the peace was always menaced. Peace is indissolubly bound up with security, with guarantees of security; they are its indispensable conditions.

In its turn the UN decided upon a "Security Council" as its principal organ. Its General Assembly, among other resolutions, invited all the nations

> to abstain from all threats and every act, direct or indirect, designed to compromise the liberty, the independence or the integrity of any State whatsoever, to foment internal struggles or to oppress the will of a people in any State (Twenty-sixth Plenary Session, held at Lake Success, December 1, 1949).

In his Christmas message of 1939 the Pope deplored the fact that his efforts and those of other men working for peace had not achieved the desired effect, "particularly because of the uncompromising and profound defiance, grown beyond measure in souls during the last years, which erected insurmountable barriers between the nations." During the same year, replying to the Belgian ambassador on September 14, the Holy Father expressed his intention of grasping every opportunity to lead nations toward the conclusion of a peace honorable for all, "a peace which protects the vital rights of everyone and which safeguards the security and the tranquility of the nations." The following Christmas (1940), while enunciating the indispensable conditions for the new order, the Pope called for "the victory over distrust, which weighs like an oppressive mass on international law and renders every true understanding unrealizable."

In the Christmas message of 1941, in stating the principles of an international order, Pius XII declared in the first place that

> in the field of a new organization founded on moral principles, there can be no place for alienation of the liberty, the integrity, and the security of other nations, whatever be their territorial extent or their ability to defend themselves. . . . Security, insofar as it can be attained here below, can have no other solid foundation than the physical and moral health of the people, good public order both internal and external, normal relations of neighborliness (Allocution to the Sacred College, June 2, 1947).

But in the Christmas message of 1956, which had exceptionally broad repercussions throughout the world, the problem of security was treated at length under its philosophical and theological aspects.

"Security! the deepest aspiration of those living today. . . ." If the message had such repercussions, it was no doubt due primarily, in the eyes of an elite, to its depth and weight; but in the case of the average man, because it went directly to the heart of the anguish under which the modern world labors, to the terrible contradiction that weighs humanity down: on the one hand, unbounded pride in the marvels of progress, marking the dawn of "the second technical revolution," and on the other, unrest, fear, insecurity at the threat of self-destruction brought on by that very progress. . . .

Why does humanity find itself in these straits?—For one thing, because modern man refuses to recognize the reality of sin and the awesome risk that the abuse of his liberty causes him and humanity. The believer, on the contrary, knows the power of human nature, but also its limits and its weakness. He is aware that original sin and its consequences "have not deprived man of his domination of the earth, but of security in the exercise of this domination." He leans confidently on the work of Redemption, which has restored his dignity as a child of God the Father and given him the strength of grace, capable of helping him to triumph, at least interiorly, over the general disorder caused by original sin and aggravated by his personal faults. Thus, without excessive optimism, but also free of a depressing pessimism, the Christian finds his interior security in the well-balanced realism of his belief.

Another error at the base of the existing contradiction in society is that modern man has had the audacity to construct alone, by his own powers and the techniques of progress, an entirely new society, while rejecting three essential values: historical reality with the traditions of the past and its social structures; the free act, the true liberty of man; and finally religion, which is accused of seeking at all costs to preserve the past under its most outmoded forms and of constituting, by its doctrine of absolute and immutable values, an obstruction on the road to the future.

How can security be re-established?—By proceeding to a reas-
sessment of the values concerned: it is necessary to rediscover
the profound meaning of these three essential values and to give
them their rightful place in the reconstruction of society.

First there is religion, "which, truly seeking liberty and security, must direct society toward its real and supreme Founder,
convinced that only the idea of society dependent on God will
protect it in its most important undertakings."

Then follows historical reality. In the name of a sense of
history some have made a *tabula rasa* of the past, rejecting the
accumulation of the positive contributions made by past generations, roughly obliterating the social structures that assured
the liberty and the security of man. Attempts have also been
made to oppose the sense of history to liberty, as though genuine
historical progress presupposed the disappearance of liberty, the
free act of man, this third value to be protected.

On the contrary, "history and liberty" must unite "in harmon-
izing the dynamism of reforms with the stability of traditions,
the free act with common security." True, man must look to the
future; he must construct a new society, and there is no question
of fixating himself in the past. He remains "capable, in accord
with his destiny, of creating history," but by way of crises and
struggles, of hopes and doubts, a mixture of security and incer-
titude. History is "a realm of human reality, in which social man
must labor not only with the forces of nature, but also with himself. Since he is responsible to men of the past and of the future,
he is charged with unceasingly fashioning the common life."

But there must be no contradiction between this free action
of man who "weaves his history" and the security that under-
girds society. On the contrary, harmony and mutual support
prevail between the two. "Thanks to personal and free action,
a dynamic evolution is always going on, but it does not suppress
the security that the individual enjoys in society and with society.
On the other hand, a certain fund of tradition and stability to
safeguard security always exists, while at the same time society
does not suppress the free and personal action of the individual."

Once more we assert that order, whose necessity Pius XII
demonstrated with such clarity, is not purely static, but dynamic.
This order of beings and of ends established by the Creator must

be viewed in all its harmony. But in its light and in order to realize it, men have the obligation of constructing a better society by free and concerted action in "a dynamic evolution," by collaborating with the free and ever beneficent action of God within the framework of the tremendous historical fact of the redemptive incarnation of the Son of God, who dominates everything—past, present and future. "In Bethlehem's manger the profound meaning of the history of man, past and future, really becomes incarnate."

In the conclusion of his 1956 Christmas message, the Pope treated directly the facts of international life. A most important passage concerns the UN. The Pope desired to see its authority strengthened, indicated its deficiencies, demonstrated the weakness of its means, particularly the absence of a military force. Reinforcement of its authority would be necessary to obtain a general disarmament and, further, to bring about the observance of the new obligations imposed by international law for the control of arms manufacture.

In a word, it is clear that for Pope Pius, the order of security on the international level is actually constituted by the UN and, for all time to come, by the community of states and nations, whatever concrete form it may assume.

In reply to a question put to him by the Italian director of the Associated Press in March, 1947, at the very moment when the Four Powers were meeting in Moscow to decide the future status of Germany, Pope Pius XII remarked that the problem of peace in Europe and in the world had till that time been considered "solely from the viewpoint of the individual security of each state." And he added, "We foster the hope that soon the United Nations will be in a position to give effective guarantees for the security of all" (*Croix de Paris,* March 28, 1947).

FUNDAMENTAL RULE OF THE INTERNATIONAL ORDER:
THE ORDER OF JUSTICE

1. *Doctrine of the Popes concerning justice in the relations among nations.* Since the time of Leo XIII all the popes have taught the obligations of justice and charity in international life.

The texts are numerous and rather similar. It may be of interest to point out a form of each pope's characteristic and original intervention in this sphere.

Leo XIII. During the pontificate of Leo XIII the Conference of Nations, whose work was described in the first chapter, was held at The Hague in 1899. The co-operation of the Holy Father's authority was first requested by Russia, which had taken the initiative in convening the congress. In two replies dated September 15, 1898, and February 10, 1899, respectively, Cardinal Rampolla, then Secretary of State, revealed how far the noble undertaking corresponded to the most ardent desires of the Sovereign Pontiff and to the Church's doctrine on peace. He re-affirmed the necessity "of opposing to the law of force the force of law," and of using mediation and arbitration as means. And in a letter of May 29, 1899, in answer to the invitation of the Queen of Holland, Leo XIII stated that he intended not only to give his moral support to the undertaking but also to co-operate actively with it, in conformity with the Church's mission of peace.

Italy alone opposed this representation of the Holy See at the conference. In his allocution of December 14, 1899, Leo XIII protested against this insult. "What subject more deserved the invitation of the Sovereign Pontiff? To promote justice, to work for peace, to forestall dissensions—these things, by God's will, are part of the role of the supreme pontificate."

St. Pius X, who was called upon to arbitrate among three South American states (Brazil, Bolivia, and Peru) and who, on August 2, 1914, at the moment when war was declared, exhorted the Catholics of the entire world to pray for peace in words filled with sorrow, decided to be represented at the inauguration of the Carnegie Foundation for International Peace. At that time (1911) the Modernist crisis had reached its peak. To combat the error, the Pope had scored as dangerous any collaboration in the moral order between Catholics and dissidents. Now, although the Carnegie Foundation was of Protestant origin, St. Pius (in a letter of June 11, 1911, to the Apostolic Delegate of the United States) did not hesitate to recommend the undertaking to Catholics and to approve it, since it sought the attainment of peace. After praising the founders, he added: "We do not doubt that these eminent men, with all their intelligence and political acumen, will seek, in order to procure peace for a disturbed age, to open to the nations the royal road to holy and general observance of the laws of justice and charity." Then he called attention to the idea of an order of justice and charity. "In effect, because peace presupposes order, he would labor in vain to achieve peace who would not employ his best efforts to have these truths, which form the principle and the essential basis of this order, duly respected."

Benedict XV.   Later we shall have occasion to speak at length of the role played by Pope Benedict XV during World War I. On September 8, 1914, in his first exhortation to the Catholic world he announced his resolution to leave no stone unturned "to hasten the end of this calamity." Too few Catholics have taken cognizance of the nobility of his mission during the hostilities. While passions were at a white heat, a campaign of calumnies against the Pope led calm judgment astray. With the passing of time, however, this Pope, who suffered so much, appears more and more as a defender of law and as a teacher of international morality.

On January 22, 1915, in an allocution to the Cardinals, he solemnly proclaimed that "no one, for whatever reason, may ever violate justice," and added that he announced this principle openly "to utter a strong reproof against all the violations of right wherever they have been committed." On June 13, 1921, again in an allocution to the Sacred College, he addressed an insistent appeal to rulers: "We beg them to induce the nations by their initiative and under their direction to give up mutual hatred for the promotion of the common good and to regulate by way of discussion the differences that still separate them, taking justice as a guide and charity as a companion."

We must devote special attention to the message of August 1, 1917, to the belligerents and their rulers, a message in which Benedict made some practical suggestions for negotiations "which appear to be the bases for a just and lasting peace, leaving to them the task of further determining and completing them."

The first point proposed must figure in all treaties and international agreements: "Above all, the fundamental point must be that the moral force of law be substituted for the material force of arms."

Pius XI. In several documents Pope Pius XI sought to clarify the idea of peace. He based it on justice, but at the same time he showed that by itself justice does not suffice to assure peace.

> The genuine peace of Christ cannot be separated from the rule of justice, since God himself judges according to the law (Ps 9:5) and peace is the work of justice (Is 32:17). But a justice rigid and hard as steel can never be the foundation of peace. Charity is required (Encyclical *Ubi Arcano*).

2. Personal contribution of Pius XII: An International Order of Justice. The motto of Pius XII is well known: "*Opus justitiae pax*" (Peace is the work of justice). His doctrinal teaching has fully revealed the necessity of an international order of justice and of law. At the end of the first year of the war, he already courageously put the question on this ground:

> At the end of the war, will the treaties of peace, the new international order, be animated by a spirit of justice and equity to all, the spirit that redeems and makes peace, or shall we see a lamentable repetition of errors ancient and modern? (Christmas message, 1940).

Further, in international morality, which he derived from the natural law and from Revelation, Pius XII enlarged the perspectives and gave justice some new and vast dimensions.

Necessity of an international order of justice and law. In the first place Pope Pius demonstrated the necessity of an international natural law and of a law of nations dictated by nature, in order that stability of relations between peoples will not depend upon the sole will of the states, but upon the order of a higher law. During the entire nineteenth century the natural law was denied. The school of the positivists, of juridical positivism, bases international law entirely on treaties, on custom, in a word, on agreements freely entered into by the states. The whole matter was restricted to the limits of contracts; practically speaking, the will of the states made the law. The interest of the nation was supreme, and no order of justice or of higher law imposing itself on the will of rulers and parliaments was admitted.

Pius XII combatted this juridical positivism. He advanced considerably the study of the problem of a higher international order and indicated the path to follow.

Constitutive elements of the order of justice. The Pope was not satisfied with demonstrating the necessity of a superior order of justice and of law; he also defined and clarified its essential elements.

To begin with, this order of justice comes into existence fundamentally as soon as states recognize effectively this principle of justice: the equality of rights and duties.

> The soul of a peace worthy of the name, its vivifying spirit, can be nothing other than a justice which, with an impartial hand, gives to all their due and demands of all that to which each one is bound (Radio message of September 1, 1944).

To render to others their due, to receive from others what they owe—this is the first rule of justice: the equality of rights and obligations.

> Justice applies an equal measure on all sides. What a nation, a state, claims for itself by an elementary sentiment of right, what it will never renounce, that it must also unconditionally grant to another nation, to another state (Allocution to the pilgrims of Pax Christi, September 13, 1952).

The rule of justice demands of all states a respect for contracts, fidelity to agreements and to the word publicly given, as Pius did not cease to reiterate. He enunciated the same rule of justice in his words:

> We hope that all of humanity . . . will recognize the reality and consider seriously putting into practice law and justice, not only when there is question of demanding the fulfillment of its own needs, but also when others' just claims must be satisfied (Christmas message, 1940).

In his homily on Easter, 1939, Pius XII recalled some of these demands of justice and added:

> It is impossible to have peace so long as matters are not in order; by the same token, order cannot exist if justice is discarded. . . . Justice has for its function to establish and preserve intact the

principles of this order of things which is the primary and principal foundation of an enduring peace.

Further, the order of justice demands that the rights and duties of states in their relations with one another and with the international community be defined and acknowledged. In chapter three we shall present a list of these rights and duties as they are reflected in papal teaching.

An order of justice also implies that the fundamental rights of the human person be respected, acknowledged, and guaranteed by the international organization. Pope Pius XII constantly asserted and defended the dignity and the rights of the human person in all spheres. We have shown this on the social plane by the exposition of the social doctrine of the Church. But the order of peace and the international common good are also directly interested in the recognition of these rights and liberties of the human person within the limits of each state. "Justice demands that all recognize and respect the sacred rights of human liberty and dignity," Pius stated in the Easter homily preached in St. Peter's on April 9, 1939. In the same homily the Pope showed that peace cannot exist as long as so many men lack work and a state of life that respects their human dignity.

In the Christmas message of 1942, Pius XII posited as the first principle of peace respect for the dignity of the human person:

> Whoever wishes to see the star of peace rise and rest on society must do his share to render to the human person the dignity which was conferred on it by God in the beginning . . . to promote respect for and the practical exercise of the fundamental rights of the person. . . .

And he then proceeded to enumerate these fundamental rights.

For an order of justice such as will affirm and organize "the necessity of a sharing by all in the goods of the earth" (Christmas message, 1941), there is required

> progressive action, balanced by corresponding guarantees, to establish an order that gives to all states the means of assuring to their citizens of all classes a suitable standard of life (Christmas message, 1940).

Finally, an order of justice and of law is one that will be sustained and guaranteed by the constitution of an organization of nations built on solid foundations, having at its head a strong authority endowed with powerful means, with military and police forces sufficient to enforce the rules of law acknowledged by all and the obligations agreed to by all.

Enlargement of the order of justice. After culling, from the doctrinal work of Pius XII the necessity of an international order of justice and the determination of the constitutive elements of that order, we must now show how he has given new dimensions both in depth and in width to international justice.

First dimension: Purely legal justice must be replaced by a justice conformable to international natural law.

The doctrine of Pius XII on this point embraces two fundamental principles, one concerned with the fidelity owed to treaties, the other with the possible revision of treaties.

First principle: Fidelity to contracts and to treaties is a demand of justice and an indispensable condition for mutual confidence.

> To regard treaties as ephemeral as a matter of principle and to attribute to one's self the faculty of annulling them unilaterally as soon as they are considered no longer useful would be to destroy all confidence among states. The natural order would thereby be overthrown, and pits impossible to fill would be created between the peoples (Christmas message, 1939).

The preamble to the pact of the League of Nations had proclaimed this same principle:

> Considering that, in order to develop cooperation among the nations and to guarantee them peace and security, it is necessary . . . to respect scrupulously all the obligations of treaties in the mutual relations of the organized nations. . . .

and the preamble to the charter of the United Nations affirms it anew:

> Resolved to create the conditions necessary for the maintenance of justice and of the respect for obligations begotten by treaties and other sources of international law. . . .

Here a very important question arises: Whence do treaties derive their obligatory force? On this point the authors are divided: for some it is custom, for others the internal constitutions of the states. The more one maintains the primacy of the rights and the sovereignty of states, the less will he be willing to seek its basis in an order of law and justice superior to the interests and the caprices of states, and consequently he will deny any obligatory character to treaties.

According to Pius XII, the foundation must be sought in an international juridical order, which respects and guarantees the principles of international natural law.

> So that harmonious and lasting contacts and fruitful relations may exist, it is indispensable that the nations should acknowledge and observe the principles of international natural law, which regulate their normal development and functioning.

Now, what do these principles demand? The Pope replies: First of all, respect for the rights of each nation, of which we shall speak in the following chapter. Then he adds that ". . . they demand, besides, fidelity to treaties stipulated and sanctioned in conformity with the rules of international law" (Encyclical *Summi Pontificatus*).

Pursuing further the study of the reason for this fidelity, Pius XII considers the international juridical order of security and justice, determines its necessary conditions, and defines the soul of the juridical relations among the nations:

> It cannot be doubted that the necessary and indispensable condition of all peaceful common life among the nations, the very soul of the juridical relations existing among them, consists in mutual confidence, in the acceptance and the persuasion of a reciprocal fidelity to the pledged word (Encyclical *Summi Pontificatus*).

In conclusion, for Pius XII there does not exist, as some have maintained, a "conditional value of treaties," in the sense that a treaty would cease to have binding force for a state when the state calculated that it would be to its interest not to observe the treaty any longer. For the Pope the obligatory force of treaties rests on the principles of international natural law and on an international order.

Second principle: Revision of treaties under certain conditions. This fidelity, however, must not be purely literal, that is to say, it must not be left imprisoned in the letter of treaties. It must remain conformable to law and be constantly penetrated by a spirit of justice, corresponding to the needs of changing situations, to the evolution of events, to the legitimate aspirations of peoples, to the moving life of nations.

Treaties are not eternal; the part expressing the past is provisional. Furthermore, they are usually made at the conclusion of a state of war. The victor imposes his will on the vanquished, who is exhausted and discouraged. Materially, the treaty has the appearance of a contractual agreement; formally, it generally is nothing more than a forced imposition.

A comparison with the wage contract in many cases, while bearing in mind the marked differences, may help in understanding the problem of law in relations between nations as in relations between employer and employee. In 1891 Leo XIII set down this great principle in the *Rerum Novarum:*

> Let it be granted, then, that, as a rule, workman and employer should make free agreements, and in particular should freely agree as to wages; nevertheless, there is a dictate of nature more imperious and more ancient than any bargain between man and man, that the remuneration must be enough to support the wage-earner in reasonable and frugal comfort. If through necessity or fear of a worse evil, the workman accepts harder conditions because an employer or contractor will give him no better, he is the victim of force and injustice.

The analogy is striking. If, constrained by necessity or driven by the fear of a worse evil, the vanquished nation accepts hard conditions, which it cannot refuse because they are imposed, it suffers violence against which justice protests. Hence a treaty represents a solution corresponding to the equilibrium of the forces at a given moment; it does not incarnate justice by the mere fact that two nations have signed the agreement. In fact, it runs the risk, "of merely being injustice under the cloak of justice" (*Summi Pontificatus*). He then describes the temptation that besets the conquerer: This is the hour when

> the angel of justice struggles with the demon of violence; the heart of the victor easily becomes hardened; moderation and foresight based on wisdom appear as weakness to him; the violence of popular passions, fired by the sufferings and sacrifices undergone, frequently blinds the rulers themselves and makes

them deaf to the counsels of humanity and of equity, whose voice
is dimmed or extinguished by the inhuman cry: *Vae victis*—Woe
to the conquered! Resolutions and decisions made in such circumstances would run the risk of merely being injustice under the
cloak of justice.

We have here a concrete application of the demands of the
natural law, about which we recalled the teaching of the Church
and of Pope Pius XII in the first chapter.

It is true that with the passing of time and with substantial
changes of circumstances, which were not foreseen and possibly
could not have been foreseen at the moment of stipulation, a
treaty or some of its clauses can become, or appear to be unjust
or unrealizable or too burdensome for one of the parties; it is
evident that in such circumstances a frank discussion looking to
the modification or replacement of the pact must be instituted
betimes (Encyclical *Summi Pontificatus*).

In the Christmas message of 1939, on the fundamental points
of a just and honorable peace, Pius XII twice returned to the
problem of treaty revision. Discussing the third fundamental
point, the Pope remarked that it would be wise to draw on the
lessons of experience in order to remedy the deficiencies and the
imperfections of the past, notably in the functioning of juridical
institutions.

Since it is so difficult for human nature—one might almost be
tempted to say, impossible—to foresee everything and to take
care of everything at the time of the peace negotiations, because
it finds it hard to shed all passion and all bitterness, the establishment of juridical institutions which serve to guarantee the loyal
and faithful observance of agreements and, in case of need, to
revise and correct them is of capital importance for an honorable
acceptance of a treaty of peace and for the avoidance of arbitrary and unilateral attempts and interpretations regarding the
conditions of the treaties themselves.

In the fourth fundamental point the Pope shows that over and
above the strict law of the treaties in force, it is necessary to study

. . . the true needs and the just requests of nations and of
peoples, as well as of ethnic minorities. If such requests do not
always suffice to beget a strict right when there are in force
recognized or sanctioned treaties or other juridical titles opposed

to them, nevertheless they always merit a cordial examination in order to satisfy them by peaceful ways and even, where this appears necessary, by the means of an equitable, wise and concordant revision of treaties.

From the papal texts cited above it is obvious that a number of conditions must be verified before proceeding to a treaty revision.

First condition: An understanding and an honest discussion between the parties; no unilateral and arbitrary decisions on the part of one state.

Second condition: At a time when the UN did not yet exist and it was not certain that a new form of international juridical institution would one day be created, Pius XII, from the beginning of the war, demanded as of "capital importance" the constitution of juridical institutions to guarantee the faithful and honest application of agreements and, should circumstances call for it, their revision and correction. Hence treaty revision must fall within the competency of the international community, of its juridical institutions. These must also take into account the degree to which disarmament will be affected, a necessary condition, concerning which Pius XII has given an entire body of firm and courageous teaching, as will be seen in chapter four.

To the extent that disarmament will be realized, it will be necessary to establish appropriate means, honorable for all and efficacious for the observation of treaties. . . . In order that reciprocal confidence be restored, it is necessary to create institutions which, meriting general respect, are dedicated to this very noble function, either to guarantee the sincere execution of treaties or to promote, according to the principles of law and equity, opportune corrections or revisions of them (Christmas message, 1941).

We should observe the prudence and wisdom with which Pius XII proposes the problem of treaty revision in the international sphere. First these are the same juridical institutions that will have the twofold task of guaranteeing the sincere execution of treaties and of promoting their timely correction or revision; then, this whole task must not be one of force or caprice on the part of an international assembly, but one of fidelity "to the principles of law and equity."

It may be worthwhile to compare the attitude of the international assemblies on this point with the position of Pius XII.

Already the pact of the League of Nations had emphasized that it might be opportune—politically opportune, that is—to reconsider treaties that had become, after their conclusion, "inapplicable," as the result of events outside the will of their authors.[2]

In its charter the UN has several articles envisaging particularly situations that can threaten the peace. The applications made of them lack force and authority, because they are not based firmly enough on the principles and demands of law. The political compromises, the tensions among various blocs, the absence of unanimity regarding the very concept of law have tended to diminish the utility or the efficacy of the articles of the Charter, which represent a praiseworthy effort—still rather timid—to find solutions, to resolve differences, to ward off menaces to peace.[3]

The problem here goes beyond the case of treaty revision. It is interesting to note that measures have been taken to prevent differences from being settled unilaterally or even between only the two parties, but through the intervention of an international juridical organization, as Pius XII had postulated—whether the Assembly, or the Security Council, or even at the request of a single member of the UN. Practically—and much will already have been gained thereby—the organ of the UN facilitates a

2. "The Assembly can, from time to time, invite the members of the League to a re-examination of treaties that have become inapplicable" (Art. 19).

3. Article 11, No. 2, authorizes the Assembly "to discuss all questions relating to the maintenance of international peace and security" and to make "recommendations." Article 11, No. 3, permits the Assembly to draw the attention of the Security Council to "situations which appear to threaten international peace and security." Article 14 enables the Assembly to pursue "the peaceful adjustment of any situation, whatever be its origin, which seems to it to be of a nature to injure the general welfare or to compromise the friendly relations between nations." Article 34 attributes to the Security Council "the right of inquiring into every difference and every situation which might cause a disagreement between nations or beget a difference" whose prolongation might menace the peace.

meeting of the two parties for examination and discussion of the treaty or the situation.

Third condition: a serious reason—"a recognized need," says the Pope. These reasons may be of different natures. First, the historical setting must be considered: "the passing of time and substantial changes in circumstances." We should note again the Pope's concern to take into account historical conditions and transformations produced by life. Then there are reasons of a psychological, sociological, and human order: "the true needs and the just demands of nations and of peoples as well as of ethnic minorities."

These are the conditions posited by the Pope for treaty revision, with the evident understanding that when the treaty was concluded, it was impossible to foresee everything and that changeable passions in the victor perhaps influenced the composition of the treaty.

Second dimension: Equity. In the passage we have just considered from the 1939 Christmas allocution, concerning the examination of true needs and just demands of nations, peoples, and ethnic minorities. Pius XII states that an "equitable" treaty revision must be undertaken when these needs and claims do not suffice "to establish a strict right."

It should be noted that habitually—or at least very frequently —Pius linked justice and equity. Thus the Encyclical *Summi Pontificatus* posed the question:

> Will the peace treaties, the new international order at the end of the war, be animated by justice and equity towards all, by that spirit that liberates and pacifies, or will they be a lamentable repetition of errors ancient and modern?

In the first of the five fundamental points of a just and honorable peace, in which he affirms the rights of nations to life and independence, he declares that, when there has been a violation of these rights, the juridical order demands reparation according "to the norms of reciprocal justice and equity."

The Christmas message of 1943 teaches that true peace, in accord with the dignity of man and with the Christian conscience, "must be the fruit of provident justice and of equity toward all."

In his radio message on the fifth anniversary of the war, Pius XII called for the establishment of international institutions capable of "safeguarding the peace, according to the principles of justice and equity, against all possible future threats."

What is equity? It is a special virtue standing between justice and charity, but leaning more toward justice.

A passage from Pius XII's Easter homily of 1939 will help in analyzing the concept of equity:

> . . . this equity, which, through a wise and benevolent application, can with order and right reason elucidate and resolve the bitterest and most complicated controversies.

We can now enumerate more definitely the elements of equity. First element: Its domain is the "application," the practical realization of juridical rules. It is a principle of action. Second element: It is "benevolence," composed of wisdom, moderation, and right reason for the resolving of conflicts. Third element: Equity helps to go beyond the letter of treaties and inspires a human usage of law, beyond "strict law," as Pius says, in striving for "order"—i.e., the common good.

Equity exercises its benevolent influence in two ways. In the first place, by a sincere examination of a juridical title, even though still imperfect and undetermined. In this text it was a question of "just demands," which, however, do not beget a strict right. In the second place, equity urges each of the parties to moderation and wisdom in claiming their rights.

We are treating here of a new dimension. Moral theology and canon law appealed to equity in relations between individuals and groups. The popes, and especially Pius XII, have extended the notion of equity to include international relations, in order to mitigate the severity of treaties and to facilitate relations between states. Pius XII himself applied equity to the grave problem of a sharing of the goods of the earth by all, in place of the monopoly of economic resources. He affirmed the principle of the need of a participation of all in the earth's goods, as we shall see in the study of the state's rights (No. 7). Then he added:

> It is conformable to equity that a solution to this question, so

decisive for world economy, be sought progressively and methodically, together with the necessary guarantees, by drawing a lesson from the failures and the omissions of the past (Christmas message, 1941).

Third dimension: International Social Justice. Pius XII extended social justice to the international community and taught that it created among the states the obligation of collaboration, in order to resolve, by the common effort of the entire international community, the social problems posed in a certain country and threatening to compromise international peace, or the social problems that confront the entire community of nations. On this occasion he applied the need of collaboration on the part of all nations and states to the problem of unemployment. "Only the concurrence of all the nations of the entire world for an action of great scope, honestly understood and in perfect accord, can supply the remedy," he told members of the International Congress of Social Studies, June 3, 1950.[4]

This text permits us to see the new dimensions that international social justice will take, corresponding to the demands of social justice on the one hand and the international common good on the other. The Pope opens perspectives of considerable breadth: ". . . the universal collaboration of peoples and states, each making its respective contribution of wealth in raw materials, in capital, in manpower."

Henceforth this principle must become a beacon and guide in all spheres: material, technical, sanitary, cultural aid to underdeveloped countries, which is not merely the result of a humanitarian effort, as we shall see in chapter three in treating the rights and duties of states. The attainment of the international common good, of peace, is at stake. In the same way he writes of the problem of unemployment, for which he summons all nations to seek a solution:

4. Away with the egotistical preoccupations of nationalities and classes, which might even to the least extent prejudice an action honestly undertaken and vigorously prosecuted by co-operation in every manner possible over the entire face of the earth, in the concurrence of all initiatives and all efforts of individuals and groups, in the universal collaboration of peoples and States, each one making its respective contribution of wealth in raw materials, in capital, in manpower."

Thus will be eliminated one of the most disturbing factors of the international situation, the one which more than any other nowadays fosters the ruinous "cold war" and threatens to bring on, incomparably more disastrous, the hot war, the burning war.

There is another sphere in which international social justice certainly will develop in the future: that of the rights of man, no longer only as a member of a national group, but as a member of the international community. It is a new thing that an international body, the General Assembly of the United Nations, published (Sept.-Dec. 1948) a "Universal Declaration of Human Rights": 1) Personal rights to life, security and liberty; 2) Family rights; 3) Public rights and public liberties; 4) Social and economic rights.

Article 28 of the Declaration shows its bearing in the international sphere and the imperative character of these decisions taken together: "Everyone is entiled to a social and international order in which the rights and freedoms set forth in this Declaration can be fully realized." Alas! how far we still are from this order. There exists likewise a "European convention to safeguard the rights of man and fundamental liberties," published November 4, 1950.

Pope Pius XII who, in his Christmas message of 1942 and in many other allocutions, drew up a list of the fundamental rights of the human person and called for a juridical order to protect these rights against every arbitrary assault, in the same message declared that international relations and the internal order of states were intimately connected. If one nation violates these rights of the human person, the equilibrium and harmony among nations are immediately menaced and peace is compromised. Hence, the order of international justice calls for an effort on the part of all nations to seek means of assuring everywhere the demands of social justice.

SUPREME LAW OF THE INTERNATIONAL COMMUNITY: THE ORDER OF CHARITY

Here we attain the summits of the Church's doctrine on peace and on the community of nations. It is particularly in the domain of charity that the fortitude, the originality, and the practical efficacy of this doctrine manifest themselves.

1. *Texts of the Popes.* Even while the first World War was raging, Benedict XV was a courageous and indefatigable apostle of international charity, despite all misunderstandings and unjust attacks upon him. Did he not say, in his encyclical *Ad Beatissimi* (November 1, 1914), when speaking of the suzerainty over souls which the charity of Christ had to regain, "This will be Our objective and as it were the special mission of Our Pontificate"?

Benedict XV advanced international doctrine considerably when he enunciated in formal terms a principle which should have been self-evident, but which in fact was very generally ignored or misunderstood:

> The Gospel does not contain one law of charity for individuals and another law for states and nations, which after all are nothing but agglomerations of individuals (Encyclical *Pacem,* May 23, 1920).

In this work the Pope already defined all the principal elements of an order of charity when he declared:

> Perhaps never so much as today has the human race had need of that benevolence for all, born of a sincere love for others and expressing itself in a joyous and solicitous dedication.

And in the same text he affirmed: "Never has it been more necessary to enlarge the frontiers of charity than at the present time."

Pius XI made an important contribution to international doctrine, basing himself on St. Thomas. He indeed shows—as we have seen in speaking of the order of justice—that peace must be the work and the fruit of justice, but he adds that "it belongs rather to charity than to justice" (Christmas allocution, 1930). After declaring that it is necessary "to temper justice with a dose at least as great of charity, this virtue that is essentially intended to establish peace among men," Pius XI recalls a profound remark of St. Thomas (*Summa Theologiae,* II-II, q. 29, a. 3 ad 3): "The Angelic Doctor notes that true and genuine peace derives more from charity than from justice; this latter removes everything that is opposed to peace, as wrongs and injuries, while peace is properly and especially an act of charity" (Encyclical *Ubi Arcano Dei*, December 23, 1922).

2. *Order of Charity according to the Doctrine of Pius XII.* The first element is an atmosphere of mutual understanding. In tracing the obligations and the task of Catholics in the face of the problems of international life in 1952, Pius XII explained how they were

> . . . in the first place extraordinarily fitted to collaborate for the creation of an atmosphere without which common international action can possess neither consistency nor prosperous development.

Here is the complete text, for our consideration:

> This is the atmosphere of mutual understanding, of which one can indicate the fundamental elements: mutual respect, reciprocal loyalty which honestly attributes the same rights to others which one demands for one's self, a disposition of benevolence toward the children of other peoples as toward brothers and sisters (Allocution to the members of the Congress organized by Italian Catholic Action, July 23, 1952).

Let us emphasize at the outset the primary importance of the atmosphere of mutual understanding; it constitutes the necessary condition for the consistency and prosperous development of common international action. Understanding depends directly on intelligence, but we ought to say an intelligence of the heart animated by charity. Charity in fact is the virtue that impels us to put ourselves in the place of others, to consider our neighbor as another self, to love him for his own sake, to "understand" him with the particular characteristics deriving from his civilization, his race, his mentality and psychological differences, his history, his difficulties, his needs and aspirations, "the healthy cultural peculiarities of each people."

Furthermore, the Pope pointed out the fundamental elements of this understanding:

"Mutual respect," which forbids everything that may offend others and which manifests itself in the attitudes of "politeness" (Christmas message, 1940), civility, and courtesy. Studying the indispensable conditions of the order of peace, Pius XII demanded that, in order to establish the victory over hatred which divides peoples, all those who desire peace "should consider it a sacred duty and an exalted mission not to permit the natural ideals of veracity, of justice, of politeness and of cooperation in good to be blotted from the thoughts and sentiments of men." International courtesy, as distinct from international morality, is defined by writers on international public law as the aggregate of the relations that the states foster among themselves by simple agreement and which are not juridically obligatory; gracious concessions, which exclude every idea of law, and hence of sanctions, of reprisals, and whose suppression cannot be considered as an offense.

Until comparatively recent times the rules of respect, politeness and courtesy were observed as a point of honor in diplomatic relations. Nowadays they are too frequently disregarded; because of the character of the propaganda of the totalitarian states they have been replaced by contrary practices (at least in public and on the speaker's platform), which entail serious consequences for the relations between nations. We speak of the injurious attacks leveled against a state, of the insolent and incendiary harangues which picture the rulers of a particular nation as warmongers. In private, indeed, the same ambassadors and the representatives of the same states, who present themselves as antagonists in public, continue to meet each other, if need be, with smiles and sumptuous receptions. Here we have a tragicomedy, which threatens peace, because the general populace does not perceive any difference, and take as literally true the defamatory accusations reported in the press and on the radio.

"Reciprocal loyalty," which honestly recognizes for others the same rights that one demands for one's self—a comprehensive work of charity which inspires acts of justice! We speak of justice, since rights are involved. Now, these rights of others must be acknowledged in the same manner as they are demanded for one's own nation. It is precisely in this sphere that egoism and excessive nationalistic blindness tend to deny these rights of others and to vindicate only those of the nation.

Thus a comprehensive charity plays its beneficent role. There is no question yet of any act of intelligence, of judgment, of appreciation to recognize the rights of others. But under the influence of charity, which is disinterested friendship, the understanding and acknowledgment of the rights of others are exercised loyally and honestly.

"Disposition of benevolence toward the children of other peoples." We shall soon discuss the important role of benevolence. There is question here of an immediate preparation, of a "disposition" to this kind of virtue, which a pioneer in the field of natural law, Taparelli, in his great work entitled *Saggio teoretico del diritto naturale* (1883), already point out as the first law of international relations and which after him theologians and jurists concerned with the international order have assigned a place next to justice.

Pius XII characterized this disposition to benevolence as a spirit of brotherhood: the children of other peoples are considered "as brothers and sisters" and must be treated as such.

> Humanity will not be able to rise above the present crises and desolation, to tread the way to a more harmonious future, if it does not repress and dominate the forces of division and of discord by a sincere spirit of brotherhood that unites in the same love all classes, all races and all nations (Christmas message, 1947).

As the point of departure there is a comprehensive love of other peoples; with an enlightened attitude they are regarded as brothers and sisters. This comprehension inclines to benevolence, which directly produces a spirit of brotherhood, under the influence of charity.

What kind of brotherhood are we speaking of? First of all, of the brotherhood that unites all men of the great human family, by reason of the unity of the same human nature and the same origin. As such, this human and fraternal love can be practiced by all men of good will. Its law extends not only to the disciples of Christ, but to unbelievers, to men far removed from the Church.

But beyond this and above all, this brotherhood unites in the family of God those who by their calling to the supernatural life have become brothers and sisters in Christ the Redeemer (the "elder Brother," as St. Paul calls Him), in order to form one body.

Second element of the order of charity: benevolence. If understanding has to do with the intellect and draws people together in a common effort, benevolence is a disposition of the will. The word itself clearly indicates as much: "to wish well." It is an essential form of charity, desiring everything good for one's neighbor.

Here an objection obtrudes. In relations with others it is already difficult for human nature—egotistical, jealous, envious, ambitious—to wish others well, to look with favor on the success of their undertakings, on prosperity in their affairs, particularly if they compete in the same profession. This demands all the strength that charity can muster. But to ask one nation to take a benevolent attitude toward another nation is to attempt the impossible. This demand of the Church's doctrine is chimerical, not to say dangerous, for in the last analysis the prosperity, the rapid development of another nation tends to compromise the interests and the future of one's own.

We have deliberately presented the objection (which has become current) in all its harshness, in order to point out more clearly the boldness and the originality of the Church's doctrine on the matter of relations among the nations.

Boldness? Yes, indeed, for it is not only the reactions of the passions and national interest which reject this doctrine. As we shall see at the beginning of chapter three, there was a tradition, a custom in the relations among the nations of old Europe, to seek to injure the others, to employ intrigue, ruse, cunning; in fact, the aim was to create anarchy in other nations. As far as doctrine is concerned, it will suffice to mention that of Montesquieu, this expert on "the spirit of the laws" of society. "Grotius was right," says Taparelli, "in castigating the doctrine of Montesquieu, who permits a declaration of war against a nation for no other reason than that this nation is prospering and developing."[5]

But the doctrine of the Church is not satisfied with recalling to nations the obligation not to injure one another. Benevolence makes it a duty of charity for them to wish other nations well

5. *Op. cit.*, II, 136 (Rome, 1900³).

positively, sincerely, effectively, to hope for their development and security—in a word, to approve their common good in accord with their jurisdiction.

International benevolence goes further. In the name of charity it inclines nations and peoples to be reciprocally well disposed, so that they may co-operate for the welfare of the entire international community—preserving, however, their individuality and their own characteristics. Love of benevolence causes them to rejoice at the place each holds within the community of nations, at the particular mission it may be called upon to fulfill there, at the riches its culture, its civilization, its scholars, its artists, its technicians can bring to the great human family.

Comparing these relations among the nations in the international community to a harmony, whether that of a melody or of classic polyphony, Pius XII declared:

> Such is the harmony that must result from the agreement of all the nations, great and small, strong and weak, differing by reason of physiognomy or particular interests, but all equally permitted to make themselves heard, because all rest on the same foundation, the personal dignity of the whole man, because all are animated by the same desire for peace (Allocution to the Diplomatic Corps, February 25, 1946).

In the same sense Cardinal Feltin used this felicitous expression: "The peace which the Church desires is a living symphony of nations" (Conference of December 21, 1951, on "The Church and the Problem of Peace").

In the field of culture particularly, Pius XII explains "how one nation excels in learned researches of the sources, another in analyzing or synthesizing the matter that has been inventoried, another in its elaboration, another in its presentation." The Pope then recalls an essential principle that must be extensively applied in the community of nations:

> Thus it comes about that the nations, far from competing with one another and opposing one another, will seek rather to work for their mutual completion, each one bringing its contributions and each one benefiting by the contributions of all the others (Allocution to the International Committee for the Unity and Universality of Culture, November 14, 1951).

We have here a striking application of the effects of benevolent love with regard to the nations both considered individually
and as members of the international community that embraces
them. In regard to the nations considered individually, it is a
matter of respecting their culture, their traditions, their customs,
their institutions. This permits them to preserve their manner of
thinking, of living, of organizing their family life and social
relations, of developing themselves in their own fashion and
according to their particular resources. On the other hand, it is
a matter of benefiting from the contributions of all the others.
The love of benevolence also benefits members of the community
of nations, which acquires a harmonious beauty, a strengthening of its unity by the communication of its own contributions
and qualities to the others and by the reciprocal exchange of
goods.

Thus is clarified the concept of the love of benevolence. At
first sight it does not always reveal its significance in its application to nations and their relations. Reciprocal communication
of contributions and goods—this may well be styled a characteristic trait of the love of benevolence.[6] But there are two other
points in the text cited: first, consciousness on the part of the
nations of the fact that they are called "to perfect one another
mutually"; then, the awareness that this solidarity is not something imposed. Benevolent love will bring it about "that they will
take pleasure" in mutually completing one another. True charity
consists in this pleasure, this joy of knowing that one is helping
to realize a more conscious and more harmonious unity.

We suggest a comparison in order to emphasize the grandeur
and the fecundity of benevolent love between nations. This will
perhaps be the most convincing refutation to the objection stated
above.

Might one not compare the love of international benevolence
to meekness in relations among individuals? Meekness is a virtue
eminently proper to Christianity. The Savior practiced it and

6. See Taparelli, *op. cit.*, "The international communication of material
goods is a general law for nations in their normal state of power and well-
being" (p. 151); and speaking of the moral goods of intellect and will, the
celebrated author writes: "The nations must labor to procure these different goods mutually" (p. 153).

communicated it to men. In fact, he defined himself by it: "I am meek . . ." This virtue is very much misunderstood; many regard it as a sign of weakness of character. It is actually a power of the soul in a human being, a mastery of self, notably of those instincts of aggressiveness and anger with respect to others, which are manifested by excessive zeal to defend one's individuality and one's rights, and by a passionate attachment to one's own ideas and points of view. The egotistical and intolerant side of the individual is always on guard to defend itself against everything that appears to interfere with his tastes, his preferences, his caprices, his plans.

Now, one can see the legitimacy of applying this to nations. If the word "nation" is substituted for "individual," scarcely anything will have to be changed in the description given above. The instinct of aggressiveness, the solicitude to defend and to reclaim the nation's rights, the fear of losing national individuality in yielding to others—all this is but a picture of everyday reality.

But what is meekness? It is a benevolent attention to the personality of the neighbor, to the real being he represents in society, to the member of the mystical body, together with the unique place he holds and the irreplaceable mission he must fulfill in the design of God.

Meekness is that disposition of charity which, instead of becoming irritated and impatient because others are not like ourselves, because they differ from us in their physical, intellectual and moral make-up, desires with good will, with "benevolence," that they retain their own character, their particular vocation, their gifts and qualities, their personal destiny. Besides that, meekness inclines a person to rejoice that this is so, to "take pleasure" in this diversity.

Here again the application to nations is easy and evident. All that we have said about the love of international benevolence proves the logic and the opportuneness of the comparison.

Meekness goes still farther and higher. It not only sets two human beings vis-à-vis in order that they may mutually reveal themselves; but it also brings them together to direct them to a higher good for which they will work together. Here we have an order of charity that transcends them in order to put them more completely in the service of God and their brethren.

The same is true of benevolent love; it inclines nations to strive together by a loyal and reciprocal collaboration, to seek the international common good and to realize "the indissoluble union of states," of which Pius XII said that, under the aspect of the common good in intrinsic relation to the unity of the human race, it was "a natural postulate."

Third element of the order of charity: effective action of collaboration, of mutual aid and solidarity, of service and devotion. In his 1940 Christmas message, Pius XII demanded that the cold egotism of nations be replaced by "a sincere juridical and economic solidarity, a fraternal collaboration among the nations." In the section of chapter three dealing with the duties of states, we shall explain the principal forms of this action, of this active charity.

A recent example will suffice here to indicate what fruits Pope Pius XII expected from fraternal international collaboration. On April 12, 1958, he received in audience an important delegation of French and Italian personalities, notably representatives of the territories of Africa and Madagascar. On that occasion he treated of the problem of exchanges between Europe and Africa for a common exploitation of the resources of the soil and subsoil of the African continent. At the end of chapter three we shall study this teaching on Eurafrica.

The wishes Pius XII expressed at the termination of the reception, which allowed him to treat with so much realism and courage a problem of international collaboration, where at the present hour material interests and national passions are at loggerheads, will furnish the best conclusion for the preceding pages. In that speech he gathered the three elements of the order of charity which we have drawn from his teaching: fraternal understanding, friendly good will, and "profound and lasting collaboration."

> We express the sincere wish that fraternal understanding and friendly good will may accompany your discussions and assure a profound and lasting collaboration among your different lands for the greatest good of all.

3. *Problem of International Charity: objections and difficulties it raises.* What is the nature of the charity that must animate

international relations and be the guarantee of peace? Pius XII answered:

> When We speak of charity, We desire to speak of that fruitful and generous charity that Christ has brought, of that charity that impelled the divine Redeemer to die for our salvation, of that charity that constrains us (Easter homily, April 9, 1939).

He then spoke of charity as a theological supernatural virtue that has its source in God: "God is love" (1 Jn 4:8), of an infused virtue diffused in our hearts by the Holy Spirit, which makes us participate in the very love of Christ for his Father and his brethren. "This is the sublime supernatural ideal of fraternal love brought into the world by Christ" (Christmas message, 1940).

At this point a number of objections present themselves with regard to states, to unbelievers and to Christians themselves.

First Objection: On the part of states. Charity touches persons who have a supernatural vocation to a life of union with God here below by the grace that is given to the soul of every human being, and eternally in the beatific vision. How can this be applied to states, which are moral persons and have only a temporary existence?

Reply. The word "state" can be understood in two legitimate but distinct senses: 1) the organized community of a nation. This work is concerned with the state in this wide sense. This does not prevent the study, within the limits of this vast conception, of the role of the state in the second sense: 2) the authority responsible for the common good of the particular nation.

In the first sense, supernatural charity has full sway in this sphere. It extends to all persons who make up a nation, whatever be their race, their color or their origin. It is universal. Pius XII explained the dynamism of Christian charity:

> It consists in this, that the Catholic Church teaches consciences to consider as one's neighbor not only this or that man, but an entire people, and not only a people, but the individuals of all peoples as brothers and sisters who profess the same faith in Christ and share the same Eucharistic table—and not only brothers and sisters of the same mother, the Church, but all men of the entire world, who, according to the precept of the only Redeemer, merit

respect, compassion and love (Discourse to the Italian Center of Studies for International Reconciliation, October 13, 1955).

Thus charity, traversing the obstacles of national egoisms, of age-old hatreds, of conflicts of interests among the nations, desires for all individuals of all these nations, for each one of them, not only their human well-being, which is a condition requisite for their development, but also their supernatural welfare, their salvation, their approach to God, their union with him.

In the second sense—the authority responsible for the common good—it is necessary to point out exactly how supernatural charity can be exercised.

In the first place, indirectly, by means of the authority serving the common good; it is after all human beings that are affected. The common good that the state must assure is the sum total of external conditions and the national public order that favors the development of the material, cultural, and spiritual life of the individuals subject to the state. In this connection, then, charity is a love for the mission of service of the common good which the state is called upon to fulfill with regard to persons: the mission "of safeguarding the intangible sphere of rights of the human person and of facilitating for him the fulfillment of his duties," (Message of June 1, 1941). Charity toward the state begets the desire that it should carry out in the most perfect manner possible its civilizing mission with regard to its own people.

Further, directly, one can consider human persons, no longer as individual objects whom the state ultimately affects in assuming the common good in their regard, but one may look upon them as living in society, in a community. Now, the role of the state in the realization of this form of collective human life is of capital importance. Here we enter the sphere of social charity.

Social charity goes beyond the natural order, the temporal common good. It considers individuals in society as oriented toward man's total destiny, as ordained toward an eternal good, the supreme Good. It desires a social order more worthy of a humanity redeemed by Christ, an order of social relations among men which prefigures here below the eternal city, where all men will love one another in God. Its principle is divine. It is the Holy Spirit who, by means of the Church, diffuses the life of charity in the members of the mystical body, and through the mediation of the Church this life is communicated to the body social. Hence, it runs like a supernatural current through human relations, everywhere inspiring the practice of a comprehensive, benevolent, active charity—the true and total love of men.

In this perspective the problem of the relations of Church and state takes on its full meaning. The Church, while respecting the autonomy of the state in its own sphere of the temporal order and pursuing its mission of supernatural charity toward all men, by the same token purifies men of their egoism, frees them from their passions, brings them together, unites them, creates or favors a climate of peace, of candor toward others, of fraternal collaboration. A state that hinders the supernatural mission of the Church does itself incalculable harm and attacks the essential rights and the fundamental liberties of its subjects, by setting itself at odds with their supernatural destiny and their life in community.

With the development of the international community, supernatural charity changes neither its nature nor its motive, but simply enlarges its scope. It desires, first of all, for each state the accomplishment of its mission of civilization, rising above everything that may tend to divide the states. Then it teaches each state its obligations over against the other states and the international community, develops in all of them the consciousness of the international common good, a will toward peace. It allows the states to share in its power and dynamism to inspire devotion, a passion to elevate humanity toward its supreme destiny. While fully respecting the functioning of the international community and leaving the international order intact, charity elevates and supernaturalizes it in order to lead it to God and to Christ the Redeemer.

Second Objection: Regarding unbelievers and those who live outside the Church. How is it possible to appeal to charity, a supernatural virtue, to animate an international order where Christians form only a minority and where the unbelievers, the indifferent, the patently hostile, the members of other religions are so numerous? The Holy Father always seems to consider the world as Christian. And yet, do not many live outside the visible Church?

Reply. On the contrary, even with his first encyclical *Summi Pontificatus*, Pius XII demonstrated his paternal solicitude for all those who do not belong to the visible organism of the Church. "Nor can we pass over in silence how pleasing to Us were the congratulations and good wishes of those who, though not belonging to the visible body of the Catholic Church, have not forgotten, by reason of the nobility and sincerity of their sentiments, all that by which they are bound to Us either by their love toward the person of Christ or by their belief in God. To all of them go Our sincere thanks!" He entrusted each and every one of them to the guidance and protection of the Lord, solemnly declaring, after the example of the Good Shepherd, that he had but one desire: ". . . that they may have life and have it more abundantly." Such was the charity of Pius XII toward those not belonging to the visible Church! He also showed in other ways that he had a bond of union even with these.

In another passage of the same encyclical he speaks of "so many brethren and sisters who, as a result of errors, of passions and of prejudices, have departed from the faith in the true God and separated themselves from the saving message of Jesus Christ." With regard to these, the charity of Christ constrains him. "What heart would not burn to come to their assistance?"

Finally, "even toward those for whom the hour of supreme enlightenment has not yet struck, Our heart knows nothing but love." In the Encyclical on the Mystical Body, he repeated to those who are outside the Church his loving invitation to listen to the appeal of the Savior.

> Without ever ceasing Our prayers to the Spirit of love and truth, We await them with Our arms opened wide, as men who knock at the door, not of a stranger's house, but of their own father's house.

This charity of Pope Pius XII—without limits, without frontiers, truly universal, entirely supernatural—ought to help Christians to discover the dimensions of charity and its mission on the international level. True, the Vicar of Christ exercises his jurisdiction as head over all the members of the visible Church, but his paternal affection extends to all men, to the whole of humanity.[7] He cannot help desiring for all of them, over and above material and cultural goods, that they may enjoy a more humane life, the supreme good of the soul; they are all called to a supernatural destiny. "God wishes all men to be saved" (1 Tim 2:4).

Why, then, is the true conception of supernatural charity resisted even by Christians? Because liberalism on the level of doctrine, and a certain tolerance in human relations, by confusing respect for the liberty of the believer with indifference with regard to the salvation of the individual outside the Church, have altered and minimized "the breadth and length and height and depth" of the Mystery of Christ and of his charity (Eph 3:18).

It is necessary to dissipate an ambiguity and to refute an error that form an obstacle to the deepening of charity. Some apparently see an attack on personal liberty in the desire to have all men join Christ and the Church. This is a serious error! Pius XII refuted it in the same passage of the Encyclical on the Mystical Body. Speaking of the desire that all the wandering sheep might soon return to the one flock of Jesus Christ, he said: "We declare, however, that it is absolutely necessary that this be done freely and entirely voluntarily, since no one can believe against his will." He went even farther. Considering the case of those who might be constrained to join the Church without believing and to receive the sacraments, he declared that "these beyond any doubt would not become true Christians," since faith, "without which it is impossible to please God" (Heb 11:6), must be "a free submission of the intellect and of the will" (First Vatican Council). Finally, without hesitating to judge contrary practices which perhaps were introduced here or there to force someone to embrace the Catholic faith in spite of himself, Pius XII pronounced this severe reprobation: "Conscious of Our duty, We cannot but condemn such a procedure" (Encyclical on the Mystical Body).

Thus freed from a preoccupation that might paralyze them

---

7. In his Christmas message of 1956, Pius XII recalled the words of Leo XIII uttered in 1899 on the eve of the first Peace Conference. "What moved [the Popes] was the impulse of a spiritual paternity, which binds men together as brothers and saves." And Pius XII added: "The same holds true today as yesterday."

with regard to their unbelieving brethren, Christians will understand, by embracing the example and the teaching of the Popes, that they must extend charity in all its strength. Then they will discover that true charity, elevated to sublime heights and drawing on the very heart of Christ, is the solid foundation of peace, and that it alone is capable of helping men to forgive one another, to subdue their individual or national egoism, to sacrifice themselves for the common good.

Third Objection: Offered by Christians themselves. "Oh, indeed, this program of international charity is very beautiful. In fact, it is too beautiful, too demanding. It seems inapplicable, too far removed from the hard realities of the struggle for life that goes on among the nations. It is unrealistic and gives the impression of appearing to ignore the actual drama of international relations."

Reply. No doubt, this ideal of charity is extremely high; it makes difficult demands. But, it is precisely this radicalism in love, in devotion, in giving that constitutes the incomparable power of Christian charity. To diminish it under the pretext of making it more bearable for humans takes away its dynamism. It must be understood, of course, that the order of charity cannot be immediately and rapidly established; this demands time, patience, and profound education for several generations. But it constitutes the ideal that must be striven for without ceasing. Christians have an obligation to try to approach it more day by day. They also have the duty, as of now, immediately, not to place voluntarily any obstacle in its progress, slow though it be, by their judgments, their omissions, their ignorance of the true nature of charity.

Far from ignoring the many obstacles that egotism and the passions of individuals and of nations place in the way of peace, such a program posits as its point of departure the tragic existence of the sin and egoism of men and of nations.

Until one has grasped precisely the nature of this obstacle of sin, he will not discover the supreme role of charity; he will not be convinced that evil belongs to the spiritual order, that it signifies a lack of love and that, consequently, the decisive remedy must be sought in the spiritual order and in love.

Apprehension is expressed that charity lacks realism. Without doubt, people are afraid that its implications may prevent them from perceiving, in international relations, the tricks of propaganda, the craftiness of diplomacy, the stratagems of politics; in a word, they fear they may be taken in.

An eminent specialist in the field of international public law, R. P. Delas, has studied very closely how the role of charity tends in fact to "humanize," to bring it about that juridical and political problems are posed by opponents in human terms, to concretize the state, administration, positive law (all of which have a natural tendency to be abstract, to empty themselves of their human substance and to be replaced by an annoying and arid formalism). He writes as follows: "Charity is a great realist that flees abstraction; it maintains contact with life because it loves life" (*Semaine sociale de Paris*, 1928, p. 415).

But let us consider particularly the reflections of Pope Pius XII; these dominate the whole problem of the international order (as explained in this second chapter) and the entire design of God (presented in the first). After showing how negligence, disorder, negation and contempt with regard to Christian thought and principles had led the world to catastrophe and the tragedy of war, Pius XII gave this teaching:

> If, then, the root of the evil lies here, only one remedy remains: to return to the order established by God Himself in the relations among states and nations, to come back to true Christianity in the state and among the states. Let no one say that this is unrealistic politics! Experience should have taught everyone that politics oriented toward the eternal realities and the laws of God is the most realistic and the most concrete of politics. Realistic politics conceived in any other manner creates only ruins (Allocution to the College of Cardinals, December 24, 1945).

The true greatness of a nation does not consist in its multiplying tanks, destructive weapons, landing fields, but rather in its fidelity to a supreme moral law, in its active cooperation with the international community, and in its will to serve always more loyally the ideal of charity among the nations and the absolute values it contains.

Throughout this chapter, charity is understood in its twofold form of love of God and love of neighbor. We have seen the role of love of neighbor in the relations among nations—and the "neighbor" is the African, the Chinese, the Japanese, the Australian, the man of every race and color. As far as the love of God is concerned, it constrains the members of every nation to respect the design of God regarding the unity of the international community, to collaborate in its realization, "to return to the order established by God in the relations among states and nations," according to the papal program elaborated above.

AN ORDER OF PEACE

In his radio message addressed to the entire world in the midst of war (Christmas, 1941), Pius XII enumerated five essential prerequisites "of an international order that assures to all nations a just and lasting peace, fruitful of well-being and of prosperity."

This order rests on a Christian conception of peace. We shall study it in the pontifical documents particularly with regard to the two principal elements: 1) the divine foundation of peace; 2) the true nature of peace.

1. *The divine foundation of peace.* "The precept of peace is of divine law." God desires peace. "He is the God of peace. He created the world as a dwelling place of peace. He has given His commandment of peace" (Christmas Message, 1948).

God's design for the world is a design of peace. He sent his Son, Jesus Christ, into the world as the Savior and Redeemer of the human race to bring it peace. Jesus is "the Prince of peace," as the prophet Isaias foretold. "His exalted and divine mission is to establish peace between each man and God, among men themselves and among nations" (Christmas Message, 1951).

In order to remain faithful to God's design, to co-operate in carrying it out in the world, Christians must have a desire for peace.

This consists of more than experiencing a feeling for humanity in the presence of the horrors of war. Unfortunately, even among Christians, confusion exists on this point. Let us listen to Pope Pius XII's radio message of December 24, 1948, addressed to the entire world:

> Supporting itself on God and on the order established by Him, the Christian desire for peace is strong as steel. It has quite a

different temper from the simple feeling for humanity, too often
based on pure sentimentality, which detests war only because of
its horrors and atrocities, its destruction and its consequences,
but not because of its injustice.

True, one cannot help feeling deep sorrow at the atrocious
tragedy of war. Many times, in gripping words, Pius XII described his feelings as a father in the face of the ravages of war
and its inhuman character. But in him all his anguish was intense
compassion for the sufferings of men, and at the same time and
above all an expression of the rending of his soul at the sight of
the "injustice" of war, at the sight of the violation of God's design
of love for mankind and of the contempt for the almighty and
eternal God's desire for peace.

The sentiment of peace, taken by itself, is fragile. It has a
materialistic origin, a utilitarian character. Regarding this sentiment, Pius XII declared in the same Christmas message of 1948:

> It prepares the ground in which take root the deceitful illusion of
> sterile compromise, the attempt to save one's self at the expense
> of others, and in every case it favors the aggressor.

On the other hand, the will for peace derives its power from
the fact that it is based on an unconditioned and indisputable
obligation, on a formal commandment of God, on the divine
precept of peace, on the redeeming message of Jesus Christ and
of the Gospel of salvation and of peace he brought to the world.
It is no longer allowed to those who, although believers, base
their doctrine of peace not on the doctrine of the Church, but
on the theses of excessive nationalism, to ridicule those Christians
who are attached to peace. "It behooves us," said Pius XII, "to
desire peace in a sincere and Christian manner."

This Christian will for peace places those who love it between
two contrary errors. On the one hand are the "pacifists," who
demand peace at any price, no matter what peace, even that of
injustice; they encourage those who are preparing aggression. On
the other are the "bellicists," who, abusing the axiom "If you
want peace, prepare for war," provoke suspicion and mistrust.
"Both of them," concluded the Holy Father, "without wishing it,
compromise the cause of peace."

The Christian will for peace reveals itself by certain characteristics: it consists in a loving submission to the design of God

and to his will; it has weapons, the principal ones being prayer and love—peaceful arms that come from God.

It never turns an issue of prestige and of national honor into war or even a threat of war. It carefully abstains from pursuing by force of arms the vindication of rights, which, however legitimate they may be, would not compensate for the risk of provoking a conflict with all its terrible consequences, both spiritual and material.

The Christian will for peace is practical and realistic. "Its immediate goal is the suppression or at least the diminution of causes of tension that morally and materially aggravate the danger of war." The Christian will for peace can be recognized by the fact that it takes an unequivocal position with regard to war; it adheres wholeheartedly to the doctrine of the Church on this point, as we shall explain it in chapter five.

2. *Definition of peace: its true nature.* What is peace? To begin with, Pius XII remarked to a group of United States senators on November 1, 1947, that it has a positive character and a noble dignity. . . . It is certainly something more than the simple absence of war and of bloodshed.

It is necessary to return to the celebrated and profound definition of St. Augustine. "Peace is the tranquility of order." Pius XII then continued:

And what is order? Order consists in an arrangement of components, equal or unequal, obtained by assigning to each its proper place. Let each and every element keep its proper place or return to it. Affirm this order in such a way that it be lasting, and its fruit will be gathered with calm assurance. You will then have introduced peace into God's world. This is an admirable formula, perfectly exact, comprehensive, elegant. No other has ever been advanced to replace it or to equal it. It echoes the divine message of the Redeemer; it expresses the immortal tradition of the Church.

Several elements of order may be drawn from this definition: first, the plurality and the diversity of the components; then, the assignment of each to its place in the ensemble (there is order in a house when everything is in its place); finally, unity in the universal harmony of human society. The character of stability is bound up with attachment to this order.

It is easy to verify and to apply this definition to peace in international public order.

Peace appears as a fruit, an effect, or even better, a synthesis of various elements which enter as components into international public order, each of the elements having its place in the unity of the whole.

The order of peace implies essentially an order of justice and of charity in relations among nations. It demands, as a necessary condition, an order of truth, of liberty, of security in the structures, the organisms, the means toward relations among the nations. To be an *order*, it must always be animated by the tendency to realize in the most perfect and most lasting manner the unity of human society in the harmony of the community of nations.

The order of peace must be constructed anew every day; it is not a tranquil, slothful, do-nothing and egotistical enjoyment of situations inherited or established by men and nations, often unjustly. On the contrary, it demands laborious, persevering efforts, replete with sacrifices on the part of men, of states, of rulers resolved to serve the common good of their nation and that of the international community. In other words, if one wishes to get to the bottom of the problem of peace, it has essentially a spiritual character.

This is a principle that Pius XII constantly stressed: "The crux of the problem is now of a spiritual order; it means spiritual deficiency or defect," as he put it in his Christmas message of 1951.

It suffices simply to enumerate some of the obstacles to peace diagnosed by Pius XII himself in his message in order to understand the serious admonition he offered to our times: hatred, lies, mistrust, utility taken as the rule and foundation of rights, might creating right, frigid egoism, the insatiable hunger for earthly goods, the overweening desire for prestige, the disordered appetite of an unleashed nationalism, forgetfulness and rejection of the law of universal morality, contempt for or negation of the supreme authority of God and the redeeming message of Christ and of the Christian order. All these causes belong to the spiritual order; they constantly place peace in jeopardy. "Everyone must be persuaded that the danger of war has primarily a spiritual character."

To neglect this spiritual aspect of the problem of peace, whether voluntarily or through ignorance, means to see only one side of the questions affecting peace. As a result, peace will be made to depend solely on the question of material arms. Undoubtedly, this calls for serious consideration. Pius XII denounced "the monstrous cruelty of modern weapons." He insistently called for disarmament, for the simultaneous and reciprocal reduction of armaments, as we shall see in chapter four. But besides these material weapons, there are those of a psychological and moral nature, which are also dangerous where the Christian sense no longer exercises its influence to dominate them and where the Christian ethic has been rejected.

Peace and force. It must of course be understood that peace is not solely spiritual and that, to establish it, the role of force must not be rejected or denied. In his 1943 Christmas message, Pius XII determined these relations of peace and force:

> True peace is not the mathematical result, so to speak, of a proportion of forces, but, in its ultimate and deepest signification, a moral and juridical action. It cannot, in fact, be realized without a deployment of force, and even its stability calls for a normal measure of power. But the proper function of this force, if its use is to be morally correct, must serve to protect and to defend, not to diminish and to suppress right.

Role of the Church in establishing and safeguarding peace. Since the problem of peace is principally a spiritual and moral problem, the Church contributes powerfully to the preservation of peace.

> The Church desires peace. She does the works of peace, and her heart is with all those who, like herself, desire it and labor for it. She desires it and for that reason she promotes everything that, within the realm of the divine, natural and supernatural orders, helps to assure peace (Allocution to the members of the Universal Movement for a World Confederation, April 6, 1951).

In particular, by revealing the spiritual character of peace, which till now has escaped an immense multitude of men and rulers, the Church fulfills a unique mission. She excites and stimulates "the practical understanding of the spiritual crux of the problem," in the words of the 1951 Christmas message.

Finally, by propagating Christian principles, the Church works for the peace of the world; for peace is dependent on the principles brought to men by Christ.

> Peace can come only from the principles and the norms taught by Christ and put into practice with sincerity and loyalty. In effect, they recall men and nations to truth, to justice and to charity. They set a curb to their cupidity. They oblige feelings to submit to reason and reason to obey God. They command all, also those who govern nations, to recognize the liberty due to religion, which, besides its primary purpose of leading souls to eternal salvation, sustains and protects the very foundations of the state (Encyclical *Summi maeroris*, July 19, 1950).

It is well known that the Scholastic philosophers, following Aristotle, have reduced the analysis of every being to four causes: material, formal, efficient and final. As far as this powerful synthesis of an international public order is concerned, which Pius XII integrated in his vision of the world, could not the metaphysics of causes suggest an application that might be fruitful of deep reflections?

In this public order to be established, the *final* cause would be peace. The end, the goal to pursue, is the object chosen by the will. The final cause is a good to acquire, the terminus that specifies the actions of men—and here of nations—by impelling them to act. Now, peace is truly the goal that all nations desire to attain by organizing their international community.

For his part, Pius XII said in 1948, in his discourse to the Ambassador of Brazil, that only the desire of making his attitude always more conformable to the precept, to the example of Christ, who entrusted to Peter and to his successors the task of confirming his brethren in the faith, had animated his untiring and persevering efforts "to lay the moral, juridical, economic and social bases and foundations for a peace in conformity with the will of God and the dignity of the human race."

The *efficient* cause is that which acts and creates. In this order of law, which must assure and guarantee the relations between nations, justice is called upon to fulfill the functions of "efficiency." Justice begets peace. *Opus iustitiae pax*—"Peace is the work of justice": this was the motto of Pius XII. Justice constructs peace with the loyal collaboration of men and of nations—of all those who recognize the natural law—in the mutual respect of rights and the mutual accomplishment of duties.

The *formal* cause is the actual principle that gives "form" to a being, specifies it and enlivens it. In the international public order charity carries out this role, because it brings about unity of hearts and spirits in seeking for God's design for the unity of the community of nations, and promotes its realization through love for him and for men. On the human plane it inspires everything that serves to bring men and nations together in understanding, benevolence and collaboration.

The *material* cause is the potential element, as the philosophers say, the element capable of being determined, of being "informed" by the formal cause.

When there is question of a particular nation, the subjects and their families constitute the material cause. In the international community, the remote material cause is the subjects; the proximate material cause, the nations that must be organized or put in order, or who must organize themselves or put themselves in order with a view to the common good; in other words, the beings and the nations to be organized in a public order and their relations.

It is customary, too, to attach to the material cause, as disposing causes, the sum total of external conditions without which the international public order would be neither possible nor stable. As a matter of fact, how can its construction be undertaken and pursued if lying propaganda incites the nations against one another (hence without an order of truth, of veracity); if a police state or a "machine" imposed by force bends all wills under the dictatorship of one man or one party, hungering for prestige, for domination, for conquest (hence without an order of liberty); if, finally, the independence and the rights of the nations are endlessly threatened (hence without an order of security)?

3

*R*IGHTS AND DUTIES OF STATES

> *. . . the meaning of a community willed by*
> *God, which includes reciprocal rights and*
> *duties, regulated by determined laws.*
> —PIUS XII, Christmas Message, 1947

FOR A long time the problem of the rights and duties of states in the international sphere did not pose itself to governments or nations. To discover the political morals of the old Europe, one should read, not without astonishment, the study of the eminent historian, Albert Sorel,[1] *L'Europe et la Revolution.*

In this purview the state is supreme. The reason of state is the foundation of all politics. Machiavelli is less a theoretician than an observer. The growth of the state by any means whatsoever, including conquest, constitutes the object of all politics. In the diplomacy of the old Europe the only rule of conduct was deceit. There was no guarantee that agreements would be respected. Preventive wars were even justified. Whatever seemed necessary was considered right.

There was no principle of order; there was no international public law based on principles. Custom, resting on empirical maxims, was taken as a rule of thumb. Reason of State was the

---

1. We stated that the problem of rights and duties did not present itself "to governments and nations." We may not pass over in silence the efforts of teachers and theologians to introduce morality into war: from St. Augustine to Taparelli (in the nineteenth century, coming through St. Thomas in the thirteenth, Vitoria and Suarez in the sixteenth). The theology of a just war will be discussed in chapter five.

ultimate motive, intrigue was the means, might supplanted right.

If there were any limits to the absolute sovereignty of the state, they were determined purely by its self-interest. It undertook to obtain by conquest only what would offer it a definite advantage and what it could retain. On the other hand, the ambition of the state had as its limit the ambition of the other nations. What is called European equilibrium is in reality nothing more than the balance of forces opposed to one another, the opposition of interests.

If neighboring states experienced difficulties, that was cause for rejoicing; that anarchy and chaos should rule there was ardently desired.[2] In fact, revolutions were favored, factions were encouraged. No idea of international solidarity existed; only the self-interests of the state counted.

The idea of rights and duties appeared in the nineteenth century with the awakening of the concept of an international society and the realization of their interdependence on the part of the states—thanks to the rapid development of means of communication and the evolution of ideas, as was noted in the first chapter. The problem of rights and duties of states now assumes enormous importance; as long as these rights and duties remain undetermined, the accomplishment of duties remains very difficult and the door lies open to unjustified claims, to the unlimited ambitions of certain states, to all the causes of conflict. But how are the rights and duties of states to be determined?

On what basis can a list of the rights and duties of states be drawn up? A great deal of hesitation exists because the principles of the natural law are not recognized. At one extreme the positivist conceptions are unacceptable—namely, that states possess only those rights granted them by the letter of treaties, that in fact they do not possess any fundamental rights.

Some authors[3] hold that fundamental rights have their origin in the common feeling of men regarding the absolute necessity

2. E.g., Choiseul said of England: "We are not desirous of seeing a solid ministry established in England. Indeed, I hope that anarchy will not soon cease. I should wish it to last a century." Louis XIV said of Russia: "Everything that serves to plunge it into chaos and to reduce it to obscurity is advantageous to my interests."

3. E.g., M. Sibert, *Traité de Droit international public* (Dalloz, 1951), I, p. 226.

of such rights for maintaining international solidarity and peace.

What are these fundamental rights? A list was presented by the International Juridical Union in its "Declaration of the Rights and Duties of Nations" of November 11, 1919. This expressly attributes to every nation three fundamental rights: the right of existence, the right of independence, the right of equality. Three years before, on January 6, 1916, the American Institute of International Law had voted a "Declaration of the Rights and Duties of Nations" which was more complete, recognizing the following fundamental rights of states: the right to existence, the right of independence, the right of equality before the law, the right of possessing an exclusive territory and jurisdiction, the right to the respect and protection of the other nations.

The enumeration of rights and duties varies according to the authors. Taken as a whole, however, their differences are slight.

The doctrine of Pope Pius XII must be set in this historical and juridical context; and then we can appreciate its high authority, its power, and its urgency.

The high authority of this doctrine derives from the fact that it was given to the entire world, rising above the bitter struggles which divided nations, at a critical time when the entire structure of international relations, built up with so much labor and difficulty by the League of Nations, seemed about to collapse for good. At a moment when one could hardly speak of rights and duties of nations without being regarded as a utopian and a dreamer and while a great head of state, Roosevelt, prepared to play a capital role in this field, a man rose above all conflicts to make himself the defender of international law, by recalling to the powerful ones of his day its absolute demands. One could say that Pius XII incarnated international morality and law, whether in the encyclical *Summi Pontificatus* (October, 1939), which contains his entire program, or in his Christmas messages during the terrible war years (1939-1945). On the very eve of war, August 24, 1939, in his radio message to governments and peoples, Pius XII delivered a most heart-rending appeal in favor of peace:

> We implore you by the blood of Christ, whose strength is Our support, conscious that all men of feeling, all those who thirst for justice, all those who suffer are with Us [here follows a mov-

ing enumeration of mothers, fathers, the laborers, the young, etc.].
With Us is the whole human race that hungers for justice, bread
and liberty, not for steel.

Truly, at this decisive hour the Pope was the voice and the
conscience of all humanity. The conversations of Dumbarton
Oaks did not begin till August 21, 1944. The Declaration of Pots-
dam on the part of the allied heads of state came only on August
2, 1945. The charter of the United Nations was signed on June
26, 1945.

The power of his teaching derives from the fact, as we have
seen in chapter one, that it is based on the natural law, the expression of this moral law ". . . whose observance must be
applied through the public opinion of all nations and of all states
with such unanimity of voice and power that no one may dare
to doubt it or to weaken its binding force," as the 1941 Christmas
message has it.

The relevance of his teaching emerges very clearly, particularly
in this chapter, when we compare his list of rights and duties
with those drawn up by contemporary authors on international
public law, or with the fundamental principles for a lasting
peace as enunciated in the resolution adopted by the General
Assembly of the United Nations in its twenty-sixth plenary session
(December 1, 1949). Let us remark, however, that Pius XII goes
farther in his appeal to the demands of the moral law; even now
these have not been entirely incorporated into the prescriptions
of positive law or international conventions. In this way again
Pius was an inspirer, he was ahead of concrete realizations; he
showed the way to follow in order to give peace a law, and a
just and lasting organization.

FUNDAMENTAL RIGHTS OF STATES

In *Summi Pontificatus,* Pius XII affirmed the necessity for nations to recognize and observe the principles of international
natural law regulating their normal development and functioning,
for these principles, he added, "demand respect for the rights of
each nation to independence, to life, to the possibility of progressive evolution in the ways of civilization."

This is the first enumeration of the essential rights of every nation: He wanted to defend three rights against the menace of the totalitarian states; but they also contain others that will be discussed explicitly later.

In his Christmas message of 1939, Pius XII stated as a fundamental postulate of a just and honorable peace the guarantee of the two essential rights to life and independence on the part of all nations, great and small, powerful and weak.

The two most complete lists of the rights of nations are contained in two of his discourses. The first, the allocution to the Union of Italian Catholic Jurists, December 6, 1953, enumerates five rights:

> . . . the right of existence, the right to respect and reputation, the right to their own character and culture, the right to develop themselves, the right to the observance of international treaties . . .

The second, to the Italian Center of Studies for International Reconciliation, October 13, 1955, repeats the same enumeration with one difference: ". . . the right of using the goods of the earth for the preservation of life." The affirmation of this right had already been anticipated in the passage in the 1941 Christmas message on "the necessity of participation on the part of all in the goods of the earth"—a protest against the monopolizing of economic resources by certain nations.

Despite the completeness of these enumerations, Pius himself pointed out that it was not exhaustive and definitive. In his discourse of December 6, 1953, after giving a list of the five principal rights, he added: ". . . and other equivalent rights."

Pius XII offered this table of the rights of states as expressing "the exigencies of the law of nations which nature dictates." We shall study them successively.

1. *The right to life:*

A fundamental postulate of a just and honorable peace is the assurance of the right to life and independence on the part of all nations, great and small, powerful and weak. One nation's will to live must never be equivalent to the death sentence of another. When this equality of rights has been infringed upon or destroyed or jeopardized, the juridical order demands reparation, whose degree and extent are determined not by the sword or arbitrary egoism, but by the norms of reciprocal justice and equity (Christmas Message, 1939).

This text calls for some remarks. Pius affirmed the right to life of *nations*. In this chapter, as in treatises on international law, the fundamental rights and duties of *states* are determined. In fact, the two terms are very often used interchangeably. In certain texts Pius joins them together.

In law, it is necessary to distinguish the two social realities, as we shall see in chapter four in dealing with nationalism. The *nation* is a natural milieu offering its members the human values of civilization. Pius XII defines national life as "the active totality of all the values of civilization which are proper to a determined group, which characterize it and constitute the bond of its spiritual unity." It is a cultural patrimony, composed of particular traditions, of mores and of a special manner of life, of language, of education. These values make up a common good of the members of the nation; they are the foundation of the duties of these members toward their nation; they are also the foundation of the nation's right to life, to self-preservation, and to development of this whole national life, a right that other nations must respect.

The *state,* on the other hand, is a political and juridical organization, whose purpose is to assure the common good of the nation. Hence it must protect the values of the national life, respect them, just as it must respect other spiritual values that transcend it. If it fulfills its mission toward its citizens and is capable of carrying out its international obligations, then it has a right to existence, and other states must recognize it in the sphere of international society.

Pius here speaks also of a nation's right to "life." This term is very rich, since there is question of the life of a nation, of national life. When there is question of the state, then we speak of the right to existence. Certain writers on international public law state that in reality states, natural and moral personalities, have only one fundamental right, the right to existence; from this flow all the other rights (right to self-preservation, right to liberty).

For a nation what must be respected is the right not to be smothered, destroyed, absorbed, the right to occupy its place in the community of nations, the right not only to physical and moral preservation, but to a dynamic development in its economic, cultural and social life.

Placed in its historical context, the text reveals its full meaning. In his Christmas message of 1939, Pius XII denounced "the premeditated aggression against a small, industrious, peaceful nation under the pretext of a threat which neither existed, nor was considered, nor was even possible." He was referring to the invasion of Finland (November-December, 1939) by Russia, then bound to Germany by a non-aggression pact. Pius XII condemned this aggression, putting it among "the acts that are just as irreconcilable with the prescriptions of international public law as with those of the natural law and even with the most elementary sentiments of humanity."

In the name of the demands of the international moral law, he then proposed five fundamental points as the basis of a just and honorable peace. At the head of the list of these five postulates he put the right to life for each nation, be it great or small, powerful or weak.

Since a nation might invoke the principle of the right to life and the will to live, of the right to "living space," as the Germany of Hitler's day did, the Holy Father fixed limits to any abusive appeal to this right. No state may invoke this right in order to attack another state's right to existence. "The will to live of one nation can never be equivalent to the death sentence of another nation." In such a situation and from that hour the Holy Father demanded reparation in justice and equity, in face of the armies that had invaded Finland and Poland.

In precisely what sense must the right to life on the part of each nation be understood? Another Christmas message, that of 1941 on "the foundations of a new order," points it out to us.

At that time Hitler's Germany was beginning to speak of a "new order." Pius XII did not want to see this term monopolized by the totalitarian states nor did he want it deprived of its true meaning. In view of the pretensions of National Socialism to aggrandizement, in view of the successes obtained by Germany and Italy in that year, the Pope, in his Christmas message of 1941, defended the rights of small nations. He showed very clearly that he did not accept as a *fait accompli* the victories of the totalitarian states which were extending their domination over southeastern Europe. In that year of 1941, small nations had been conquered and occupied: Jugoslavia, Greece, Crete. Others—Hungary, Bulgaria—were drawn into the tripartite pact.

Already at this time the Pope was turning to the future. He was thinking of a "new organization," but one that would be "founded on moral principles." He affirmed the right of the small nations "to respect for their political liberty, to the effective maintenance of their neutrality in the conflicts between states, according to natural and international law, to the protection of their economic development."

> In the purview of a new organization founded on moral principles there will be no place for the violation of the liberty, the integrity, and the security of other nations, whatever be their territorial extent or their ability to defend themselves.

Specifically, this entails the right of a nation to liberty, the right to live freely and freely to preserve its religious, spiritual and cultural traditions, without being at every instant exposed to threats by an invading state that wants to impose its own philosophical system and totalitarian doctrines. The liberty to choose the form of government that it wants, its constitution, its internal legislation, always respecting the rights of other nations, without having to fear the interference of other states through force or threats. The right also for a nation to organize and to administer its public services freely according to the policies it has adopted, and finally, the right to exercise its judiciary powers over persons and things.

This also involves the right of a nation to integrity, the right of a nation to take all the necessary measures to protect its territorial integrity and its intellectual, spiritual and moral integrity, by organizing its internal police, by defending the inviolability of its territorial integrity against an unjust aggressor, by preserving its neutrality in the conflicts between two or more other nations. The Pope made it clear, however, that it must do these things "according to natural and international law"—there will be other cases in which, in the name of the same natural and international law, a nation will have the duty not to regard itself merely as a simple spectator in an attitude of impossible neutrality. This also holds true when higher interests of humanity are threatened by an unjust aggressor, as we shall see in chapter five, regarding the question of war.

Furthermore, there is the right to security. In the absence of the very far-reaching reforms that the Popes have proposed in order to substitute the force of law for the material force of arms, each state has the right and the duty to organize its security for the sake of self-defense and not for aggression: military defense (troops, armaments, fortifications, etc.); defensive alliances with other states; non-aggression pacts. A state likewise has the right to protect its security against the menace of bellicose propaganda that creates dangerous complications for peace within the country.

It is interesting to note in the resolution adopted by the General Assembly of the UN on December 1, 1949, a passage that reflects the thought of Pius XII, but with an essential difference. The Pope quite simply affirmed these rights; the Assembly rather timidly invited all nations "to abstain from every threat and every act, direct or indirect, calculated to compromise the liberty, the independence or the integrity of any state, to foment intestine struggles or to oppress the will of the people in any State whatsoever."

2. *The right to independence.* Together with the right to life, Pius XII asserted, as a fundamental postulate, the right to independence, in the passage of the Christmas message of 1939 as well as in the Encyclical *Summi Pontificatus.*

The term is used in order to define the nature of the relations of one state with another, hence it is concerned with the external order. The right to independence implies that a state may fulfill its own mission with complete adequacy recognized by international law, without being subjected to the interference of other states in this sphere and without being placed in a position of juridical dependence to any state whatsoever.

The word "sovereignty" is likewise employed to define the state's exercise of its mission with complete adequacy, but it has need of being clearly defined.

In this community of nations, each state is then inserted into the organization of international law and thereby into the order of the natural law, which supports and crowns the whole. Consequently it is not—and never was—"sovereign" in the sense of a total absence of limits. In the true sense of the word, "sovereignty" signifies autarchy and exclusive competence with regard to the handling of the affairs of a particular territory, always within the realm of international law, without, however, becoming dependent on the juridical system of any other state. Every state is immediately subject to international law. States which would lack this fullness of power, or whose independence of the power of any other state would not be guaranteed by international law, would not be sovereign. Yet no state could complain about a limitation of its sovereignty, if it were denied the power of acting arbitrarily and without regard for other states. Sovereignty is not a divinization of the all-powerful state, more or less in the Hegelian sense or after the fashion of absolute juridical positivism (Discourse to Italian Catholic Jurists, December 6, 1953).

Three ideas stand out in this text. First, there is a condemnation of the state's absolute sovereignty, independent of all moral law.

There does not and there cannot exist an absolute sovereignty of the state, in the sense of "a total absence of limits," or a total liberation from every higher law, from every moral law, from every international authority. In chapter four, on the obstacles to the community of nations, we shall study this doctrinal error.

Second, there is a statement of the true meaning of sovereignty. A sovereign state is one that is not subordinated to any other state. It is sovereign if, possessing fullness of power, it is in a position to reject the interference of other states in the exercise of its own functions. "Sovereignty" in the true sense of the word signifies self-government and exclusive competence—without being subject to the juridical organization of any other state.

The first condition of true sovereignty, then, is fullness of power. There is a second: a guarantee, by international law, of this independence with regard to the authority of any other state. States lacking these two conditions would not be sovereign. Thence comes a third idea enunciated by the Pope, as a logical consequence of the second condition: the independence of states within the framework of international law.

In the text we are studying Pius XII lays great stress on a third idea: the insertion of each state into the order of international law and, through it, into the order of the natural law which supports and crowns the whole. Hence every state is directly subject to international law, which acknowledges, guarantees and protects its independence. But the state has the obligation of respecting international law and, in co-operation with all the other members, to promote the common good of the community of nations.

3. *Right of equality before the law.* "Every nation is a member, with equal rights, of the family of nations." In these terms Pius XII, in his Christmas message of 1948, affirmed the right of equality for all nations, whatever be their territorial extent or their ability to defend themselves.

Here again the position taken by the Holy Father manifested a noble and unvaried tradition. He constantly showed himself the defender of the rights of small nations in the face of powerful states. In order to understand better both the courage and the realism of the papal teaching on this point, it suffices to place it in its actual setting.

For a long time—and this held true even in the nineteenth century—the equality of the rights of states was denied. The great powers readily presumed to possess a higher authority in settling conflicts. Not a few were even of the opinion that the existence of small states was an obstacle or at least a disturbing factor in the harmony of international life. But on the contrary, it must be recognized that they are an element of equilibrium, of wisdom, in the great international assemblies; they have no ambition of conquest; they are the sure defenders of international law, because they place their weakness under its protection; they are concerned about justice and rights.[4]

The principle of the juridical equality of nations was proclaimed at the first Peace Conference in 1899, as well as at the second in 1907. It has been accepted in international jurisprudence in matters of arbitration. Article 1, § 2, of the charter of the United Nations, solemnly proclaims it.[5]

4. *Code de Morale Internationale* (Paris, Spes, 1951), p. 29.
5. The United Nations propose "to develop among the nations friendly relations, based on respect for the principle of the equality of rights of nations."
Several practical consequences flow from this principle: every State's

On this particular point, the teaching of Pius XII can be summed up in a few principles:

Equality of rights of all nations, large and small, must be admitted; that is to say, every nation, no matter how weak, enjoys equal rights with every other nation, so far as law is concerned.

This principle is simply the application of the fundamental equality of nature and purpose which all nations possess, as was stated in chapter one in dealing with the foundation of the community of nations.

Accidental inequalities do in fact exist, and these must be kept in mind. The great states, for example, possess vast political and economic power. Quite naturally they will take the initiative in forming economic groups into which the small nations will necessarily be drawn. Pius XII, whose doctrine is always realistic, examined these cases, but even there he discovered a way to recall the demands of the principle and to protect the liberty and the rights of small nations, their legitimate neutrality, and their economic development for the common good of their people. Thus, in his Christmas message for 1941, he said:

> If it is inevitable that the great states, because of their greater possibilities and their power, should lead the way in the formation of economic groups among themselves and the smaller and weaker nations, one can still maintain, in the field of general interest, the right of these weaker ones (as of every nation) to respect for their liberty in the political sphere, to self-preservation, to their neutrality in the conflicts between states by reason of the natural law and international law, to the defense of their economic development, since only in this way can they adequately attain the common good, the material and spiritual well-being of their own people.

---

right to have a seat and to speak at international assemblies and diplomatic congresses; the right to an equal voting power (in fact, there is a violation of this principle affirmed by the charter in the veto which the five great powers have reserved to themselves and which creates constant obstacles to decisions); the right of each state to participate in the establishment of necessary organs of international institutions; the right of a state to escape from the interpretation of a treaty which another state would seek to impose, etc. As a matter of fact, however, the large nations exercise superior power.

If absolute equality is difficult to attain, the solidarity that must exist and in fact does exist among nations demands the disappearance, as soon as possible, of the great disproportions in the standard of living of the nations, their investments and the employment of their manpower.

Patently the Pope here went beyond juridical equality. He reached to the plane of international solidarity and showed forth its demands, and its obligatory character in the movement toward economic equality or at least toward a cessation of a lopsided disparity. As he said in his Christmas message of 1952:

> While it is true that the perfect realization of international solidarity can only with difficulty lead to an absolute equality of nations, still it is urgent that it be practiced at least to the extent of definitely changing existing conditions, which are far from reflecting a harmonious proportion. In other words, the solidarity of nations calls for the cessation of the enormous disproportions in the standard of living and, correlatively, in investments and the degree of productivity of human labor.

4. *Right to respect.* International law upholds the principle that states have a right to respect for their moral dignity, their material prosperity, their political and administrative personality. They may not treat each other offensively, but must exhibit the conventional honors. They may not interfere unduly in the economic development of other states nor violate their territorial integrity. They may not injure each other in the functioning of public services, but must reciprocally respect their civil personalities. Sanctions for offenses in this field are provided for in the law.

The right to respect and to the reputation of a nation includes "reciprocal esteem" and forbids contempt for a nation. Pius XII here struck at the root of numerous violations of this right:

> Reciprocal esteem . . . no contempt for a nation because, for example, it may appear less richly endowed than one's own nation. Contempt of this kind would manifest purblindness. Comparison of national aptitudes must take into consideration the most diverse fields, and to make such a comparison demands deep knowledge and long experience . . . (Discourse of Pius XII to the pilgrims of Pax Christi, September 13, 1952).

". . . respect for the right of every nation to exercise its activity. This right cannot be artificially limited or hamstrung by forcible measures" (*ibid.*).

In other circumstances, too, Pius stressed this respect for the economic activity of a nation. There, too, the Pope was thinking of small nations, too often the victims of politics, of prestige or political and economic pressure on the part of a powerful neighboring state.

> It behooves the nations not to permit themselves to be drawn along by motives of prestige or outmoded ideas to create political or economic difficulties for the interior development of other nations, while they ignore or take no thought for the common peril (Christmas message, 1950).

Pius XII was always solicitous about the defense of the small nations and for their right to respect on the part of the larger nations. In his allocution to the Sacred College of June 2, 1943, he said:

> Our thought and Our affection go out to the small nations, those, namely, which, because of their geographical or geopolitical position—considering the present disrespect for both international juridical and moral norms—are exposed more readily to be drawn into the conflicts of the great powers until they see their lands, become the theater of devasting struggles, afflicted with unspeakable horrors which do not spare noncombatants and destroy the flower of their youth and of their intellectual classes. You do not expect Us to describe here, even partially, all that has been attempted and tried by Us to diminish their sufferings, to ameliorate their juridical and moral situation, to defend their basic religious rights, to help them in their distress and their need.

Several days after this discourse, Pius XII returned to the subject of the rights of small nations when speaking to the new ambassador of one of them, Finland, June 26, 1943. It is necessary, he said, that ". . . the need of living space and the demands of the relations of neighborliness be equally applicable to the great and small, to the strong and to the weak."

5. *Right of a state to self-development.* A state has the right to develop and "to have the possibility of a progressive evolution in the ways of civilization," in the phrase of the *Summi*

Pontificatus. It has a right to develop its economic, industrial, commercial and agricultural life, always observing, be it understood, the rights of other nations and the demands of the international common good. Besides, international solidarity has an interest in this development of nations. The 1952 Christmas message states

> . . . that every nation, as far as the standard of living and the employment of its labor force are concerned, must develop its possibilities and contribute to the parallel progress of other nations less well endowed.

In particular, a state has the right to population growth.

In the light of this right, one will be able to judge more clearly a very real problem that will tend to become more acute with the passing of time—that of demographic Malthusianism, presented by international propaganda as the remedy to the problem of famine in underdeveloped countries. According to this doctrine, population must be brought into line with the quantity of foodstuffs available in a country. No doubt, we are here faced with a serious problem, one in which morality must also play a part with its concept of the person and of society. But the problem is illusory if it allows of only one alternative: either diminish the number of human beings or aggravate still further the tragedy of famine.

Another solution remains—a solution of progress, of solidarity of nations and of humanity; a collaboration of the entire community to supply sufficient foodstuffs for the whole world population.

In any case, one cannot help condemning the nations that would impose on them a policy of birth control while keeping the underdeveloped nations in political or economic dependence. They would thus violate these nations' right to self-development and do grave injury to their public morality by introducing or promoting contraceptive methods among them.

In taking up the defense of the rights of national minorities, Pius XII declared that, in a new organization founded on moral principles, there could be no place for "the limitation or the abolition of their natural fecundity" (Christmas Message, 1941). In the same spirit he took issue with the pressure exercised on emigrants to induce them to adopt birth control: "An attempt is being made to mechanize even consciences, in this instance, public measures for conception control" (Christmas Message, 1952).

On the occasion of the Social Week of Palermo (September 27, 1953), an important document was issued by Msgr. Montini, (now Pope Paul VI, then substitute Secretary of State). It expressed the mind of Pope Pius XII on the problem of the growth of world population, its economic, social, moral and religious character, together with its repercussions on the family as well as on the international order and peace. It is not by means of the violation of the laws of life and the rights of the family that a solution may be sought, according to this letter. Such a course would be immoral and humiliating to the noble demands of the spirit. Rather it is necessary "to educate consciences to the value and the responsibility of human life, to promote a more equitable distribution of goods, to exploit the resources of nature, always observing the most reasonable procedure. . . ."

Finally, in a discourse of January 20, 1958, to the Italian Federation of Associations of Large Families, Pius XII forcefully stigmatized the illicit practices of birth control, which a widespread propaganda canonizes as the remedy to overpopulation. The Pope denounced the avarice and egoism, whether of nations or of individuals, that inspire such pretended solutions. He appealed to modern society to reform its own conduct and to apply itself to find solutions that are reasonable, practical, and beneficial for the whole of humanity.

> Overpopulation, then, is not a justification for broadcasting illicit practices of birth control, but rather a pretext to legitimatize avarice and egoism, either on the part of nations which see in the expansion of others an attack on their own political hegemony and a lowering of the standard of life, or on the part of individuals, particularly the rich, who would selfishly prefer to enjoy the world's goods rather than to share in the glory and merit of bringing forth new lives. In this manner the certain laws of the Creator are violated, under pretext of redressing imaginary errors of His Providence. On the contrary, it would be far more reasonable for modern society to strive more resolutely and universally to reform its own conduct by removing the causes of famine in the "depressed" or overpopulated regions, by using

modern discoveries more actively for peaceful purposes, by adopting a more generous policy of collaboration and exchange, an
economy wider in scope and less nationalistic, particularly by
reacting to suggestions of egoism by charity, of avarice by a more
concrete application of justice. God will not demand of men an
accounting for the general destiny of mankind, which is His
affair, but of each of their actions which they shall have per-
formed either in accord with or contrary to their conscience.

Thus Pius XII indicated the direction in which the solution
must be sought, in a positive and concrete manner.

First means: Removing the causes of famine in depressed or
overpopulated regions. These causes have been analyzed: outmoded methods of production, low yields from cultivated land.
Hence there is question especially of developing the crops necessary to feed the population of these underdeveloped regions.
Tremendous acreages still remain uncultivated.[6] Furthermore,
land must be brought to yield more. Through the use of selected
seeds and proper fertilizers, the production of the greater part
of foodstuffs could be increased fifty percent in twenty years,
according to the estimates of UN experts. Besides, the construction of dams on rivers and streams would allow India, for example, not only to nourish its own population adequately but
even to export a certain quantity of food products. Where dams
have already been constructed, two crops a year are harvested.

Together with the use of better agricultural methods, the underdeveloped countries must also be assured of an increase in
the exploitation of the raw materials they possess in important
quantities. Lastly, these countries must be industrialized; they
need technicians, financial aid to build up their economic and
social infrastructure by means of highways, railroads, canals,
port facilities, universities, schools, hospitals.

Second means: Using modern discoveries more effectively for
peaceful purposes. Already in the 1954 Easter message Pope

---

6. "Of the sixteen billion arable acres, only two billion are actually being
cultivated." Conference of Raymond Scheyven, former president of the
Economic and Social Council of the United Nations, at the eleventh plenary
assembly of Pax Romana. Other statistics given in this paragraph are drawn
from the same conference.

Pius XII had expressed the wish that nations and scientists would use modern discoveries exclusively for peaceful purposes, instead of exploiting them as a preparation for war.

> When shall we see the wise men of this world turning the wonderful discoveries of the deep forces of matter exclusively to the purposes of peace, in order to give human activity an inexpensive source of energy to supply the lack of sources of wealth and labor, or to correct their unequal geographical distribution, as well as to offer to medicine and agriculture new weapons and to open to the nations new paths to prosperity and well-being?[7]

Third means: Adopting a more generous policy of collaboration and exchange, an economy wider in scope and less nationalistic. An entirely new spirit, generous and open to everything, must animate the policy of states and their economy in view of the needs of underdeveloped countries. Instead of national aggrandizement, the states must practice a policy of honest and generous collaboration, in order to put to use all the resources of the world for the benefit of all, and particularly of the underdeveloped countries. In place of canonizing the negative, restrictive and immoral measures of birth control as the means of resolving the problems of economically underdeveloped countries, they

7. Atomic energy can transform the conditions of life by increasing considerably the power at man's disposal. Thus, at a time when resources in natural fuels (coal, petroleum) are diminishing, a new source of energy appears, and that precisely at a time when the world's need of energy is increasing considerably. As of now, applications of atomic energy have been made with regard to ships, submarines and aircraft. But, as Pius XII noted, it is particularly in the field of medicine and agriculture that remarkable progress is being made.

In agriculture, radioisotopes are being used to study the changes—mysterious until now—which take place in animal and vegetable life, and to learn nature's processes. By means of the intense rays emanating from the pile, it is possible to irradiate all sorts of substances and, in plants, to follow the path of various substances. For example, the moment when phosphate injected into the soil is absorbed by the plant or how it enters into the plant can be determined. In this manner it is possible to obtain useful and practical information regarding the best time for fertilizing the soil, the quantity of seed required, and the proportions of mixtures necessary to obtain the best results. In his book *Des atomes et des hommes*, M. Leprince-Ringuet explains: "How many elements there are favorable to the production of foodstuffs! How could one have foreseen that the hunger

must seek to organize the great strength of their economy for the greatest good and the common benefit of all mankind.

To the promptings of egoism the nations must reply with charity. To avarice they must oppose the most concrete applications of justice.

Pius XII called for a more generous attitude, for a rejection of the narrow confines in which the nations had hitherto boxed their economy, in the name of the moral doctrine of which he was the guardian and interpreter, in the name also of God's design for the community of nations.

Some eminent economists, on the strength of their observation of facts and analysis of economic realities, already proclaim this as the way of salvation in the world plan: an economy of giving in place of the avarice of nations, an economy of service to the whole range of the human species—in concrete terms, "an official proposition of internationally controlled disarmament, addressed to Soviet Russia by the United Nations, with the allotment of a large percentage of the present armament expenditures to go to a common fund for world-wide development . . . , as François Perroux summarizes the plan.[8] Of this very specific proposal the

---

of undernourished countries would probably be allayed through powerful reactors that are only now beginning to be constructed?" (p. 181).

In medicine, results of the use of radioisotopes are steadily gaining in importance, since it becomes possible to learn where and how the doses of various substances (iodine, calcium, etc.) act on the organisms attacked by disease. Radioisotopes are a great help to physicians in both the diagnosis and the treatment of various ailments. For the first time in the history of medicine it is possible to observe at close range the route followed by certain elements in the human body, to ascertain whether circulation is good or bad, and to localize the spots in the circulatory system where symptoms of disease appear. Thanks to radioisotopes, great progress has been achieved in the examination of the heart, in the treatment of cancer, in the diagnosis and treatment of cerebral tumors, and in the diagnosis of thyroid conditions.

8. *Europe sans rivages*, p. 409. On the same page the eminent writer, calculating the benefits that would accrue to underdeveloped nations from reductions in armaments, says: "With a fourth of the monies now spent on armaments, the free world could increase by two percent annually the national per-capita income of the underdeveloped nations; with half of the armament expenditures, a far more ambitious policy could be put into effect."

author writes: "Should it succeed, it contains in germ the greatest happening in the world's history. Poised on the brink of the abyss, mankind takes hold of itself and transforms an awful threat into an immense benefit."

6. *Right to a particular character and culture.* On several occasions Pius XII insisted on the need of respecting the individuality and the diversity of nations in the world community.

It is necessary to utilize always "the endowment of the human person and of the individuality of nations as a natural and fundamental point of support" (Christmas message, 1952).

Conversely, he warned against the danger of excessive uniformity and of a forced leveling process, "since respect for the cultural characters of the various nations would, by reason of their harmonious variety, produce a more flexible and stable union" (Discourse to the European Union of Federalists, December 11, 1948).

The Pope here alluded to the pitfalls to be avoided in the formation of a European Union. But the rule he enunciated possesses a general character of wide application.

Pius XII was thinking not only of the international common good, but also its harmonious union, when he called for "a respectful caution and consideration for the healthy cultural peculiarities of each nation," in his Allocution to Italian Catholic Action, July 23, 1952. In this instance he was defending a right against the tendency and the practice of the totalitarian states, which seek to force nations, particularly the small or medium-sized satellites which move in their orbit, into their own political and cultural system.

> The nations, and notably those which are small or middle-sized, claim the right to take their destinies into their own hands. They can be led to assume, with their full and willing consent, and in the interest of common progress, obligations that will modify their sovereign rights. But after sustaining their share—their large share—of suffering in order to overthrow a system of brutal violence, they are entitled to refuse to accept a new political or cultural system that is decisively rejected by the great majority of their citizens (Discourse to the Sacred College, June 2, 1945).

7. *Right to use the goods of the earth.*   In his Christmas message of 1941, Pius XII declared:

> Within the purview of a new organization founded on moral principles, there can be no room for the narrow calculations of egoism, which tend to monopolize the economic resources and the materials destined for common use in such a manner as to exclude the nations less favored by nature.

Here the Pope invoked "moral principles" on which the new organization of the community of nations must be founded. He condemned the egotistical hoarding of economic resources and of materials intended for the use of all on the part of certain nations to the detriment of others.

A fundamental principle of the Church's social doctrine here comes into play—namely, that the resources of the whole of creation and all the goods of the earth are destined for the whole of mankind. They are at the disposal of all nations according to the principles of justice, of equity and of charity, for the common good of all.

In this same 1941 message the Pope stated that he found it very consoling to see affirmed "the necessity of a sharing by all in the goods of the earth, even on the part of those nations which in the fulfillment of this principle belong in the category of 'givers' and not in that of 'receivers.' "

We are dealing here, Pius XII continued, with a question that is "decisive for the economy of the world." Without an equitable solution on the point, "there would persist in the relations between peoples a deep and far-reaching root, blossoming forth into bitter dissensions and burning jealousies, which would eventually lead to new conflicts."

The simple fact is, as the Pope asserted in his allocution to the members of the International Bureau of Labor, March 25, 1949, that there exists "an imbalance between creditor nations and debtor nations, . . ." or as he put it in his 1940 Christmas message, "glaring differences in the field of world economy."

8. *Right to observance of international agreements.*   It would be superfluous to comment on this right. The second part of this

chapter, which is concerned with the duties of states, will supply the best commentary. This right is nothing else than a guarantee, rendered practicable in an international organization, that other states will fulfill their reciprocal duties and will be faithful to their commitments.

DUTIES OF STATES

The duties of states are embodied in the international public order, discussed in chapter two. They consist of duties of justice, duties of equity, duties of charity, whether in their relations with one another or with regard to the international community. We shall distinguish three kinds of duties: 1) Juridical duties, sanctioned by law. Besides the obligations deriving from general morality and international natural law there is also a juridical obligation for the states that are members of the UN. 2) Duties with regard to certain problems proper to themselves: national minorities, emigration and immigration, development of young nations held in trusteeship. 3) Duties of joint responsibility among the states: a) in the field of social justice and social charity: unemployment, refugees, health, famine and destitution in underdeveloped countries; b) in the defense of a nation unjustly attacked; c) in the establishment of continental and intercontinental alliances designed to build up progressively the community of nations.

1. Juridical duties sanctioned by law:

In order that harmonious and lasting contacts and fruitful relations may exist, it is indispensable that nations should recognize and observe the principles of international natural law, which govern their normal development and functioning. These principles demand respect for the rights of each nation to independence, to life, and to the possibility of a progressive evolution in the ways of civilization. . . . Furthermore, they demand fidelity to treaties stipulated and sanctioned in conformity with the rules of international law (Encyclical *Summi Pontificatus*).

This text of the Encyclical *Summi Pontificatus,* already quoted earlier, specifies three kinds of duties imposed on states:

First, states must respect the fundamental rights of each nation.

Then, states must respect the binding force of treaties and fidelity to the pledged word. Few rules of law have been so forcefully stressed by Pius XII as this one. There are needed, he stated in the 1939 Easter homily, ". . . agreements in which fidelity to the word publicly pledged is the unfailing rule of all right-minded parties." And in his Christmas message of 1941, it was his belief that—to the degree that disarmament will become a reality—

> . . . means must be found which are appropriate, honorable and effective in order that the norm "treaties must be observed" (*pacta sunt servanda*) will once again enjoy its vital and moral function in the juridical relations between states.

Finally, states must respect all the other general principles of international law, notably with regard to war. Before war breaks out they must have recourse to all the procedures of arbitration and mediation capable of avoiding it (thus the states that signed the UN charter have undertaken, with a moral obligation, the juridical duty of having recourse to the procedures for peaceful settlement); during war they must observe these principles in its conduct.

2. *Duties of states with regard to certain problems proper to themselves.*

Rights of national minorities and their cultural and linguistic characteristics must be respected by states. In the same 1941 Christmas message he said:

> Within the purview of a new order founded on moral principles, there is no room for open or concealed oppression of the cultural and linguistic characteristics of national minorities, for the hindrance or restriction of their economic resources, for the limitation or abolition of their natural fertility. The more conscientiously the government of the state respects the rights of minorities, the more confidently and the more effectively can it demand from its subjects a loyal fulfillment of those civil obligations that are common to all citizens.

For a long time national minorities, which differ from the rest of the population of the state in which they live by reason of race or language or religion, were subjected to oppressions, either open or occult. With the League of Nations a step forward had been taken by acknowledging in their populations certain rights to life, to liberty, to security, to the free use of their language, to nationality. But the peace treaties of 1919–1920 subjected only certain states, not all, to the obligation of assuring the rights of minorities. The UN has been concerned especially about religious or racial persecution and discrimination. Nevertheless, these continue to take place in certain countries.

As early as his Christmas message of 1941, Pius XII drew attention to this very serious problem of minorities. He undertook the defense of their rights and specified the fields in which only too often the oppression of minority populations occurs: their cultural and linguistic characteristics, their economic life, their demographic problem, and the natural fecundity of their race.

True, he stressed the fact that to these rights of minorities correspond duties of loyalty on their part to the state: the faithful fulfillment of the civic duties "common to all citizens." On the other hand, the state's conscientious fidelity to respect the rights of the minorities will also bring about their loyalty more surely and more effectively.

In the 1954 Christmas message, Pius XII again came to the defense of ethnic minorities:

> It would certainly be an erroneous policy of unification—if not an actual betrayal—to sacrifice ethnic minorities to nationalist interests, minorities that are deprived of the power of defending their faith, and their Christian culture.

Problems of emigration and immigration. Among the many problems that stand in the way of the organization and the functioning of a genuine community of states, particularly if it is a community that embraces all nations, Pius XII has cited "the question of the right of immigration and of emigration," as he terms it in the Allocution to the Union of Italian Catholic Jurists, December 6, 1953. There exists a right of emigration: the right of an individual to leave his country in order to seek in another the means of assuring his right to life and of realizing his human destiny—for the usual causes of emigration are lack of space and lack of the means of existence.

Pope Pius XII also predicates a "right of the family to living space." He refers to it precisely when speaking of emigration. "Where this exists, emigration will attain its natural purpose, as experience amply proves." And what is this purpose? "A better distribution of men over those parts of the earth's surface suitable for agricultural colonization," as he explained in the Pentecost message, June 1, 1941 (to commemorate the fiftieth anniversary of the Encyclical *Rerum Novarum*).

Certain duties on the part of states correspond to these rights: the duty of encouraging emigration to regions still insufficiently populated; duties of the interested states—the one permitting the departure of the emigrant and the one receiving him—to have a mutual understanding in order, he says in the same message, "to avoid anything that might hinder the initiation and development of genuine trust between the two countries."

This collaboration, he continued, will be to everyone's advantage:

> . . . families will accept a country which will be for them a fatherland in the true sense of the word; countries with a dense population will be relieved and their citizens will create new friends in a foreign territory; finally, the states that welcome the emigrants will be enriched with hard-working citizens.

In this collaboration, and not in the annexation or conquest of new territories, the states must seek the solution of the problem. Thus, the two states will contribute to the increase of human well-being, to the progress of human civilization, to a certain economic and social equilibrium between the nations—provided, of course, that the emigration is accomplished with due respect to the needs of the human person and of the family.

Conversely, if no attempt is made to resolve this grave problem, the peace of nations runs the risk of being compromised. In his allocution to the members of the World Congress of Organizations of Catholic Women (April 24, 1952) the Pope cited "misery, unemployment, obstacles to emigration" among the material causes of conflicts.

Development towards autonomy of peoples in trusteeship. To peoples subject to one of the colonizing powers and to members of these colonies, the Church has always preached the same doctrine regarding the dignity of the human person, whatever his color, his race, his social weakness in the eyes of men. The same doctrine is hers concerning universal brotherhood, transcending everything that divides men or sets them in opposition, men against men, nations against nations, since all are children of the same Father in heaven. Hers is the same doctrine regarding the equality of races and the condemnation of racial discriminations and the Nazi theses about racial superiority; the same doctrine on the respect due to civilizations and cultures; the same doctrine on social justice necessary for all and on a rule of justice equal for all. For having preached this doctrine, missionaries often have run into opposition from government administrations and private interests. And in many regions, particularly in the Far East, the missions have become the victims of atrocious persecutions, the missionaries "treated as enemies of the public welfare, banished from society, condemned to prison and to death" (Message of October 15, 1953), and obliged to abandon their missionary work, simply for being fearless witnesses of their fidelity to the faith and to the doctrine of the universal charity of Christ.

For a long time the Church foresaw the movement of emancipation which today is in full flower. The directives she gave to her missionaries—that their apostolic and pastoral ministry be maintained free of any attachment to a country's politics and material interests—attest to her desire to safeguard her independence in the face of pressures from the colonizing state and to her concern to fulfill her mission of announcing freely and without omission the message of salvation to all men of all races and peoples. The providential creation of an indigenous clergy came as a result of this clear papal vision. The establishment of a hierarchy, "chosen from among the inhabitants of the place," as the Encyclical *Evangelii Praecones* (June 21, 1951) worded it, crowned this entire program of Christianization.[9]

Suppose that a war or other political events replace one regime by another in a mission territory and that the departure of the missionaries from such a nation be demanded or decreed; sup-

9. In order to understand better the farsightedness of the Church, which had searched the future and foreseen the events that today are a reality, one should reread in this Encyclical the reproduction of the directives given by Pius XI regarding "the indigenous clergy" in 1926:

pose—certainly a thing that will occur with greater difficulty—
that the natives, after reaching a certain degree of culture and
a certain political maturity, decide, in order to obtain their autonomy, to expel from their territory the functionaries, the troops
and the missionaries of the country to which they are subject, and
cannot obtain this goal without the use of force. What disaster,
We ask, would not threaten the Church in those regions, unless
steps had been taken betimes to provide for the needs of the new
Christians by spreading a network, as it were, of indigenous
priests over the entire territory?

At the present moment in all the lands that have known a
regime of colonization under one form or another, there is unrest, ferment, a demonstration of aspirations of independence.
The territories formerly under colonial rule are rapidly arriving
at the age of autonomy. Since 1945, more than thirty countries
have obtained their independence in Africa and in Asia.

Through her visible head the Church is present in this development. In three very important documents Pius XII treated of
this complex and delicate problem: the Christmas message of
1954, on coexistence in the truth; the Christmas message of 1955,
on Christ in the historical and social life of mankind; the Encyclical *Fidei Donum,* of April 21, 1957, on the situation in the
Catholic missions, particularly in Africa. The teaching contained
in these three documents is centered on the following points:

a) Facts. Among the peoples hitherto regarded as colonial
"a process of development toward political autonomy" is taking
place (Christmas Message, 1954). "The greater part of the territories [of Africa] is undergoing a phase of social, economic and
political evolution that is of the greatest importance for their future" (Encyclical *Fidei Donum*).

b) Seriousness of the situation. Cells of opposition have been
formed between the European nations and those who, outside of
Europe, aspire to full political independence. Furrows of hatred
crisscross the populations. Enmities are being created. There
are explosions of nationalism, and hunger for power.

c) Responsibilities. The proponents of a policy of nationalism, which was not foreseen in time, today see themselves
forced to retreat before adversaries who have adopted their own
methods. It serves no purpose for the peoples of the West, particularly of Europe, to consider the past with sterile regrets, to

remain passive, or to reproach one another with colonialism. A great deal remains to be done. Duties must be fulfilled.

d) Duties. Pius XII pointed out their duties to both sides: to the nations that practiced colonialism and to the new peoples aspiring to independence.

He asked the first to safeguard true values: ". . . to apply themselves in a constructive manner to extend, where this has not yet been done, the true values of Europe and of the West, which have borne such good fruit on other continents." The Pope's words must be well understood; he does not speak of methods, of mores, of customs of Europe and of the West, but of true values. On a number of occasions he asked that the mores and customs proper to the various peoples be respected. But side by side with material and technical progress, sometimes truly remarkable, and the achievements in the field of schools, hospitals and hygiene, which colonial administrations have brought to native populations, how often, alas! have they not introduced among them alcoholism and drugs, immorality, injustice, forced labor, break-up of the family, a laicism denying all spiritual values and certain nationalist and socialist ideologies.

In the civilization of the nations of the West, on the other hand, Pius XII denounced the danger of "materialism, which at least implicitly puts its ideal in the enjoyment of the comforts of life" (Discourse to the Fifth Congress of American-European Associations, September 18, 1955). It is driven by the forces of demoralization, which glorify egoism, the spirit of pleasure or of domination.

The "true values" of Western civilization are those which have come to it from Christianity: a concept of man, of his dignity, of his rights, of his liberty; a concept of society which demands the virtues of justice and charity; a concept of life, and the meaning of objective truth. These are the true values of a civilization inspired by Christianity, basing itself on the natural law inscribed in the heart of man, on the natural law deriving from God. These are the values that must be brought to the peoples of Africa, of Asia, of the various continents, so that their civilizations may be penetrated by them.

Then in the Christmas message for the same year (1955), the

Pope indicated the spirit with which these problems connected with the creation of new nations must be treated: first, a spirit of "preventive pacification," which seeks to anticipate, eliminate, or reduce in good time the opposition between peoples; a spirit "of impartial justice and even of generosity, always remaining within the limits of a healthy realism."

A healthy realism must likewise "guide the steps" for the welfare of the peoples (*Fidei Donum*). Education toward liberty is a gradual process. The Pope spoke of "progressive" liberty. But events come quickly, precipitously, and they do not always allow even the wisest rulers the possibility of using a method that demands time, patience, moderation. They must take into account nationalist passions and the irresistible impulse of the legitimate aspirations of young nations.

But above all, the great duty of European states with regard to the new nations is specified in these terms: "That a political, just and progressive liberty be not denied to these peoples and that no obstacle be placed in its way" (Christmas Message, 1955; Encyclical *Fidei Donum*).

> The Church which, in the course of the centuries, has seen many nations born and thrive, necessarily must be particularly attentive today to the accession of new peoples to the responsibilities of political liberty. (*Fidei Donum.*)

On the other hand, at the same time that he pointed out to the European nations their duty of understanding and assistance, Pius XII asked the new nations "to credit to Europe some merit for their advancement; without its wide influence in all fields, they might be drawn by blind nationalism to throw themselves into chaos or into slavery."

From both parties, finally, the Pope asked "the desire of peace and reciprocal understanding" (*Fidei Donum*).

Here again, as always, Pius XII's teaching forms a whole, marked by wisdom and courage, by balance and an open mind toward human progress. To isolate only one passage from this ensemble would mutilate his thought. He was above political quarrels and partisan positions. To all he preached the truths necessary to achieve peace through justice and fraternal understanding. If one were to emphasize merely his attention to the

accession of the new peoples to political liberty, without re-
membering his concern, in the face of Communism, to safeguard
the true values of Europe and of the West, to see the influence of
Christian civilization extended to all spheres, to have the new
peoples grow progressively in liberty and to protect themselves
against the errors and seductions of a false nationalism and the
Communist ideology—such an attitude would not only violate the
truth; it would also serve to line up against the Pope's teaching
those who, whatever their intentions, are always ready to seek
only those parts of this teaching which appear to confirm their
position. This attitude, considering the complexity and the touch-
iness of the problems involved, would result in hindering the
papal program from working for the welfare of all.

We might well ponder, too, the concluding words of *Fidei
Donum,* where he addresses both parties:

> In renewing this twofold exhortation, We express the wish that
> there be pursued in Africa "a work of constructive collaboration,"
> free of prejudices and mutual recriminations, preserved from the
> seductions and pitfalls of false nationalism, capable of extending
> to those populations, rich in resources and with a bright future,
> the true values of Christian civilization, which have hitherto
> brought forth such good fruits on other continents.

Pius XII himself also reminded missionaries of the stringent
duties that these problems impose:

> There are no new nations in which there are not awakened new
> aspirations and pretensions that are occasionally untimely, that
> create stringent duties for pastors who have a sense of responsi-
> bility and are concerned about the true welfare of their peoples
> (Message to the missionaries of the whole world, October 15,
> 1953).

3. *Duties concerned with the joint liability and solidarity of
states.*

Duties of social justice and social charity. Pope Pius XII
posed the problem of juridical, economic, social, charitable and
cultural solidarity among states and nations not only when he
enunciated the principles governing these obligations of international solidarity, but also when he applied them to three con-

crete cases: unemployment, refugees, economic aid to under-developed countries.

Unemployment. We need point out here only that the Pope makes it a duty of social justice incumbent on states and the community of nations to seek to resolve, through the concerted effort of all, this pressing problem of unemployment, which continually puts the peace of the world in danger.

Refugees. Another problem the Pope placed before the consciences of states and nations is that of refugees.

On October 2, 1949, when the Pope received a delegation of United States congressmen, who had come to investigate the problem of war refugees (displaced persons), he showed how urgent was the solution of this problem, not only because any delay would bring with it dangers of a political, economic, and even social nature, but for much deeper reasons. And the appeal to conscience and to moral duty thus becomes all the more pressing.

> Our prime anxiety—as We are sure it is yours deep down in your hearts—touches the judgment of history and of history's Lord on the fulfillment of that gravest duty of man to man and of nation to nation, which demands respect for the image of God in even the weakest and most abandoned of His children. No reason of state or pretext of collective advantage . . . can avail to justify the contempt of that human dignity and the denial of those elemental human rights that the Creator has imprinted on the soul of each of His creatures.

Problem of health. The solidarity of states imposes upon them the duty of seeking to resolve by organized action questions relating to public health. The League of Nations achieved appreciable results in this field. The UN has undertaken a concerted effort through the World Health Organization.

On June 27, 1949, in an audience granted to more than four hundred delegates of the World Health Organization from more than sixty countries, who were meeting in Rome at the time, Pius XII expressed to them his joy at seeing

> . . . on a point of major importance, the large number of nations, despite the tensions that still remain in relations of an economic, social, political and moral order, nevertheless uniting to work in common for progress of world health, urged forward not only

by a very justifiable preoccupation of reciprocal defense, but by a praiseworthy spirit of mutual help and solidarity.

The Pope then described the extent of the evil and examined its causes:

> Among a great many peoples, either as a result of their poverty and their weakness, or because of the backward state of their civilization, their science and their technique, the level of hygiene and of health is far below that of other countries. The epidemics that recur periodically and the permanent endemic diseases little by little bring about their ruin, and recent statistics, however imperfect they may still be, attest to the ravages that threaten the disappearance of entire tribes and clans.

Thereupon Pius XII specified the duty of joint responsibility that follows as a result:

> Would it be tolerable to see our brethren suffer sicknesses and physical deformities, which at times lead to their extinction, while at the same time, in the rest of the world, many other societies have reached such a high degree of sanitary perfection that infant mortality diminishes progressively and the most stubborn plagues are gradually being conquered?

Pius XII congratulated the World Health Organization for bringing ". . . to this eminently humanitarian and social enterprise the most universal, and concerted co-operation, which consequently possesses the surest and most rapid efficacy. . . ." Finally, he unfolded the doctrine of the Church on the question of health, which, he said, "goes beyond the limits of biology and medicine; it necessarily has its place in the sphere of morality and religion."

The Church has always stressed the importance of moral and religious forces in maintaining health. "She has always considered it among the conditions required for the dignity and the total welfare of humanity, for its corporeal and spiritual, its temporal and eternal well-being."

Assistance to underdeveloped countries. On several occasions Pius XII instructed the more favored nations on their solemn duty to come to the aid of underdeveloped countries; a duty of international solidarity, a duty of social justice, a duty of collaboration in welfare, a duty of humanity. We treated this problem above under the aspect of a state's right to its own development. Here we shall examine it from the standpoint of the joint liability of states.

The Holy Father recalled the principles of the social doctrine of the Church.

"The necessity of a participation by all in the goods of the earth" (Christmas Message, 1941). This is a condition for peace and for an international organization founded on moral principles.

It is indispensable that "The goods created by God for all men should be equitably distributed to all, observing the principles of justice and charity" (Encyclical *Sertum Laetitiae,* November 1, 1939). This is a demand of God's design for the universal purpose of created things.

What is the ultimate meaning of this purpose of the earth's resources? What purpose are the natural riches of a country to serve? The betterment of the living conditions of human groups.

> The natural riches of a region, of a country, of a continent, are destined not for the exclusive economic profit of a few, but for the betterment of living conditions, material first of all, but also and principally moral and spiritual, of human groups who must live by exploiting the resources of the soil (Allocution to the delegates to the Fourth World Congress of Petroleum, June 10, 1955).

This presupposes an economic organization on a world scale, in order to obtain the best distribution of all resources. The Holy Father continued:

> The world-wide character of economy, coming more and more to the fore, and the duties incumbent on privileged nations toward those less favored will have their influence on the division of goods produced.

As Msgr. Montini, Subsecretary of State (now Paul VI), wrote to the Social Week of Palermo, September 27, 1953, "a better ordered worldwide circulation of peoples, of capital, of material goods, is needed for the realization of a more rational and more equitable utilization of the earth's resources for the whole human community, thanks to an international solidarity better understood by the more favored nations toward the others that lack the necessities of life."

Studying the problem of population growth, he wrote: "It follows that the adequate study of the relations between density of population and means of subsistence must be developed on a world-wide level, and the problems connected with it can only be solved in the same manner, in the active solidarity of all nations, so that, once the artificial barriers that now divide them are lifted, a better ordered circulation of peoples, of capital and of material goods may result."

"More than half of the world's population is undernourished; in order to satisfy the needs of mankind, food production would have to be doubled." This is the tragic problem Pope Pius XII treated in an allocution on the tenth anniversary of the Food and Agriculture Organization (FAO) of the UN on November 10, 1955.

A billion and a half men suffer hunger. Two out of every three. Only the joint liability of the more privileged nations and those underdeveloped can confront this gigantic problem.

After expressing his interest in FAO the Pope set forth the duty of collective responsibility with regard to this problem:

> The nations favored by nature or by the progress of civilization run the risk of a rude awakening one day, if they do not undertake, as of now, to assure to those less fortunate the means of living decently, in a human manner, and of developing themselves as well. To stir up among a large number of individuals and of nations this sentiment of collective responsibility and especially to bring about enlightened and generous assistance by this means is a high and noble task. In these times of suspicion, of division, of revolt, the moral result of such an undertaking will far surpass its material consequences.

Finally, he specified the order of virtue to which such a world-wide action of solidarity in the struggle against misery and hunger belongs.

> We take pleasure above all in recognizing, in a world-wide action destined to affect not a privileged order, but the great multitude, often powerless and without means of self-defense, a genuine aspect of the charity which Christ manifested in His life and in His death, and which He wished to make the distinctive characteristic of His disciples.

Two years earlier, December 6, 1953, in addressing the members of the same organization, Pius XII had said: "An action of this kind obliges the nations to feel themselves, with a sense of solidarity, the beneficiaries and the benefactors one of another." Solidarity calls for a true fraternal collaboration and conforms to the designs of God, as the Pope indicated in another place.

> May the victory over the spirit of cold egoism bring about that sincere solidarity, both juridical and economic, which is fraternal collaboration, following the principles of the divine law among nations thus assured of their autonomy and independence (Discourse to the members of the Congress of International Exchanges, March 7, 1948).

As a conclusion which, at the same time, constitutes a magnificent program, we shall quote these words of Pius XII to the representatives of the European Community of Coal and Steel, November 4, 1957:

> Europe feels—and all the world feels with it—that all men are brothers and called to unite in the task of mitigating the misery of mankind and of bringing to an end the scandal of famine and ignorance.

Duties of solidarity in the defense of a nation unjustly attacked. We shall see in chapter five that one of the two instances cited by the Pope for a legitimate defensive war is that of the military intervention of states in the name of their solidarity and of charity. As he insisted in his radio message to the world, December 24, 1948,

> This defense [of a nation unjustly attacked] imposes itself equally on the solidarity of nations, which implies the duty of not abandoning the victim of aggression.

After that date Soviet tanks snuffed out the uprising of the Hungarian nation seeking to reclaim its liberties. In this connection, on November 10, 1956, the Pope addressed a radio appeal "in favor of peace and liberty" to the nations and rulers of the entire world:

> Can the world disregard its brethren and abandon them to a fate of degrading slavery? Assuredly the Christian conscience cannot withdraw itself from the moral obligation of using all permissible means to restore their dignity and to return their liberty to them.

Every word of the Pope should be weighed. There is question, he said, of a "moral obligation" resting on the Christian conscience. "All permissible means" must be employed. The UN here had a mission to fulfill by the means at its disposal; at least observers should have been sent to make an impartial investigation.

Pius XII expressly referred to the case of Hungary in his 1956 Christmas message: "No one expects or demands the impossible, not even of the United Nations, but one might have expected that its authority would have some weight, at least through the intermediary of observers in the places where essential human values are in extreme peril." Soviet Russia obstinately refused to admit observers.

For his part, the Pope also called for a pact among nations sincerely looking toward peace and liberty:

> Let the ranks be soon closed again and let all those nations and governments that wish the world to follow the path of the honor and the dignity owing to the children of God be grouped in a solid pact—a pact capable of effectively defending its members from every unjust attack directed against their rights and their independence (Appeal of November 10, 1956).

One month later in the Christmas message Pius XII pinpointed his thoughts on this point by envisaging the effective means the UN ought to have at its disposal to bring about respect for law:

> It ought to have the right and the power of preventing any military intervention of one state in another, under any pretext that might be advanced, no less than of assuring, through the use of sufficient police forces, the protection of order in the state that is threatened.

Duties of juridical and economic solidarity in the establishment of continental and intercontinental unions for the purpose of building up progressively the community of nations. The first "Congress of Europe" was held at The Hague, May 7-10, 1948. Pius XII judged it opportune to send a "special personal representative" to this congress. On June 2 following the feast of St. Eugene, his patron, in an allocution to the Sacred College, he explained the reasons for his decision.

> In the midst of repeated attempts at reconciliation, at rapprochement, between nations only lately engaged in war with one another, they [i.e., those, namely, to whom the Pope referred in a

preceding passage as "far-seeing and courageous spirits," who "are seeking tirelessly for new ways to a road of security"] are laboring to re-establish a Europe shaken to its very foundations and to make of this hotbed of chronic agitation a bulwark of peace and the providential promoter of a general advance on the face of the whole earth. For this reason, while at the same time not wishing to draw the Church into the entanglement of purely terrestrial interests, We thought it opportune to name a special personal representative to the "Congress of Europe" recently held at The Hague, in order to demonstrate the solicitude of the Holy See and to add its encouragement of a union of the nations.

And we do not doubt that all Our faithful will be mindful that their place always is at the side of those generous souls who prepare the way for mutual understanding and for the re-establishment of a sincere spirit of peace among the nations.

Four salient ideas emerge from this text, and clarify Pius XII's whole attitude with regard to the European community, an attitude frequently misunderstood and presented in a false light by political propagandists.

1. Nature of Pope's intervention. Pius XII did not desire "to draw the Church into the entanglement of purely terrestrial interests." Faithful to the Church's traditional stand on political and economic problems, which are concerned with purely earthly matters, the Pope clarified the nature of his intervention. This is surely not to say that he did not take an interest in the concrete problems studied by the assemblies of Europe, in their accomplishments, in their institutions. On the contrary, he followed closely and with lively interest the efforts being fostered by the federations. On June 13, to the participants of the Congress of Europe of 1957, he related the history of the European community and described its first accomplishments.

From the very beginning, however, he made it clear that he intended to respect completely the autonomy of the statesmen responsible for the institutions they were creating in their proper sphere of temporal interests.

2. Motive of the Pope's intervention. What is the profound reason for the Pope's interest in this project of a European community? He himself put it in these words: "The union of nations." Hence he took a universalist view of the European community, a view that embraces all nations. In the construction

of an international community of nations, the European community is a first stone, a first rung.

On June 13, 1957, when he spoke to the participants of the Congress of Europe, he also replied to some objections that pictured the European community as a closed preserve or as directed against outside powers. He spoke of an extension of the association to Africa, and then added:

> Thus [Europe] will prove that its intention to form a community of states does not constitute an egotistical move, that it is not dictated by a reflex of defense against outside powers which threaten its interests, but proceeds above all from constructive and disinterested motives.[10]

3. The goal to pursue.   Finally, what is the supreme objective that the Pope wished to see pursued increasingly by means of all this effort at the reconstruction of Europe by the interested states? Peace among the nations, among all nations.

Already in his 1947 Christmas message Pius XII had declared: "The pacification of Europe is the primary condition for the other steps leading to universal pacification."

What drew the Pope's solicitude, as he stated clearly in his discourse of June 2, 1948, was precisely the task incumbent on the statesmen responsible for the enterprise to put an end to those age-old struggles that have made Europe "a hotbed of chronic agitation" and to transform it instead into "a bulwark of peace and a providential promoter of a general advance on the face of the whole earth."

Moreover, several sentences later, when he asked the faithful to support this great movement, he again proposed the same goal of international peace: to support those who prepare the way "for a mutual understanding and a re-establishment of a sincere spirit of peace among the nations."[11]

10. See also his words to the German delegation on his eightieth birthday: "We welcome everything that signifies rapprochement, mutual understanding, and collaboration among the nations and states of Europe, not indeed in a spirit of hostility toward outside states, but rather with a view to incorporating a strong Europe into a world which seeks true peace and a healthy order."

11. Pius XII expressed the same idea in his Christmas message of 1956: "It is a concrete demand of the present hour, one of the means of assuring

4. Spiritual and human aspect of the values at stake. Side by side with these great motives of the union of nations and of peace, Pius XII pointed out two others, in order to explain his interest in the solidarity of Europe.

First of all, there are "the fruits of a spiritual and human order which can flow from the common enjoyment of the rich patrimony of Europe." As he said to the delegation of the European Community of Coal and Steel:

> When We speak of patrimony, We purposely use a word with a wide connotation, a word which above all embraces intellectual and moral values. Without doubt it is necessary to base the project of political union on economic and concrete considerations, but even more account must be taken of the enrichment and the stimulation which without doubt the fusion of ancient and deep cultures, the meeting of complementary temperaments and traditions, the common exploitation of the peaceful conquests have produced—conquests over the forces of nature, which have developed, enriched and beautified the land, conquests over ignorance and error, which have given birth to the culture, the science and the spiritual life of the West. There is no question of abolishing national states or of arbitrarily mixing the races.

Furthermore, the spiritual and human values which form the patrimony of Europe must be called by their proper name: they are Christian values.

In his 1954 Christmas message, Pius XII declared that Europe must again become conscious of the eminently Christian foundations of its civilization.

> In any case, what must remain and no doubt will remain is the true Europe, that is to say, the sum total of spiritual and civil values which the West has accumulated by drawing on the riches of each of the nations which compose it, in order to spread them over the entire world. In the disposition of divine Providence, Europe can again become the generator and dispenser of these values, provided it becomes conscious anew of its own spiritual character and rejects the divinization of its power. Just as, in the past, the sources of its power and of its culture were eminently Christian, so it must, if it wishes to rediscover the foundation and

---

peace and a fruitful heritage of good to the entire world, a force that embraces equally the peoples of Asia and Africa, the Middle East and Palestine with the Holy Places, to reaffirm the solidarity of Europe."

bond of its unity and of its true greatness, decide to return to God and to Christian ideals.

Today and tomorrow—as yesterday—it is this Christian message that can guarantee all human values in Europe and aid it to fulfill its mission.

If it is true that the Christian message was for it like yeast put into the dough, which penetrates the mass and causes it to rise, it is no less true that the same message remains, yesterday as well as today, the most precious treasure of which Europe is the depositary. It is able to preserve in their integrity and their vigor, with the concept and the exercise of the fundamental liberties of the human person, the functions of the family and national societies, and to guarantee, in a supranational community, respect for the cultural differences, the spirit of conciliation and collaboration, together with the acceptance of the sacrifices which this implies and the commitments it calls for (Allocution to the participants of the Congress of Europe, June 13, 1957).

As we have just indicated, the Congress of Europe of June 13, 1957, had attacked the problems of the association of Europe and Africa, for which the Common Market treaty reserved a prominent place. Stressing this fact, Pope Pius XII declared:

It seems necessary to Us that Europe maintain the possibility of exercising its educative and formative influence in Africa, and that, as a basis for such action, it deploy extensive and comprehensive material aid to help lift the level of life of the African peoples and to put to use the natural riches of that continent.

The problem of exchanges between Europe and Africa was treated in an audience granted April 12, 1958, to an important delegation, to which we referred in chapter two (order of charity). First the Pope underlined the benefits of collaboration between Europe and Africa for the establishment of an effective rapprochement through a task undertaken in common:

We are pleased to see the increases of exchanges between Europe and Africa which serve to unite so many geographical and historical bonds. By the common exploitation of the immense riches which the Creator has placed at the disposal of human industry on and below the surface of the African continent, a more effective rapprochement will be produced than by the protestations of friendship. Working together always has been a providential means of coming to mutual understanding and esteem. If the divergences of immediate interests can stir up temporary conflicts, a reasonable concern for the general welfare, an exalted view inspired by far-seeing prudence and the sentiments of mutual confidence, will lead to a loyal accord, which will respect the rights and aspirations of all.

He then showed how the economic development of the countries of Africa, thanks to the collaboration of Europe, is not only a necessity but also a duty:

> The contribution of European capital and technique is an imperative service to hasten the development of the countries of Africa. This development is urgent, as everyone knows, since in the modern world economic interdependence has become such that an underdeveloped country cannot enjoy complete liberty. The unequal distribution of the gifts and riches of nature imposes on men a moral obligation to help one another, each one according to his rights and the powers he has received.

Such a duty rests even more heavily on the more privileged nations, as their conscience and their enlightened self-interest make it a duty:

> This obligation takes on ever-growing proportion in accord with the greater powers at the disposal of the social or national group. No one can deny that nowadays the more favored nations are conscious of it and seek to fulfill it, despite internal opposition and the considerable material difficulties they necessarily encounter. There is cause to rejoice at the sight of all the efforts that tend to a realization of what the united voices of conscience and self-interest, understood in a wide sense, urge them to undertake without further delay.

Observe the foundation on which Pius XII established the moral obligation on the part of the more favored nations to assist the underdeveloped countries: first, the unequal distribution of the gifts and riches of nature, and second, the impossibility for the underdeveloped countries to enjoy complete liberty, by reason of the economic interdependence that exists in the present-day world.

CONCLUSION

States are true moral personalities with an end proper to themselves, distinct from the personal end of the citizens: to assure the common good of their peoples. What are called their natural rights comprise everything they need to carry out this mission. Thus, in the first place, they must be able to exist, to live their own lives, independent, free, secure. Then they must be able to develop themselves, to perfect themselves in the various spheres of their economic, cultural, and technical life, if they desire to contribute to the human and personal development of their citizens. Finally, there must be respect for their reputation, their character, their culture, as well as for the basic equality of nature that exists among the states and derives from their function in the pursuit of the same end, whatever be their inequalities in the material elements of which they are composed (territory, population, economic wealth, institutions). These rights must be recognized and respected by the other states in the community of nations to which all belong. On the other hand, if they have rights, they likewise have duties with regard to the other states.

These fundamental rights and duties derive from the very nature of states and of their mission. They have not been created arbitrarily by the will of men.

Positive law has been added in order to determine these rights more exactly and to apply them to the different circumstances of time and place, whether this is done by custom or by treaties and agreements.

Authors vary considerably in the enumeration of the fundamental rights and duties of states.

In this field, too, Pius XII rendered a novel service to states and the community of nations by drawing from the principles of international natural law a list of fundamental rights of states. Thus an entire juridical array of rights and duties in the relations among states comes to help in the formation of a community of nations.

Moreover, in organizing the principles and rules we have culled from the teaching of Pius XII in this chapter on the rights and duties of states, the first outlines of an economic and social order become apparent.

Pius XII had the progressive organization of this economic and social order in mind when in the 1940 Christmas message he called for

. . . the victory over the seeds of conflict which consist in the extreme differences in the sphere of world economy, demanding a progressive action, balanced by corresponding guarantees, to establish an order which gives to all states the means of assuring their citizens of all classes a suitable kind of life.

Some of the steps are: the necessity of promoting a more equitable distribution of goods, a participation of all nations in the goods of the earth, the right of access to raw materials; the duty of promoting international collaboration in order to wipe out the enormous disproportions existing nowadays in the standard of living of nations, in investments, in the degree of productivity; exploitation of natural resources in the most reasonable manner; adoption of a farsighted economy, less strictly nationalistic, with extensive changes; a more reasonable distribution of human beings on the face of the earth and the organization, with regard to persons and the common good, of a policy of emigration and exchange of population; the employment of modern discoveries for works of peace and as a means of opening to nations new sources of prosperity and well-being.

Furthermore, the very formal encouragement given by Pius XII to the establishment of common markets is based on the repercussions they will have on a freer circulation of merchandise, of capital, of workers, of services, on an improving standard of living, on the development of relations of exchange, of collaboration, of mutual aid, of friendship among the states, and the elimination, by progressive steps, of the obstacles to the unification of their economies.

This was Pius XII's teaching, inspired by the principles of social justice and social charity, studied in chapter two. It is quite evident that in several fields the Pope makes it a duty of juridical and economic solidarity on the part of states and the community of nations to seek, by united effort and on the vast scale of an international plane, the solution of serious problems that go beyond national capabilities to an extraordinary degree.

Among these are, in the first place, problems of labor and of unemployment, of national minorities, of emigrants, of refugees, of the growth of world population.

Then there are the urgent and trying problems of aid to underdeveloped nations in their struggle against hunger, disease, misery, and ignorance, and in addition, the problem of the evolution of the young nations and of their aspirations to political freedom and independence.

Finally, there is the problem of the continental and intercontinental unions and communities, which must serve as the foundation stones for the community of nations.

In all these problems affecting the peace of the world, Pius XII was personally present, watchful and attentive. Tirelessly he recalled the demands of justice, of equity, of charity, laboring to bring the nations together, to unite them in a common enterprise "to take in hand all the misery of mankind, to bring to an end the scandal of hunger and ignorance," to save and organize the peace.

4

OBSTACLES TO THE COMMUNITY OF NATIONS

> *We do not fail to recognize the grave diffi-*
> *culties which interpose themselves against*
> *the accomplishment of the aims which We*
> *have outlined in a desire to lay a founda-*
> *tion for, to put into effect and to preserve,*
> *a just international peace.*
> —PIUS XII, Christmas Message, 1939

> *We are well aware of the tremendous diffi-*
> *culties to be overcome.*
> —PIUS XII, Christmas Message, 1941

THE CONSTITUTION of the community of nations in accord with international public order, as described in the preceding chapters, will be a task of long duration, of patience, of courage and of farsightedness on the part of statesmen and nations.

Numerous obstacles, which at times appear unconquerable, stand in the way of this grandiose and necessary undertaking. They have been described by the Popes. We may group them into three principal categories: obstacles of an ideological and doctrinal order, obstacles of a psychological and historical order, and obstacles of a military and technical order.

OBSTACLES OF AN IDEOLOGICAL AND DOCTRINAL ORDER

These are the principal errors inspiring the conduct of statesmen and of parties that are influential in the political life of a nation.

Absolute sovereignty of the state. Pius XII denounced this capital error from the time of his first Encyclical *Summi Pontificatus*. In order to understand the significance of this condemnation, let us place it in its setting. The Encyclical is dated October 20, 1939. Borne away by his insane ambition, Hitler had just unleashed war on Europe. Four consecutive times he had imposed his will for domination respectively on Austria (1938), on Czechoslovakia (1938–1939), on Danzig (August, 1939) and finally on Poland (September 1, 1939).

Nazism, which was the very incarnation of the doctrine of the absolute sovereignty of the state, enjoyed a manifest triumph, and no one could foresee at that moment how far this dictatorship of a totalitarian state would extend.

Now, just at that hour Pope Pius XII lifted his voice in the face of the entire world in order to pronounce a scathing judgment on this doctrine. In like manner, nine years later, when Nazism had gone down in disaster, the Holy Father felt justified in recalling his unchanging attitude with regard to an erroneous conception of the sovereignty of an absolutely autonomous state.

> The Catholic doctrine on the state and civil society has always been based on the principle that, in keeping with the will of God, the nations together form a community with a common aim and common duties. Even when the proclamation of this principle and its practical consequences gave rise to violent reactions, the Church denied her assent to the erroneous concept of an absolutely autonomous sovereignty divested of all social obligations (Christmas Message, 1948).

Pope Pius XII, in speaking of a doctrinal position of the "Church," in this place calls to mind the attitude of his predecessor, Pius XI, over against National Socialism, which was persecuting the Catholic Church because it refused to submit to the doctrinal pretensions of an all-powerful state.

> Whoever takes the race or the nation or the state or the form of the state or the depositaries of power or any other fundamental value of the human community—all things that hold a necessary and honorable place in the terrestrial order—whoever takes these notions in order to withdraw them from this scale of values, even religious, and divinizes them by an idolatrous worship, re-

verses and falsifies the order of things created and ordained by God.[1]

Here is Pius XII's judgment on the idea of the absolute sovereignty of the state:

> The concept which assigns to the state an unlimited authority is an error which not only is harmful to the internal life of nations, to their prosperity, to the growing and ordered increase of their well-being; it likewise causes harm to the relations between nations, since it injures the unity of the supranational society, uproots the foundation and the value of international law, opens the way to the violation of others' rights and makes difficult both a common understanding and life in peace (Encyclical *Summi Pontificatus*).

Pius XII thus condemned as an "error" the concept of the absolute sovereignty of the state under the double aspect, national and international.

On the national level, it is harmful to the state itself, to the nation, since it has the mission to promote the common good. The Pope here envisages two fields. First, "the internal life of nations," because the totalitarian state necessarily becomes tyrannical; through its absolutism it attacks the rights and liberties of human persons, of families, of the intermediate entities between itself and the citizens; hence it not only does not assure the common good, but on the contrary compromises it.

Second, "The prosperity and the growing and ordered increase of well-being" of the nation, since the state which does not recognize the rights of other nations and the existence of a supranational community ends by isolating itself, separating itself from others, enclosing itself in an autarchy and thus goes directly contrary to the development of the economic interdependence of nations, which has become a necessity for the well-being of each of them.

But it is particularly on the international level that Pius XII showed the annoying and harmful consequences of this erroneous concept.

"It injures the unity of supranational society."

1. Pius XI, Encyclical *Mit brennender Sorge*, to the bishops of Germany, March 14, 1937.

How can the unity of the supranational society be formed, develop, exist in a stable manner under the permanent menace of such a concept? It cannot be formed, since a state that declares itself an absolute and autonomous master recognizes no authority above it, neither that of a universal moral law nor that of a community of states. It cannot develop, since the totalitarian state will always endeavor to determine its own manner of conceiving of the unity and of the common good of the supranational society, according to its self-interest and in relation to its own ambitions of political and economic imperialism. It cannot exist in a stable manner, since the state that follows such a concept will continually be an obstacle to the unity of the community of nations by its threat of leaving if its demands are not satisfied, as the totalitarian states did in the case of the League of Nations.

"It uproots the foundation and the value of international law."

Such a concept radically denies the immanent and natural law on which international law is founded and therefore also all the principles of international natural law and the universal common good of the community of nations.

"It opens the way to the violation of others' rights."

Since there no longer exists any guarantee that treaties will be respected, the rights of individuals and nations safeguarded and the freedom of communications assured. The state may indeed sign contracts, make alliances, but it will feel bound to such agreements only to the degree and for the time it will judge them useful to its own interests. It will tear up these treaties as so many scraps of paper as soon as it thinks itself sufficiently strong to impose its will on others.

As is evident, the weakest nations will be the victims; they will have no further protection, no defense. Such a doctrine necessarily leads to the supremacy of the strongest, to the triumph of force over right.

"It makes difficult a common understanding and life in peace."

Common understanding and life in peace demand as a necessary and permanent precondition mutual confidence, fidelity to the pledged word, the conviction that war and recourse to force are evil and that there are other human means to resolve conflicts, to settle differences.

In his Christmas message of 1948, Pius XII considered as threats to peace and to life in common

> . . . the narrowness of a self-centered mentality, a mentality that has been largely responsible for the conflicts of the past which, unless finally overcome or at least held in check, could lead to new conflagrations that might mean death to human civilization.

To this concept of the absolute sovereignty of the state should be joined—for they are intimately connected—the erroneous postulates legislators must purge themselves of in order to create a juridical organization destined to assure concord, whether among individuals or among societies.

Pius pointed out the three principal ones:

1. Juridical positivism, which attributes a deceptive majesty to the making of purely human law and leaves the way open for a fatal divorce from the laws of morality.

2. The concept which claims for particular nations or classes the juridical instinct as the final imperative and the norm from which there is no appeal.

3. Finally, there are those various theories which, differing among themselves, and deriving from opposite ideologies, agree in considering the state, or a group which represents it, as an absolute and supreme entity, exempt from control and from criticism even when its theoretical and practical postulates violently lead to the formal denial of essential tenets of the human and Christian conscience (Christmas Message, 1942).

Intensified nationalism. From the teaching of the Sovereign Pontiffs, and particularly that of Pope Pius XII, three principles regarding patriotism, national life and nationalism come to the fore.

First Principle: Concerning Patriotism. Love of one's country is a virtue, one of the forms of charity and filial piety. Considered from this standpoint, patriotism is a duty.

Love of the fatherland is a love of preference, but not exclusive. It flows from the Fourth Commandment of the Decalog. It calls for dedication to the fatherland, for service to the fatherland, its defense in case of unjust attack; it may go so far as to demand the sacrifice of life. Leo XIII stated that this obligation was based on the natural law.[2]

Pius X taught this traditional doctrine to the French pilgrims present at the ceremonies of beatification of Joan of Arc on April 19, 1909: "Yes, it is worthy not only of love, but of a special love —this fatherland whose sacred name awakens in your mind the dearest memories and causes all the fibers of your soul to vibrate; this common land, where you had your cradle, to which the bonds of blood and that other nobler community of affection and tradition attach you."

In this text are found assembled the elements of patriotism, of the love of country, which is "a special love." First there is the community of territory, of the common soil of our ancestors, where we were born and where we live; then, the community of blood; and finally the community of cultural, moral, spiritual traditions and of affections.

Benedict XV, commenting on the examination of the cause of Joan of Arc in 1919, refuted the "calumny" broadcast by the enemies of the Church, who accused Catholics of being opposed to the love of country, and showed that such an objection contradicts the commonly taught doctrine of the Church. In support of his argument, the Pope cited a passage of St. Thomas Aquinas which explains how it is a function of piety to pay due worship, after God, to parents and the fatherland.[3]

In the radio address directed to the people of France on the occasion of the fifth centenary of the rehabilitation of Joan of

2. "The natural law obliges us to give the best of our love and of our dedication to the fatherland; in case of need the good citizen will not hesitate to face death for his country" (Encyclical *Sapientiae Christianae*).

3. "Man is in various ways a debtor to others, according to the different degrees of perfection they possess and the different benefits he has received from them. From this twofold point of view, God occupies the first place, because he is absolutely perfect and because he is the first principle of our existence and government. Secondarily, however, this title also belongs to our parents and to our fatherland, of whom and in which we have received our life and education. Hence, after God, man is especially indebted to his parents and the fatherland. As a result, just as it is the function of religion to render worship to God, so, in a lesser degree, piety must pay worship to parents and the fatherland" (II-II, q. 101, art. 1).

Arc, and the celebrations commemorating the restoration of the cathedral at Rouen on June 24, 1956, Pius XII spoke

> . . . of the generous soil of this garden of Europe which is France, producing heroes of the fatherland and of the faith, who, for love of their mother, if her defense demands it, are ready to battle, to suffer and to die, in the knowledge that the crown of triumph will never be wanting to those who are willing to sacrifice themselves for a great and just cause.

Pius XII called attention to the fact that a lessening of love of country is a sign—and not the least significant—of a confusion of mind:

> Occasionally nowadays there are citizens who feel a sort of fear of showing themselves particularly devoted to the fatherland. As if love for one's own country necessarily implied contempt for other lands, as if the natural desire of seeing one's fatherland beautiful and prosperous internally and esteemed and respected externally inevitably begot aversion with regard to other nations. Some go so far as to avoid use of the word "fatherland"; they try to replace it with other words more adapted, as they say, to our times. Without doubt this diminution of love of country, of this great family which God has given us, is not the least sign of confusion of mind (Allocution to the pilgrims from the Marches, March 23, 1958).

Then in the Encyclical to the Church of China, June 29, 1958, Pius XII called attention to the fact that Catholic doctrine exhorts "Catholics to foster a deep and sincere love of their fatherland."

Second Principle: Concerning National Life. National life is distinct from the political reality, and attachment to the national life is entirely legitimate.

The Christmas message of 1954 on coexistence enunciates a very enlightening principle of distinction:

> The root of the error consists in confusing national life in the strict sense of the word with nationalist politics. The first, which constitutes the right and the glory of a nation, may and must be developed; the second, the source of innumerable evils, can never be sufficiently rejected. National life, by its nature, is the active sum total of all the values of civilization proper to a determined group—the values that characterize it and constitute, as it were, the bond of its spiritual unity. At the same time it enriches the

culture of all of mankind by its own contribution. In essence, therefore, national life is something non-political. This is so true that, as history and experience show, it can develop side by side with others within the framework of the same state, as it likewise can exert its influence beyond the frontiers of a given state.

Three salient ideas are contained in this text: 1) the definition and the nature of national life; 2) its excellence; 3) its non-political character.

We are dealing here with a delicate matter. In order to understand the thought of Pius XII better, let us consider the example of a true democracy which he himself proposed; namely, Switzerland, where the problem existed and found its solution (message broadcast by Radio-Lausanne, September 14, 1956).

Pius began by pointing out that in this day and age two ideas which must be kept distinct are frequently confused: nationality and state. We speak of "a national state." The case of Switzerland will help to clear up the question. "Situated geographically at the point of intersection of three powerful national civilizations, Switzerland embraces all three in the unity of one people. At a time when nationalism seems to have the upper hand almost everywhere, Switzerland, which is a transcendent political community rather than a national state, enjoys the quiet and the power to procure union among its citizens."

Might one not perhaps be tempted to ask if a regime of this kind does not do violence to the sentiment of patriotism or to the feeling of unity? The Pope replied: "Possibly no other people has such a love for the home and for the fatherland as the Swiss; no other has a livelier and more profound consciousness of civic duties."

No doubt, the defenders of nationalism will insist in affirming that nothing can replace the dynamism of the national idea. Pius XII pointed out: "The creative vigor and power which others may find in the national idea, the Swiss discover, at least to the same degree, in the cordial emulation and in the collaboration of their different national groups."

With the movement and the emigration of people, with the need of certain states to import laborers, this problem will become more acute in the future. But frequently in the past there have been states which, alongside a predominant ethnical group, also contained other ethnical groups which preserved their own customs, language and aspirations.

A brief review of the tenets of international law will also help to clarify this question.

Public international law distinguishes nation and state. Numerous international acts have proclaimed the right of protection and of equality of ethnic groups within the framework of one and the same state, and in 1919 special treaties recognized the principles relative to the protection of national minorities: protection of life, of liberty, of language, without distinction of nationality, of race or of religion. These treaties assured national minorities equality of right and of fact before the law, the right to the nationality of the state (excluding manifestations that would threaten the life of the state).

These advances in international law were all the more necessary since, as a matter of fact, respect for these incorporated national groups had not always been practiced in the past. Toward the end of the nineteenth and the beginning of the twentieth century Germany had subjected the Poles in its empire as well as the inhabitants of Alsace-Lorraine to discriminatory treatment. We may recall, too, the massacres of the Armenian Christians by the Turks of the sultanate (1894 and 1916). Before the days of atrociously cruel anti-Semitic measures of Hitler, the Jews had received extremely unfavorable treatment in czarist Russia, Austria-Hungary and Roumania.

Twice already we have referred to the intervention of Pius XII in favor of ethnical minorities; he demanded that states respect their aspirations and just demands.

Thus is posed the problem of the nation against the state, of the distinction of national life and the political reality of the state.

Definition and nature of national life: National life is the active totality of the values of civilization which are proper to a country, which characterize it and give it a particular physiognomy in comparison to other peoples. It includes cultural, psychological, moral and religious values. They are the things that constitute the bond of its spiritual unity, as it were, rising above the diversity of nationalities or ethnic groups which compose it and the social classes it embraces.

Excellence of national life: National life is "the right and glory of a people." It may and must be developed. Above were cited the papal texts demanding respect for the specific cultural characteristics of every nation and showing how much this diversity contributed to the enrichment of the unity and culture of the human family. Pius XII reaffirmed the same point in speaking of national life: "It enriches at the same time by its own contribution the culture of all mankind." His unceasing defense of the rights of small nations is well known; at the same time he recalled their duty to cooperate for the welfare of the community of nations.

> All nations have the duty of reinvigorating the flame of their natural energies . . . and to make them so effective on the economic, social, cultural and religious level that they serve not only for their own well-being, but also permit them to participate to the greatest possible extent in a world-wide undertaking to obtain the progress and the well-being of the entire human family (Address of May 24, 1949, to the ambassador of Bolivia).

By essence national life is non-political. The nation is distinct from the political reality, and national life is distinct from the political society of the state. Pius XII here mentions examples drawn from history and experience: on the one hand, there exists, within the framework of one and the same state, a national life which develops side by side with others; on the other hand, the national life may extend beyond the political frontiers of the state.[4]

From the national point of view, the sum total of the values of civilization which make up national life are essential elements of the common good of the nation. Now, the political state must serve the common good; it does not have the right, for its own advantage, in order to satisfy political ambitions, to dispose of these values of civilization by exploiting them, dominating them,

---

4. In his book, *Enquête sur la nationalisme* (1956), Marcel Clément cites the following examples: "The French nation extends far beyond the limits of the French political territory. There are six million persons who constitute 'the French nation of America' and who are citizens either of Canada or of the United States. Contrariwise, federal states like Belgium, Canada, Switzerland, unite within one political framework various national traditions; it goes without saying that such a situation poses delicate problems of unity in diversity" (p. 207).

suppressing them, as they may seem to be either an advantage or a hindrance to its imperialist appetite or to its drive for expansion. A political state cannot claim the right to impose on a nation a cultural, ideological or religious system; there are certain values that go beyond it and that it must respect if it wishes to fulfill its mission.

Third Principle: Concerning the Nationalist State and Nationalist Politics. When the state, instead of serving the values of civilization in national life, tries to dominate everything, to monopolize everything, to assume all responsibility, to centralize all activities under its totalitarian authority, to turn to its own advantage all vital forces of the nation, when it makes nationality the foundation for its urge to expand and tries to make the ethnic unity of the nation coincide with the political unity of the state —to the point of becoming a state-nation and entirely absorbing the nation—then it is a nationalist state, it carries on nationalist politics. The regimes of Mussolini and Hitler were states of this kind.

> National life became a dissolving principle for the community of nations only when it began to be exploited for political reasons, namely, when the domineering and centralizing state made nationality the basis of its drive for expansion. Thus came about the nationalist state, the seedbed of rivalry and the source of discord (Christmas Message, 1954).

Pope Pius XII, in his allocution to the College of Cardinals, June 2, 1945, described the ravages caused by National Socialism in Germany:

> You thus behold the results of a concept and an activity of the state that do not take into account the most sacred feelings of humanity, which tread underfoot the inviolable principles of the Christian faith. Today the entire world gazes thunderstruck at the ruin that ensued.

Pius XII recalled how his predecessor, Pius XI, on Passion Sunday, 1937, in his Encyclical *Mit Brennender Sorge*, had revealed to the world what National Socialism really was: "... the arrogant apostasy from Jesus Christ, the denial of His doctrine and of His redemptive work, the cult of might, the idolatry of race and of blood, the suppression of liberty and of human dignity."

The National Socialism of Hitler went to the limit in its application of the principle of the nationalist state and of nationalist politics; time has shown the errors which they contained. Such errors make these principles dangerous in themselves and at the same time are a condemnation of the nationalist state and of nationalist politics.

Within the state: the nation is an end in itself and is regarded as an absolute. It is taken as the foundation for the totalitarian politics of the state, which considers itself the mandatary of the nation and as an end to which everything must be subordinated. Self-interest is its sole guide. It does not have to take into account any interests superior to those of the individual states. It need not submit to a law of universal morality binding on individuals, societies or nations. Neither does it have to recognize its essential dependence on God. It is its own master. The political values of the state take precedence over everything else. Here we have the deification of the state and of the nation.

Already in the Encyclical *Summi Pontificatus*, Pius XII had denounced this very grave error:

> To consider the state as an end to which everything must be subordinated and directed can only do harm to the true and lasting prosperity of nations. And this is what happens either when such a sovereignty is attributed to the state, considered as the mandatary of the nation, of the people, of the ethnic family, of a social class, or when the state arrogates to itself this sovereignty as absolute master, independently of any mandate.

The Pope here distinguishes two cases: that in which the political state, apart from any mandate, attributes to itself such absolute sovereignty; and that in which it is considered as the mandatary of the nation (or of any other entity), in order to make of the nation the base of its totalitarian politics, of its political, economic and cultural imperialism.

Outside the state: nationalist politics, the nationalist state, are a tremendous obstacle to the community of nations. At the beginning of this chapter we considered the exceedingly harmful consequences of the doctrine of the sovereignty of the state in the international sphere. Now, nationalist politics, the nationalist state, rest on this doctrine. Pius XII pronounced a severe judgment on "this type of nationalist state, self-sufficient, centralizing its powers and unstable in the choice of its alliances. Far too quickly the enormous accumulation of lives and of goods demanded by this kind of state, as well as the crushing economic and spiritual burdens it imposed have been consigned to oblivion . . . a principle ruinous for the community of nations . . . the nationalist state, a seedbed of rivalry and a source of discord" (Christmas Message, 1954).

The Pope anticipated the objection which partisans of a nationalist policy might offer by saying: "These dangers need no longer be feared nowadays. In order to satisfy its ambitions, the nationalist state would require an economic and a military force; in the majority of cases it is deprived of them. It is scarcely conceivable that nationalism would now express itself in acts of this kind; that it manifests itself in feelings no longer presents the same dangers."

Pius replied:

Let no one say that, given new circumstances, the dynamism of the nationalist state does not represent a danger for the other nations, because of the fact that it is deprived, generally, of true economic and military power. In reality, the dynamism of an imaginary nationalist power, even though expressing itself in feelings rather than in acts, equally offends individuals, fosters contempt and suspicion of alliances, hinders mutual understanding, and consequently loyal collaboration and mutual assistance, no more and no less than if it were supported by a strong power (Christmas Message, 1954).

Not only acts of nationalist policy, not only the abuses of the nationalist state are a danger to the community of nations; the feelings which the egocentric nationalist policy stirs up and nourishes must also be considered. Thus, when nationalism becomes an exaggerated attachment to the nation, it carries within itself the principles of those deviations and of those abuses of which the nationalist state can be guilty, as well as of the seeds of conflict and threats which compromise the peace of the world and the community of nations.

For this reason, Pius XII, addressing the entire world in his

Christmas message of 1948, laid down the duty of Christians with regard to this intransigent kind of nationalism which endangers the solidarity of nations:

> A convinced Christian cannot withdraw himself into a convenient and egotistical "isolationism," when he is aware of the deviations of an intransigent nationalism, which denies or treads underfoot solidarity among the different nations, a solidarity which imposes on everyone manifold duties with regard to the great family of nations.

Somewhat later, Pius XII, recalling the Catholic doctrine on the community of nations, namely, that "every nation enjoys equal rights as a member of the family of nations," concluded with the assertion that every Catholic Christian has the duty of cooperating with all his heart in the generous efforts "which serve to free each of the nations from the trammels of an egocentric mentality" (Radio message of December 24, 1948).

At present we are assisting at a reawakening, an unleashing of nationalism. Now, nationalism can become one of the most stubborn obstacles to the community of nations. Pius XII condemned it in the nationalist policy which it inspires and in the nationalist state in which it finds expression. He denounced the feelings which it engenders as well as the egocentric mentality which it fosters.

OBSTACLES OF A PSYCHOLOGICAL AND HISTORICAL ORDER

In two outstanding discourses Pope Pius XII treated of the opposition and the conflicts between nations as constituting obstacles to the international community: that of December 6, 1953, to the Fifth National Congress of the Union of Italian Catholic Jurists, and that of October 13, 1955, to the Italian Center of Studies for International Reconciliation.

He remarked first of all that, in the course of the first half of the present century, the face of the earth was profoundly transformed in the national, economic, social, cultural and ideological spheres.

On the one hand, the mutual interdependence of nations developed exceedingly. On the other hand, and at the same time, the national sentiment reawakened in certain areas; in fact, there was a flowering of nationalism.

Formerly conflicts between nations existed, but they were limited to time and space. Nowadays, however, tensions between the nations have a tendency to spread out and to have an influence on the peace of the entire world.

And still, as we saw in the first chapter, there also exists among the nations a deep-seated tendency toward the formation of a community of nations.

For this reason it is necessary to study the nature and the psychology of nations, in order to foresee the conflicts which the secret and opposite movements they reveal might provoke.

There is need, likewise, to observe the changes of thought and sentiment which affect the nations.

The Pope then described the many obstacles which stand in the way of an international community. They belong to various categories; we shall try to classify them in accord with the two discourses.

Obstacles that affect "basically both men and nations." These are "natural or acquired dispositions, different and often opposed dispositions of the spiritual or physical character which act in the intellectual, affective or dynamic sphere," goals and intentions, sentiments and desires, which may indeed be upright, but also vicious.

To this first category must then be added "the natural or passionate tendencies which play so large a part in the daily life of individuals": self-love, ambition for power, tendency to expansion, to assimilation and to absorption (Discourse of October 13, 1955).

In the Discourse of December 6, 1953, the Pope had pointed out how account must be taken of the innate tendencies of particular individuals and of communities in their mutual contacts and relations; he calls it "the dynamism of conquest or of defense":

. . . the tendency of adaptation and of assimilation often pushed to the point of absorption; or, on the contrary, the tendency of exclusion and of destruction of everything that appears unassimilable; the tendency of expansion and, again on the contrary, the tendency of self-sufficiency and self-segregation; the tendency of giving one's self by complete self-renunciation and, opposed to it, attachment to self and exclusion of any altruistic tendency; the will to power, the strong desire of keeping others in subjection.

Attention must be called again to the very important place Pius assigned to the psychology of individuals and nations in a realistic study of the problems of peace. He enumerated certain tendencies by way of example, but the list is not complete. In no nation, he said, "does one find together everything that is good and just."

Pius XII here applies the law of Original Sin, the limitations and miseries of human nature; this law should remind us that sentimentalism with regard to certain international attitudes is dangerous and opens the way to many illusions. In his Christmas message of 1956, in which he denounced the errors regarding human nature, Pius XII called for a return "to true realism, to Christian realism, which determines with the same certitude the dignity of man, but also his limits; his capacity to go beyond himself, as well as the reality of sin."

Obstacles which affect milieu and civilization: These are "questions of race and blood, of soil and climate, of education and custom, of language, history and culture—everything that surrounds and influences a man or nation."

One of the present-day phenomena most pregnant with consequences is the attainment of political and cultural autonomy on the part of civilizations other than the Western. How many obstacles does not this ferment and this confrontation of different civilizations or cultures present to the community of nations! In the future, it is true, this may bring about an enrichment, a rapprochement, a strengthening of unity. But how difficult it is for a Frenchman, a European, to grasp the culture of a Chinese or of a Hindu! Happily, efforts are being made to bring about a knowledge of Oriental cultures, an understanding of the civilizations of India, China and Africa. It is of the utmost importance that Christians lead the way in this "meeting of mankinds," to quote the title of a well-written work of Dom Lou, the Chinese

Benedictine,[5] and to follow the line of conduct which Pius XII laid out in his Encyclical *Evangelii Praecones:*

> From her beginning till the present time, the Church has always observed the very wise norm, according to which the Gospel does not destroy or extinguish among the peoples who embrace it anything that is good, decent or beautiful in their character or in their genius. . . . The Church accepted with good will their arts and their culture which not rarely attained great heights, cultivated them carefully and brought them to a degree of beauty which they had perhaps not reached before.

Already in 1939, Pius XII had written in the Encyclical *Summi Pontificatus:*

> Innumerable researches and pioneer investigations, carried out in a spirit of sacrifice, of dedication and of love by missionaries of all times, are offered, in order to facilitate a deeper understanding and respect for the most varied civilizations, and to make their spiritual values fruitful for a living and vivifying preaching of the Gospel of Christ.

The economic conditions in which a nation lives or is forced to live exercise a great influence on all its thoughts, aspirations and activities: These are "conditions of ownership and possession, of freedom or of economic dependence."

Increasingly economic and social problems tend to dominate the lives of nations and international relations. They give rise to conflicts of interests and they are bound up with definite ideologies. This difference of interests and this opposition of ideologies often beget bitter tensions between nations and occasionally lead them to seek a solution in armed conflict.

No one will have any difficulty in applying these things to our times. Reference may simply be made to the competition of interests and the struggle of ideological propaganda on the part

5. Dom Peter Celestine Lou Tseng-Tsiang, *La rencontre des humanités et la découverte de l'Evangile* (Desclée, 1949). In his introduction, the former Chinese statesman, who became a Benedictine, writes: "The problem of international relations is not primarily of a political nature; it is above all of an intellectual and moral order. Fundamentally, the problem is one of bonds and of divisions among men, of resemblances and differences which unite or separate civilizations, of resemblances and differences between the 'mankinds' that are the cornerstone of each one of them."

of the two great blocs in their assistance to underdeveloped countries.

Religious problems: Religion "can exercise an exalted function of conciliation and of appeasement on the relations between states, but sometimes also cause division and tension."

Pius XII did not hesitate to call to mind the wars of religion: "Inspired by a profound spirit of religion and a sincere enthusiasm, they could lead to heroic sacrifices. But once the religious ideal was no longer maintained in all its purity, then, in many instances, only too worldly aspirations injected themselves."

In relation to this subject and other circumstances, Pius XII treated of the very delicate problem existing in a community of nations: the practical coexistence of Catholic and non-Catholic communities. This was in his Discourse of December 6, 1953, to the Union of Catholic Italian Jurists.

Two propositions must be distinguished:

1. "Objective truth and the duties of conscience with regard to what is objectively true and good."

This proposition can only with difficulty be made the object of a discussion and of regulation between the states and their citizens, especially where a number of religious confessions exist in the same state.

2. "The effective attitude of the community of nations over against each sovereign state and of each state over against the community of nations in matters of religion and of morality."

The Pope then explains the two principles which clarify the reply to the second proposition. First principle:

> What is not in accord with the truth and the moral law objectively has no right to existence, to propagation, to action. Consequently, no human authority, no state, no community of states, whatever be their religious character, can give a positive mandate or a positive authorization to teach or to do what is contrary to religious truth or moral good. Why? Because it is contrary to nature to oblige the soul and the will of man to error or to evil, or to take an indifferent attitude with regard to these two.

Second principle: The fact of tolerating or of not impeding error or evil by civil laws or coercive measures "can nevertheless be justified in the interests of a superior and more comprehensive good."

Despite the fact that God disapproves of error and sin, he allows them to exist. The parable of the weeds in the grain shows forth the merciful patience of the Lord (cf. Mt 13:24-30).

Therefore the obligation of suppressing moral and religious deviations cannot be an ultimate norm of action. It must be subordinate to higher and more general norms which, in certain circumstances, allow error or even make it appear preferable not to impede error, in order to promote a greater good.

The Church herself practices this tolerance for the sake of a higher good; she has

. . . the desire of protecting the common good, that of the Church and that of the state in every state on the one hand; the common good of the universal Church, of the kingdom of God on the whole earth, on the other.

These are the principles. For the Catholic jurist, the question of their application to a concrete case is extremely delicate. He must weigh the harmful effects arising from this tolerance and compare them with those which this same tolerance spares the community of nations; then he must consider the good which may result for the community as such and indirectly for the state which is a member of that community. As far as the religious and moral sphere is concerned, he will also ask the opinion of the Church, of the Pope, alone competent in the last instance in these decisive questions affecting international life.

What attitude ought to be taken with regard to the obstacles mentioned in the preceding pages, especially the difficulties and tendencies which appear to be opposed to the community of nations? Pius XII offered the following advice:

Within the limits of the possible and the permissible, to promote what will facilitate and make the union more effective, to abate what disturbs it, to tolerate at times what cannot be abolished and for which, on the other hand, one could not permit the community of nations to suffer harm in the interests of a higher good which one expects from it.

OBSTACLES OF A MILITARY AND TECHNICAL ORDER

How many men throughout the world sincerely regard themselves as initiators and pioneers when they denounce the armament race as a danger for mankind! They would be very much surprised to learn that all the Popes, without exception, have courageously and firmly condemned this insane race and called for disarmament in the clearest terms, ever since this danger became threatening. How many Catholics are ignorant of the constant teaching of the Sovereign Pontiffs in this matter!

Leo XIII. Beginning with 1889, Leo XIII declared that armaments are not only powerless to bring about a secure and stable peace but that they compromise it and place a heavy yoke on the nations.

> Large standing armies and unlimited warlike preparations may indeed for a time command the respect of an enemy disposed to attack, but they cannot bring about a secure and stable peace. Armaments that are built up with aggressive intentions tend rather to increase than to diminish rivalries and enmities. They disturb men by reason of the disquieting prospects of the future and offer the serious inconvenience of imposing on the nations such a heavy yoke that it may often be asked if they are more tolerable than war itself (Allocution to the Sacred College, February 11, 1889).

Already in the second chapter we called attention to the lively interest which Leo XIII had taken in the first conference of The Hague, held as a result of the initiative of Czar Nicholas II. It had as its objective the organization of international peace and the reduction of armaments.

Finally, in a letter of 1902 addressed to all the bishops of the Catholic world, Leo XIII deplored the abandonment of the great principles of morality and justice in the relations among the nations and the substitution of utility in their place. He thus described the consequences:

> Disastrous principles, which have consecrated material force as the supreme law of the world, to which must be attributed this progressive and unlimited increase of military preparations or this armed peace, comparable to the most disastrous effects of war, at least under some aspects (Apostolic Letter *Parvenu,* March 19, 1902).

Pius X. We already had occasion to point out how Pius X endorsed the Carnegie Foundation for International Peace in

1911. He gave the following reasons: "To bring about understanding, to suppress manifestations of hatred, to remove the dangers of war, even to remove worries about what is called the armed peace—this is a very generous undertaking." And the Pope added:

> This is all the more true today, when the size of standing armies, the murderous power of armaments, the notable advances in military science point to wars capable of putting fear even into the most powerful rulers.[6]

Benedict XV. In his great message of August, 1917, to the belligerent nations and their rulers, Benedict XV offered his good offices to bring about peace. He made some concrete and practical proposals, inviting the governments of the belligerent nations to come to an agreement on a number of points which appeared as the necessary bases for a just and lasting peace.

The first proposal of the Pope is based on the following principle:

> First of all, the fundamental point must be the substitution of the moral force of law for the material force of arms; then a just agreement of all for the simultaneous and reciprocal reduction of armaments, according to rules and guarantees to be established, in the measure necessary and sufficient to maintain the public order of each state (Message of August 1, 1917).

Benedict XV considered reciprocal and simultaneous disarmament as "the true foundation of peace and prosperity." We know this from a letter of Cardinal Gasparri to Lloyd George, dated September 28, 1917, which uses this expression and informs us of the only practical means,[7] easily employed, which the Holy

6. Letter *Libenter abs te,* June 11, 1911, to Archbishop Falconio, Apostolic Delegate to the United States.

7. This sole practical means would be: "For the nations, the neutrals included, to come to an agreement for the simultaneous and reciprocal suppression of obligatory military service and for the erection of a tribunal of arbitration empowered to settle international conflicts, including as a sanction the boycotting of a nation which would attempt to reëstablish obligatory military service or which would refuse to bring international litigation before the tribunal and to accept its decision." According to the letter, obligatory military service would be replaced by voluntary military service, which certainly would supply the manpower necessary to maintain public order.

Father envisaged. Benedict XV, however, did not desire, by an official document, to propose a program of a technical and political nature, since, as he was at pains to point out, he wished to leave to governments "the work of defining and completing" the concrete proposals he had made.

A very remarkable text of Pope Benedict XV ought to be known by all. In the Encyclical *Pacem*, May 23, 1920, he considered it "very desirable" that "the aggregation of states, putting away their mutual suspicions, unite to form but one society, or rather one family, both for the defense of their own liberties and for the maintenance of the social order." This society of nations would have as its primary object to respond "to the universally recognized need of making every effort to suppress or to reduce military budgets, whose crushing burden the states can no longer bear."

Toward the end of 1921, when the Naval Conference of Washington was convened (November 12, 1921 to February 6, 1922) to seek means to reduce the military budgets that had become too burdensome, Benedict XV publicly expressed his "deep satisfaction" in an allocution to the Sacred College, November 21, 1921. Shortly before, on the eve of the Conference, he had sent a telegram to the President of the United States, assuring him that the Pontiff would pray fervently for the success of the enterprise initiated by the President "with a view to bringing relief to agitated mankind."

Pius XI. Several times Pius XI declared that peace could not be assured by armaments: it "cannot be based on arms . . ." (Christmas Allocution, 1931), "the best guarantee of tranquility is not a forest of bayonets, but mutual confidence and friendship,"[8] ". . . armaments lead to an impasse" (Christmas Allocution, 1931).

In his first Encyclical *Ubi Arcano Dei*, December 23, 1922, Pius XI had deplored the fact that all the nations were obliged "to live on a war footing, a thing that exhausts the public finances,

8. Letter of April 7, 1922, to the Archbishop of Genoa, on the occasion of the international peace conference.

absorbs the living forces of the race and disturbs both intellectual culture as well as religious and moral life."

In 1931 the Pope called attention to a grave crisis, the result of a sharper rivalry among the nations and the cause of exhausting public expense. This twofold plague, he said, "is primarily caused by the excessive and progressively heightened pursuit of military preparations and armaments" (Apostolic letter to the Catholic Hierarchy, October 2, 1931).

1933 was a Holy Year. The Pope saw with sadness how the international situation was worsening. He requested prayers for the conferences that would be held in the course of the Holy Year "in order to bring about a better order in the economic situation of the whole world, an effective diminution of military preparations" (Allocution to the Sacred College, March 13, 1933).

Teaching and activity of Pius XII. The Christmas message of 1939, delivered four months after the outbreak of the war, squarely faced the problem of the armament race in the following terms:

> So that the order, reëstablished in such a manner, may be tranquil and durable—the cardinal principles of true peace—nations must be liberated from the heavy slavery of armaments and from the danger that material force, instead of serving to protect rights, become the tyrannical violator of them. Conclusion of peace which would fail to attribute fundamental importance to disarmament, mutually accepted, organic and progressive both in letter and spirit, and would fall short of carrying out this disarmament loyally, would sooner or later reveal their inconsistency and lack of vitality (Christmas Message, 1939).

In this passage three ideas come strongly to the fore:

1. The obligation of "liberating" the nations from the armament race. The Pope offers two reasons: first, because it imposes a "slavery" on the nations; despite themselves, the nations are drawn into this race, so ruinous for their budget and so burdensome for their economy; second, because this race begets a serious "danger," that of seeing material force become a tyrannical instrument for the violation of rights, instead of protecting them. Pius XII spoke of the relations between rights and force on

October 8, 1947, to a group of civil inspectors of the United States Army:

> Law and order may have need of the solid arm of force. The enemies of justice can be brought to terms only through force. But force must always act within the limits of law and order and be exercised solely for their defense.

But the guiding thought of Pius XII in this field is the substitution of respect of law for the worship of force, the force of law for the force of arms, in the conduct of nations.

> What We have always had in view in all the expressions of Our thought and Our will is this: to convert the nations from the worship of force to the respect of law and to promote peace among all—a just and solid peace, a peace capable of guaranteeing to all at least a tolerable life (Allocution to the Diplomatic Corps, February 25, 1946).

He was reiterating a fundamental point of the constant doctrine of the Sovereign Pontiffs.

Leo XIII had already said: "Nature is not opposed to the defense of one's rights by force and by arms; it does not permit, however, that force be the efficient cause of rights" (Allocution to the Sacred College, February 11, 1889).

We have given above an utterance of Pope Benedict XV to the same effect: "First of all, the fundamental point must be that the moral force of right be substituted for the material force of arms" (Message of August 1, 1917).

2. The basic importance to be given to the problem of disarmament in the future conditions of peace. Not only must this problem be discussed frankly and courageously, but steps must be taken to realize disarmament loyally. This is necessary in order to avoid inconsistency and lack of vitality in the treaty of peace. Otherwise, the order established by the peace will not be tranquil and durable.

3. The conditions and the nature of disarmament are clearly defined. The Pope enumerates four of them:

"Mutually accepted disarmament." It would evidently be very imprudent for one or several nations to disarm unless they had the certainty that all the other nations would do the same. To act differently would offer a premium on aggression.

"Organic disarmament." This is a new condition which did not apparently occur among those mentioned by the predecessors of Pius XII nor among those commonly accepted by states.[9] Manifestly, from this moment, since the UN did not yet exist, the Pope foresees that disarmament cannot be carried out except within the framework of an international organization. He will develop his thought on this "organic" character at greater length in the Christmas message of 1956, as we shall see.

"Progressive disarmament," by successive steps in accordance with the dictates of prudence necessary to insure the protection and the public order of the states.

"Disarmament both in the practical and in the spiritual order." A purely material and military disarmament would not suffice to bring about peace. It must be accompanied by a moral and spiritual disarmament, by the abandonment of sentiments of hatred, of vengeance, of contempt, of fear.

In the Christmas message of 1941, Pope Pius XII again spoke insistently of the need of a limitation of armaments. He returned to the same condition of progressive reduction, once the most dangerous causes of armed conflicts had been eliminated.

In this message the Pope presents two new ideas relating to the problem of disarmament.

In the first place, this limitation is demanded as a necessary condition for the avoidance of the scourge of a third war with all its terrible consequences.

Furthermore, this limitation must be "ample," that is, extended, vast, on a large scale; it must be "adequate" and "proportioned." The Holy Father here had in mind the flagrant disproportion between the exaggerated armaments of the powerful states and the insufficient armament of the weak ones. Such a situation constitutes a constant danger to peace: as far as the powerful states are concerned, they may be tempted to employ threats and, by abusive pressure, to demand grants and concessions to satisfy their thirst for power and their desire of expansion; on

9. In its resolution of December 1, 1949, the importance of which we have already called attention to, the UN invited all the nations "to collaborate for the establishment of an effective system of international regulation of armaments of the classical type."

the part of the weak states, there is fear, worry, suspicion and mistrust.

Here is the text of the Christmas message of 1941:

> Within the framework of a new organization founded on moral principles, once the more dangerous causes of armed conflicts have been eliminated, there is no place for total war or for a mad rush to armaments. The calamity of a world war, with the economic and social ruin and the moral dissolution and breakdown that would follow in its train, must not be permitted to envelop mankind for a third time. In order that mankind be preserved from such a scourge, it is essential to proceed with sincerity and honesty to a progressive limitation of armaments. The lack of equilibrium between the exaggerated armaments of the powerful states and the limited armaments of the weaker ones is a menace to harmony and peace among nations, and demands that an ample and proportionate limit be placed upon production and possession of offensive weapons in accordance with the measure in which disarmament is effected.

The Christmas message of 1951 deplores "the monstrous cruelty of modern weapons" and recalls that the Pope had always desired and called for disarmament, "that is to say, the simultaneous and progressive reduction of armaments."

But the dominating idea of the message was that of the primacy and spiritual aspect of all danger of war. Were one to imagine that the question of the peace is solely or principally dependent on the question of arms, he would be running the risk of dangerous illusions or of falling into "a kind of practical materialism, of superficial sentimentalism." For this reason the Pope called above all for a spiritual disarmament, consisting "of the abolition of the arms of hatred, of cupidity, of the limitless desire for prestige." This is still a negative aspect. Positively he demands that consideration be given to the decisive role which "the Christian order" can play; it alone is "capable of assuring peace."

The Easter message of 1954 describes in impressive terms the ravages which would inevitably follow from the use of the new offensive weapons. We shall study this matter in the chapter on war.

The Christmas message of 1954 on coëxistence demonstrates that if it is based on fear the treaties on the limitations of armaments will be futile. "No nation could support indefinitely the armament race without feeling its disastrous effects on normal economic development. Vain would be the very treaties intended to impose a limitation on armaments."

In the Christmas message of 1955, Pope Pius XII attacks the problem of nuclear weapons and of the control of armaments in a very concrete manner. He ties together three questions: a) renunciation of experiments with nuclear weapons; b) renunciation of the use of such weapons; c) general control of armaments.

He did not hesitate to affirm that "these three measures taken together are a matter of conscience for nations and their governments." He clearly indicated the motive of this moral obligation: "the establishment of equal security for all the nations." As a matter of fact, as far as the first two measures are concerned, he accurately described from the scientific point of view the effect of experiments with atomic explosions and the effects of the use of nuclear weapons on the atmosphere, on the surface of the earth, on human lives and for the annihilation of entire cities.

Concerning the third measure, control, the Pope enumerated the various means that have been proposed, without pronouncing on their technical aspect.[10] But he did affirm that these three measures form one whole. Hence it does not suffice to stop the experiments; the security of all the nations would not be assured. If that were all, "there might be sufficient reason to doubt the existence of a serious intention to make the other agreements."

In problems of this kind, where the fate of the human race hangs in the balance, the Pope decided to speak frankly. It is necessary that everything be exactly determined, because inadequate proposals always run the risk of putting peace in danger in a climate of suspicions among the powers, which would

10. Pius XII mentioned the two means of control that had been proposed: a) inspection by means of aircraft that had been suitably equipped; b) a world-wide network of centers of observation, staffed by scientists of different nations and guaranteed by international agreements—centers fitted out with instruments for meteorological and seismic observations, for chemical analyses, for spectographs of masses. On July 21, 1955, at the Geneva Conference, President Eisenhower had suggested aerial inspection as a means of control.

accuse one another of a lack of sincerity or of pure opportunism. The message of 1956 brought new clarifications. After expressing his regret regarding certain defective aspects of the UN, the Pope desired to see the authority of the great international organization reinforced, notably in order to bring about a general disarmament.

> If We make reference to these defective aspects, it is because We desire to see the authority of the United Nations strengthened, particularly to bring about a general disarmament, which is of so great concern to Us and of which We have spoken already on other occasions. After all, it is only within the framework of an institution like that of the United Nations that the pledge of each of the states to reduce its armaments, and especially to cease the production and use of certain weapons, can be made the matter of a common agreement and thus be transformed into a strict obligation of international law. By the same token, only the United Nations are at present in a position to see to the observance of such an agreement, by assuring the effective control of armaments of each one without any exception.

The thought of the Holy Father thus becomes very clear. "Only within the framework of an institution like that of the United Nations" can an action of the totality of the states be seriously and effectively envisaged, as well as the pledge of each of them "to bring about a general disarmament."

Hence more is demanded than the renunciation of nuclear experiments and of the use of nuclear weapons. Pius XII repeated his thought regarding general disarmament, as he had presented it in the Christmas message of 1955, and then he added two important points in the Christmas message of 1956:

1. The necessity of the framework of the UN, not only for the commitment the states should make by common agreement, but also for the effective control of a disarmament. Only under these conditions would the commitment be transformed into a strict obligation of international law, sanctioned by inspection. Here become apparent the hopes the Pope placed in the great international institution and the reason why he desired to see the authority of the UN strengthened.

2. Regarding inspection, in view of a general disarmament already envisaged in 1955, the Pope clarified his thought by two further points:

On the one hand, concerning the means of inspection: he showed the advantages of aerial photography, thanks to the "prodigious" technical progress made in this field, which the message described with scientific precision. Besides, this means would avoid the difficulties which inspection by commissions might present, as was verified after 1918 in a defeated Germany and in 1940 in France.

On the other hand, concerning the test which the acceptance of inspection would constitute as a proof of the sincere desire for peace: "Acceptance of control—that is the crucial point; thereby every nation will show its desire for peace."

An event of considerable importance in this struggle against armaments took place in November, 1957, at the General Assembly of the UN.

On November 14, 1957, in its 716th plenary session, the General Assembly was called upon to decide on a projected resolution.

Already on November 4, 1954, the UN had had to pronounce on a projected international agreement for the reduction, the limitation and the free inspection of armaments and armed forces. In November, 1957, the UN began by recalling its resolution of three years before.

It then stated with satisfaction that agreements on points of view had been realized in the subcommittee of the Commission on Disarmament.

It went on to ask the interested states to give their opinions on the following dispositions:

a) Immediate suspension of nuclear explosions, accompanied by a system of effective international inspection. The UN indicated where control stations, equipped with suitable scientific apparatus, might be installed.

b) Cessation of production of fissionable matter for military purposes; future production of such material, under effective international inspection, to be destined exclusively for non-military purposes.

c) Reduction of stocks of nuclear weapons, under inspection.

d) Reduction of armed forces and of armaments, by means of suitable arrangements accompanied by guarantees.

e) Progressive introduction of a system of free inspection, both terrestrial and aerial, destined to safeguard against the eventuality of a surprise attack.

f) Common study of a system of inspection which would supply assurance that the sending of projectiles into outer space is being done solely for peaceful and scientific purposes.

This very complete resolution, which seems to envisage all the hypotheses for a lasting peace and to shut out the dangers of war also presents, besides technical means, two characteristics of a general order which merit attention in our study.

1. The primary place assigned, by means of inspection, to an effective control in each of the six articles enumerated; hence not only for the suspension of nuclear explosions and for the cessation of production, but also for the reduction of armaments.

The most beautiful proposals concerning the cessation of nuclear experiments or the use of such weapons would not suffice, they would remain chimerical, unless they were guaranteed by control and a system of inspection.

2. The very human concern which the UN manifests by inviting the interested states to study the possibility of using the savings effected through disarmament and the progress realized in this field "for the betterment of living conditions in the entire world and particularly in underdeveloped countries."

On these two essential points it is clear that the resolution of the UN agrees with the measures indicated by the Sovereign Pontiff in his messages of 1955 and 1956.

This resolution was adopted in the General Assembly of the UN on November 14, 1957. Seventy-one nations voted in its favor; nine—Russia and its satellites—voted against it; there was one abstention, Syria.

Why did Russia and its satellites take this negative attitude, especially since on several points the resolution affirmed the necessity of measures which these countries themselves had demanded—notably the cessation of nuclear experiments and of the production of nuclear weapons, as well as the reduction of armed forces?

The resolution was rejected by them because it provided for the institution of inspection for all the measures of disarmament.

And why does inspection call forth such bitter opposition on the part of Russia and the "popular democracies"? Because these governments are dominated by the demands and the slavery of propaganda. On the one side, they protect themselves by secrecy regarding activities within their own boundaries; the discovery, on the part of strangers, of situations and facts in flagrant contradiction with the slogans of propaganda might seriously compromise their prestige in the eyes of their own peoples, from whom so many things have remained hidden for years behind the Soviet Iron Curtain.

On the other hand, these governments, which must wrap themselves in a cloak of silence, have need of grasping every occasion to organize their propaganda outside, particularly in the great international assemblies. They must do this to demonstrate their will to power. Here they find a platform which supplies them with the means of accusing other nations of warlike designs and proclaiming to the whole world that they alone sincerely desire peace. For this reason the many meetings of the Subcommittee on Disarmament held between 1946 and 1956 produced but one final result—they had to be suspended. Instead of the private and restrained sessions of the subcommittee, the Soviet delegate preferred the great assemblies, where propaganda can be given free tongue in interminable discourses.

We had to mention this categorical refusal of inspection in order to point out the obstacle which Soviet Russia and its satellites raised against the extraordinary effort made by the UN to bring about effective disarmament.

Besides, from what has been said, we arrive at a better understanding of the meaning and the importance of the Christmas message of 1957.

The Christmas message of 1957, which treats of the order and harmony in the world as willed by God, contained two considerations on the problem of armaments.

1. Once again the Pope denounced the dangers, the sacrifices and the losses involved in the armament race, bringing with it, as it does, a dangerous weakening of the national economy, even in the richest nations.

But Pope Pius XII, analyzing the competition among the states that want to make a show of their progress in armaments (the right of self-defense always being safeguarded), discovered in the beginnings of this insane race the signs of pride, "of that pride which digs pits between peoples, nourishes hatreds and prepares the way for catastrophe."

It is necessary to return to a more objective appreciation of events and to reduce facts to their just proportions by making a large view of things inspired by wisdom and the Christian spirit.

2. The Pope addressed an urgent appeal to all governments of nations in the name of the divine law of harmony in the world:

> The divine law of harmony in the world strictly obliges all governments of nations to hinder war by international institutions capable of putting armaments under an effective surveillance, to keep in check, by means of the solidarity of the nations who sincerely desire peace, those who would want to disturb it.

Pius XII imposed on governments an imperative duty in particularly energetic terms: "The divine law . . . strictly obliges to hinder war."

Then he mentioned two means of preventing war:

International institutions, but with effective control and surveillance, as he had stated in his two preceding messages;

Then he adds something new: the moral and pacific power of "solidarity" among the nations that sincerely desire peace, in order "to keep in check," by means of this solidarity, those who would want to disturb the peace.

In all this teaching of the Sovereign Pontiffs concerning the problem of armaments, which seems at first glance to be confined to the purely technical order, we must distinguish three elements: 1) a doctrine; 2) the motives invoked by the Popes; 3) the solutions of a practical order proposed by them.

1. Doctrine. From all the successive pronouncements of the Popes in this sphere, a doctrine of the Church comes into full light with an impressive constancy and continuity.

If they denounce the armament race, if they call for progressive and simultaneous disarmament, if they ask for a tendency toward general disarmament, they do so because they are teaching a doctrine—that of the Gospel—on the dignity of the human person, on the brotherhood of men, on the design of God who desires a community of nations living in peace, justice and charity.

The principal argument in the doctrinal order on which the Popes rely is that of the superiority of the moral force of right, which must gain the upper hand over the material force of arms and be substituted for it. Force of arms does not create rights. The respect for rights must supersede the worship of force. War of aggression is a violation of God's design concerning mankind. The normal state of the community of nations must be that of peace.

For this reason Pius XII made it a matter of conscience for governments to do all in their power to prevent war and to assure a just and lasting peace.

This doctrine must be embraced by every Christian who wants to remain faithful to the teaching of the ordinary magisterium of the Church; it demands of him an interior assent and practical obedience. In this connection the Popes are acting as defenders of the truth and as guardians of the moral law.

2. The motives employed by the Popes to justify their position with regard to the armament race.

Besides the motives that proceed from the doctrine of the Gospel, it is remarkable that the Popes advance reasons on the levels of the natural, human and social order: the intolerable burdens for the national budgets which competition in the armament race beget; the tremendous killing power of modern weapons and the horrible ravages which they have produced and which they will again be able to produce to an even greater extent on the life of mankind; the disturbance caused to nations by the preparation and the manufacture of new weapons, the fear and anguish into which they plunge the peoples, who hold them in horror; the certitude that armaments, far from guaranteeing peace, only compromise it.

As far as these arguments are concerned, the Popes ask of the faithful that they accept them respectfully, examine them loyally and give them their serious attention. The Church here presents herself as a mother who loves her children and protects them from threatening dangers. The Popes appear as the intrepid defenders of man and of humanity. In fulfilling her doctrinal and apostolic mission, the Church safeguards the temporal order even from the natural standpoint.

3. The solutions of a technical order which the Popes present correspond to the needs and to the material and scientific progress of an epoch. Hence they vary with the times. In this field of armaments and of means of control, new discoveries are being made with prodigious rapidity.

The Pope does not speak here as a teacher propounding a truth. Sometimes he enunciates several practical solutions without committing himself. On other occasions he sets forth a specific solution and recommends it, for example, inspection, first because this means appears to him to correspond most effectively with the goal sought, and then because—in the technical order, it is true—such a solution has direct bearing on the moral behavior of statesmen, who either accept or reject it. Furthermore, the Pope himself has, in this case, pointed out the connection; it is a test of sincerity and the will for peace.

This part of the papal message, therefore, must not only be received with respect, but it puts into action the virtue of prudence on the part of the faithful; it reflects the prudential judgment of an authority better informed than private persons.

5

DISRUPTION OF GOD'S DESIGN—WAR

The time seems to have come for humanity, which has reached a certain degree of progress, to ask itself frankly whether it is necessary to resign itself to what, in the past, appeared as a hard law of history, or whether, on the contrary, it ought to try new ways and make generous efforts in all spheres of life, in order to free the human race from the repeated nightmares of wars.

This, then, must be the most pressing concern of the responsible public authorities.

—Pius XII, Allocution, October 13, 1955

IT WAS necessary first to consider God's design with regard to the community of nations, then the international order which men and nations have to construct in order to organize the world more conformably with the loving intentions concerning the human race which the Father in heaven has made known to us.

In this international order it next behooved, both to satisfy reasons of a psychological and pedagogical nature as well as to correspond more directly with God's design, it seemed best to place peace next, the organization for peace, a primary and fundamental will for peace in the forefront of the researches, the efforts, the preoccupations of states and nations. In place of the constant obsession with war, as if it were the sole and inevitable problem of international morality, it was necessary to substitute the passion, the tenacious striving for peace.

The study of war follows, therefore, not as the other face of an indissociable diptych, war-peace; but rather as the overthrow of God's plan, as the disruption of all that international order which ought to be the positive goal of humanity's progress.

Seen in this light, all the horrors of war and the extent of its criminality become apparent.

This chapter will contain three sections:

1. First, the false concepts of war must be rejected and refuted, whether they attempt to explain war as inevitable or seek to justify it or to minimize its effects.

2. Then we shall present the Church's doctrine on war of aggression and war of legitimate defense.

3. Finally, it will be worthwhile to point out the rules laid down by the Sovereign Pontiffs for the conduct of war, once it has broken out, to make it less inhumane.

FALSE CONCEPTS OF WAR

First false concept: War is unavoidable, inevitable and necessary. The Popes have demonstrated—and they have demanded that this capital fact be kept in mind—the growing aversion of nations for war and their ardent aspirations for peace. Already in 1889, Leo XIII declared: "The aversion of the nations for war manifests itself more and more every day" (Allocution to the College of Cardinals, February 11, 1889). Pius XII, speaking in 1951 of the formal wishes of peace which the peoples had expressed with irrefutable evidence both by words and deeds during the course of the Holy Year, cried out:

> Of all the manifestations which the Holy Year inspired, there is none more important, more significant in the order of human relations than the loudly proclaimed affirmation of the will of peoples, unanimously tending toward peace. . . . All are looking for this peace, all desire it, all pray for it. All have demonstrated with the same energetic clarity their horror of war (Allocution to the Diplomatic Corps, January 1, 1951).

Now, while the peoples have resolutely pronounced themselves in favor of peace, nevertheless it must be recognized that in certain circles there are many who continue to think that war is an implacable necessity, a harsh law of history and that it is necessary to submit to the inevitable. The Popes condemn this attitude of defeatism, really one of cowardice, because it stops up all springs of the action to which men and nations must unceasingly have recourse with courage and with perseverance, in order to build up peace, despite all the obstacles standing in the way. No, the Popes do not think that war imposes itself on humanity as the only and the inevitable means of settling conflicts between nations; there are other means. They must be sought and used.

In his very first Encyclical, Benedict XV, addressing heads of states, said:

> Let those who hold in their hands the destinies of nations heed Our words! There are certainly other means, other ways of obtaining redress for rights that have been injured. Let them have recourse to these after they have laid down their arms.[1]

In 1935, when the Ethopian war was about to erupt, Pius XI declared that if the reasons alleged were true (need of expansion, necessity of assuring frontiers), he only wished

> . . . that the solution of all the difficulties might be arrived at by means other than war. How? It is certainly not easy to say, but We do not believe that it would be unthinkable. This possibility must be studied (Allocution to the Congress of Nurses, August 27, 1935).

The excerpt at the head of the present chapter contains the vigorous appeal of Pius XII to the responsible public authorities to free the human race from the repeated nightmare of war. The time has come to try new ways, to seek for new forms to settle differences, to put forth generous efforts in all spheres of life. One may not resign himself to what, in times past, "appeared as a harsh law of history."

In an allocution of May 20, 1958, Pius XII stated that "the Church does not accept the doctrine of those who believe that humanity is governed by the law of war of all against all," just

1. Encyclical *Ad Beatissimi,* November 1, 1914; the above passage was repeated in a letter of May 25, 1915, to the dean of the Sacred College.

as she refuses "to admit any doctrine which considers war as a necessary effect of cosmic, physical, biological or economic forces."[2]

The Pope energetically opposed any theory which looks upon war as an inescapable necessity. He lifted his voice against "the absurdity of the doctrine which has held sway in political schools during the past decades, namely, that war is one of the many admissible forms of political action, the necessary and quasi-natural outcome of incurable dissensions existing between two countries" (Christmas Message, 1954). No less absurd is "the actual political practice [which], while indeed regarding war as the supreme catastrophe, nevertheless pays obeisance to it, as if it were the only expedient for survival, the sole regulator of international relations. In a certain sense, that becomes the object of confidence which is abhorred above everything."

Second false concept: War exonerates from all moral responsibility. For a long time the doctrine that war was a fact free of all moral responsibility had been widely accepted. This was the consequence of the admission of a kind of inevitable law of war: men were no longer responsible. War was simply the play of blind natural forces.

Pius XII rejected this false concept. He desired that wars be considered "as an object of the moral order, whose violation constitutes a real fault that will not remain unpunished . . . as a fact of a higher and Christian responsibility before God and before the moral law." Peoples live under the fear which the cold war generates. There is a "fear" which is salutary—one that acts as a curb to war and as a stimulant for peace, namely, the fear of God that protects and guarantees the moral order.

The problem of moral responsibility before God and before the moral law affects particularly the statesmen who declare war.

Absurd and inadmissible has equally appeared the principle, likewise of long standing, according to which the statesman who

2. Allocution to the ladies of the Roman section of the patronage for the spiritual assistance to the armed forces of Italy, May 20, 1958.

declares war is only judged guilty of a political error if he loses it; but he could in no case be accused of a moral fault for not having kept the peace when he was in a position to do so (*ibid.*).

The Pope then stated that it was this absurd and immoral concept of war which, in the course of the fateful weeks of 1939, rendered futile all the efforts he had undertaken to maintain in the two camps the desire of continuing negotiations. "War was then looked upon as a die, with which one plays with a prudence and a skill more or less cultivated, but not as a moral fact which calls into play conscience and higher responsibilities." Thereupon Pius XII set the problem before the good sense and the reason of the nations in a striking manner. How? Everyone is morally responsible for his most ordinary actions. Is he who begins a terrible war exempt from this responsibility?

How is it possible that "the horrible fact of war, which is still the fruit of the free determination of a person, should be withdrawn from the realm of conscience and that there should not exist a Judge to whom the innocent victims can have recourse?"

The Holy Father concluded: It is necessary that

. . . practically, all political figures, before evaluating the advantages and the risks of their decisions, should personally recognize their subjection to the eternal moral law and treat the problem of war as a question of conscience before God (*ibid.*).

A great step forward in the recognition of the moral and penal responsibility of statesmen before the international conscience, as far as war is concerned, was taken, at least in principle, with the institution of the Nuremberg trial. This is not the place to discuss either the conduct of the trial or the composition of the court.[3]

3. The Nuremberg trial lasted from November 14, 1945, to October 1, 1946. More than a dozen other trials followed the precedent in the American zone of occupied Germany.

An agreement signed at London on August 8, 1945, by the United Kingdom, the United States, France and Russia decided to set up a tribunal empowered to judge the great war criminals. The indictment was framed on three counts: 1) the crime of war: the crime of having prepared, unleashed, directed war of aggression or war in violation of international understandings (treaties, pacts, etc.); 2) the crimes of war: acts which constitute a violation of the laws and practices of war (assassination, de-

With regard to such trials, Pius XII remarked that they raised a twofold problem of penal responsibility and of culpability:

1. The problem of those who ordered others to commit a crime or who did not hinder the crime though they were able to do so and obliged to prevent it.

2. The problem of those who committed the acts in question only on orders of their superiors or were even forced to perform them under threats of dire punishment, often including that of death. Very frequently in these trials the accused invoked as an excuse that they had only acted at the command of "higher authorities."

The Holy Father asked that international agreements fix positive juridical rules, binding on states, to obviate a juridical dilemma, where an inferior finds himself faced with an order commanding him to commit a crime. Either he does not obey, and then he finds his position, his property, his very life jeopardized; or he does obey, and then he is pursued by the fear that when the hostilities are over, the injured party, if victorious, will force him to stand trial as a "war criminal."

The Pope then proposed this principle:

> However clear the moral norm may be in every case, no higher authority is empowered to command an immoral act; there exists no right, no obligation, no permission to perform an act immoral in itself, even if it is commanded, even if refusal to act brings with it the direst personal loss.

The Pope added that this moral norm did not enter into discussion for the time being, that at present there was question of putting an end to the aforementioned juridical dilemma by international agreements. In what way?

> Will it be possible to obtain by international agreements, on the one hand, that the authorities be made juridically incapable of

---

portation, execution of hostages, etc.); 3) crimes against humanity: acts outside of war operations which attacked the fundamental rights of the human person.

Thus the heads of state, the rulers, will no longer escape the penal responsibility of the international order. Futhermore, it will not only be individuals who will incur this penal responsibility, but groups and organizations as well.

ordering crimes and that they be held responsible for having given such orders, and on the other hand, that subordinates be exempted from executing these orders and be held responsible if they obey them?

In the same discourse Pius XII also broached the problem of purely collective guilt. He did not choose to examine it from the ethical and philosophical point of view. But he asked that an effort be made "to find and to fix juridically a formula which can be used practically in case of conflict, particularly international conflict, where collective guilt may be of decisive importance in determining culpability, and there has been such more than once." It is necessary to withdraw the action of governments and of courts from purely personal caprice and opinion. To guarantee a regular juridical procedure, there is required "a solid foundation of clear juridical norms in accord with sound reason, with the universal sense of justice, to the execution of which the contracting governments can add their authority and their coercive power" (Allocution to the International Congress of Penal Law, October 3, 1953).

Third false concept: War is an adequate and proportioned means of settling conflicts. In his Christmas message of 1944, Pope Pius XII envisaged the formation of an organism for the maintenance of peace, an organism invested by common accord with supreme authority, which would also be empowered to quench in its beginnings every menace of aggression, be it isolated or collective. The Pope immediately added:

> No one would greet such a development with more joy than he who for a long time already has defended the principle that the theory of war as a suitable and proportioned means for settling international conflicts is nowadays passé.

It is permissible to interpret the thought of the Holy Father in a double sense, when he declares that war is no longer a suitable and proportioned means for the solution of conflicts.

In the first place, the Pope puts his judgment in the perspective of the existence of an international organism charged with repressing in the bud every threat of aggression. Henceforth two nations in conflict can no longer pretend to settle their differences by war. There exists, there will exist more and more, a community of nations. In the future no war can interest only the two nations in conflict. Nowadays the entire international community is involved in a conflict that starts anywhere on earth. It has the mission and the power to resolve such differences by suitable and proportioned means other than war. In this sense, war must be regarded as an outmoded means.

Furthermore, the Pope declares that "for a long time" he had defended this thesis, hence even independently of the establishment of an international organism. War is not by itself a "suitable and proportioned" means of settling conflicts. What does war prove? It is undertaken in principle to repair an injury, the violation or the rejection of the rights of a nation. To reëstablish the situation, the parties have recourse to arms. The victor will be considered to have gained his point.

As a matter of fact, however, there will be simply a modification of the juridical status existing between two or more nations. Rarely does such a modification produce reparation of injustice or recognition of a right that was rejected. On the contrary, only too often the stronger gains the victory, the one who prepared for war for a long time and planned it. War is simply a solution by force without any relation to rights; in this sense, too, it is not a suitable and proportioned means for resolving conflicts. Speaking of the horror of war which all the nations manifest, Pius XII added that they have the conviction "that it is now, less than ever, a proper means for settling conflicts, for reëstablishing peace" (Allocution to the Diplomatic Corps, January 1, 1951).

Fourth false concept: War is a school of virtue and of progress. Fascism and the totalitarian states have exalted war. They have presented it as a school of the highest civic virtues. According to them, war brings to their peak all human energies, while perpetual peace depresses and negates the fundamental virtues of man.[4]

4. "War alone brings to a peak all human energies and impresses a mark of nobility on the nations who have the courage to face it. . . . I do not believe in perpetual peace; not only do I not believe in it, but I consider

Pius XII condemned in severe terms every apotheosis of war:

> After the horrors of two world conflicts, We have no need to remind you that every apotheosis of war must be condemned as an aberration of the mind and of the heart. No doubt, strength of soul and bravery, even to the sacrifice of life when duty demands it, are great virtues, but to want to provoke war because it is a school of great virtues and offers an occasion for practicing them must be considered crime and folly (Allocution to military physicians, October 19, 1953).

Finally, in May, 1958, the Pope rejected some expressions which would attribute to war imaginary qualities:

> For the Church war is not "a crucible of manly virtues" and still less "a promoter of fruitful enterprises." War does not at all contribute to the progress of civilization, even if at times it provides an occasion and a stimulus for the development of science and technique.[5]

Fifth false concept: The right to make war is a natural right of the state. The theory of the absolute sovereignty of the state has been applied in all spheres of international life. It has begotten a doctrine of war which has been accepted for a long time and which has penetrated the domain of public law.

According to this theory, the state is sovereign. Hence it is the sole judge of its rights and of its interests. It does not depend on anyone. It is bound only by obligations which it has freely accepted. It alone decides the question of war. It considers the right to make war a natural right in all circumstances, the ultimate means of making its claim prevail. Hence the war it undertakes is legitimate in itself, whatever may be its causes, whether they be legitimate or illegitimate, fictitious or just.

This amply demonstrates to what extremes a theory as erroneous as that of the sovereignty of the state can lead.

Pope Pius XII replied: "As far as the Church is concerned,

---

that it depresses and negates the basic virtues of man" (Benito Mussolini, Discourse, 1924, quoted by *Information catholiques internationales*, June 15, 1958).

5. Discourse for the spiritual assistance of the armed forces of Italy, May 20, 1958.

war is not a juridical right which remains so in every hypothesis."
War is subject to international morality and to law. In some cases
it must be condemned; in others it may be undertaken for reasons of a higher nature, under determined conditions and in a
certain form.

VARIOUS FORMS OF WAR

1. *War of aggression.* A duty binding on the conscience of all:
to proscribe and banish war of aggression.

In his Christmas message of 1944 on true democracy, Pius XII
pronounced an extremely severe sentence of condemnation on
war of aggression. He summoned all men to do their utmost to
proscribe and banish it once and for all—and that immediately.

> There is a duty that rests on everyone and that allows of no delay,
> no procrastination, no hesitation, no subterfuge. It is the duty to
> do everything possible to ban once and for all war of aggression
> as a legitimate solution of international controversies and as a
> means of realizing national aspirations.

Every word of this statement deserves study.

"Everyone": The Pope appealed to the conscience of all of
mankind. He wished to stir up a true crusade of peace against
war of aggression. He made his appeal in a radio message where
he defined the role of the citizens in a true democracy, their
right of expressing their personal opinion and of not being
obliged to obey without being heard. The importance which
Pius XII attached to the free expression of opinion on the part of
the citizens should be noted. He counted on the good sense, the
reason and the resolution of those who make up, not an amor-
phous "mass," but a true "nation," "the sanest part of the human
race," in order to bring about the triumph of peace and the out-
lawing of war of aggression forever.

"A duty": A little later on the Pope specified: "a duty of
conscience . . . a mission."

In the past, attempts have been made to outlaw war of aggression. "All have failed." Why? Because this mission was not
undertaken with "sufficient seriousness and determination."

In order to succeed, the sanest part of the human race must

be "firmly resolved and holily obstinate, as becomes a duty of conscience," to fulfill this mission. And there is an urgency about this duty. Note the accumulation of terms: ". . . no delay, no procrastination, no hesitation, no subterfuge."

The objective: ". . . to proscribe and to banish war of aggression once and for all."

Therefore the Pope envisaged the suppression, the definitive disappearance of this form of war, inasfar as it was hitherto chosen by the nations, for two reasons:

"As a legitimate solution of international controversies." War must no longer be considered as a "solution" of international conflicts, nor as a "legitimate" solution. Henceforth, in a society organized on the international level, as the Pope envisaged it in the following paragraph, there are other solutions that will be obligatory, the solutions of peace.

"As a means of realizing national aspirations." Likewise, in order to have its legitimate aspirations respected and to realize them, it behooves that henceforth a nation will no longer have to choose war nor resign itself to it because it has no other means at its disposal. The organization of the community of nations, if it is truly animated by a spirit of justice, of equity and of charity, will have to take into account the just aspirations of a nation, as the Pope expressly states.

Immorality of war of aggression. "Every war of aggression against these goods which the divine ordinance of peace obliges to respect and to guarantee unconditionally, and then also to protect and to defend, is a sin, a crime, an offense against the majesty of God, the Creator and Governor of the world" (Christmas Message, 1948).

What constitutes the "immorality" of war of aggression? It is a violation, an overturning, a disruption of God's design with regard to the world; as a "sin" it is a revolt against God's will and his law in several senses.

First, because it is a serious attack against God's plan regarding the unity of the human race and the community of nations. In the Christmas message of 1944 on democracy, the passage summoning all men to banish war of aggression comes, as a logical application, immediately after the paragraphs demonstrating that the absolute order of beings and of ends implies the unity of the human race and of the family of nations. "On the recognition of this principle depends the future of peace," declared Pius XII. Now it is precisely this principle which war of aggression condemns and violates.

The Holy Father repeated this doctrine again in his discourse for the spiritual assistance of the armed forces of Italy, May 20, 1958: "Since Christianity considers humanity as a single great family, it must be firmly opposed to war of aggression."

Then, the divine ordinance of peace, the precept of peace, which is of divine law, has as its purpose the protection of the goods of humanity inasfar as they are goods of the Creator: material goods necessary for the life of men and of nations, but also moral and intellectual goods, higher and spiritual values, the fullness of that human endowment which constitutes the true wealth and the progress of civilization. Now it is against this plan of God, "the Creator and Governor of the world," that war of aggression with all its crimes, its terrible ravages, its tremendous destruction is directed.

Finally, in a third sense, war of aggression appears as an overturning of God's design. According to this design, "the progress of human inventions ought to mark the arrival of a greater well-being for all of humanity." But "it has been directed away from its goal in order to destroy what the centuries have built. By the same token, the immorality of war of aggression becomes progressively more manifested" (Christmas Message, 1944).

Sanctions and punishments which war of aggression deserves. Before the representatives of the International Congress of Penal Law, October 3, 1953, Pius XII, while examining the categories of crimes for which international penal law ought to provide sanctions, placed war of aggression at the head of the list.

> In first place stands the crime of modern war, which does not demand the unconditioned necessity of self-defense and which brings in its train—We can say it without hesitation—ruin, suffering and unimaginable horror. The community of nations must reckon with conscienceless criminals who, to realize their ambitious plans, do not fear to unleash total war. . . . Unjust war must be placed in the first rank of the gravest crimes which inter-

national penal law must pillory and afflict with the heaviest penalties, whose authors must in all cases be regarded as culpable and liable to the punishment provided.

Beyond the penal sanction of the courts, the Pope also counted on the unanimous reprobation on the part of the community of nations, conscious of its duty of solidarity in the defense of peace:

> Every violator of right, as a disturber of the peace, ought to be exiled to a defaming solitude under the ban of civil society. May the Organization of the United Nations become the full and the pure expression of that international solidarity of peace (Christmas Message, 1948).

Finally, there is required

> . . . the threat of a juridical intervention on the part of nations and of a punishment inflicted on the aggressor by the organization of states in such a manner that war is always regarded as under the ban of proscription and always under the surveillance of preventive action (Christmas Message, 1944).

State of the question in international law. What is the attitude of international public law regarding the problem of war of aggression? It meets with two great difficulties: the definition of war of aggression and that of sanctions.

Here we shall refer only to the difficulty that has been encountered in practical cases.

It would seem that a definition of aggressor might have been drawn from the pact of the League of Nations, namely, one who on the occasion of a conflict with another member of the League of Nations would have had recourse to the force of arms, without making use beforehand of the means for a peaceful solution that were foreseen and organized.

The Treaties of London (July 3, 1933) contained a list of cases of aggression and presented a definition of the aggressor in objective terms. A state would be an aggressor if, as the first one, it would commit one of the following acts: 1) declare war against another state; 2) invade the territory of another state with its armed forces, even without a declaration of war; 3) attack the territory, the vessels, the aircraft of another state with its military, naval or air forces, even without a declaration of war; 4) set up a naval blockade of the coasts or the ports of another state; 5) give support to armed bands which, formed on its own territory, would invade the territory of another state, or refuse, despite the request of the invaded state, to take all the measures in its power on its own territory to deprive the aforesaid bands of all aid or protection.

This effort showed real progress in the definition of aggression, but the weakness of the Treaties of London consisted in the fact that they did not provide sanctions against the aggressor.

It is important to mention, in the sense of the directions given by Pius XII (Christmas Message, 1944), the progress manifested by the Kellogg-Briand Pact (1928) which sought to shut out recourse to war as a means of regulating international conflicts and also to renounce it as an instrument of national policy in their mutual relations.[6]

In November, 1950, and again toward the end of January, 1952, the General Assembly of the UN was occupied with the problem of defining aggression. The commissions (juridical commission, commission of international law) did not at that time arrive at an understanding on the question, namely, whether it was possible or desirable to give this definition.

2. *Defensive war: theology of a just war.* The Christian thought on the problem of war was expressed long centuries ago by the Church's doctors and great theologians. There exists a theology of just war.[7]

Just war presupposes certain conditions; these were formulated originally by St. Augustine:

1. The decision belongs to the public authority;

2. The motive must be reparation of an injustice. War may be waged only with a view to peace and the common welfare—in a word, a just cause is required;

3. It must be necessary;

4. There must be a proportion between the terrible means of war and the injustice whose reparation is sought.

6. Article 1. "The high contracting parties solemnly declare, in the name of their respective nations, that they condemn recourse to war for the regulation of international differences and renounce it as an instrument of national policy in their mutual relations."

7. *La Théologie de la guerre juste,* by Msgr. de Solages (Desclée, 1946).

St. Thomas leans on St. Augustine. In the *Summa Theologiae*
(II-II, q. 40), he asks the question: "Is it always sinful to wage
war?" He repeats St. Augustine's conditions for a just war: 1)
the authority of the ruler; 2) a just cause. He adds also the right
intention. He passes over in silence the two other conditions
given by St. Augustine, which nevertheless will pass into the
theological systems of the sixteenth century.

It may be remarked that St. Thomas speaks of the "common
good." He is referring, however, only to the common good of a
state governed by a prince. He makes no allusion to the international common good, since at his time this universal perspective
did not yet exist.

In the sixteenth century, Francis de Vitoria was the great
theologian of war. He sets the question of the just war on the
plane of the natural law and of the law of nations. He repeats
the four conditions, giving particular attention to the last two:
necessity, that is, war must appear as the sole means of repairing
an injustice; proportioned means, that is, war must not be a
worse remedy than the evil it wishes to cure.

It is worthwhile to call attention to the wide wisdom of Vitoria
on the world, on the community of men and of nations, on
the common good of the world. He already foresees an order of
universal justice and, generally, the community of nations conceived as a universal organism.

In the second half of the sixteenth century, Suarez depends
on Vitoria's teaching with regard to this problem in particular.
He differs in this, that he sees in the law of nations a contract
between states, while for Vitoria it is a law. Msgr. de Solages
points out a practical difference: a contract obliges only the contracting states, while a law approved by the majority also binds
the minority.

In the nineteenth century, Taparelli, whose authority in the
field of international law we have already mentioned, had the
merit of bringing the law of war into connection with the progressive organization of international society. He foresaw this
society of states in a manner at times truly prophetic; he defined
its nature and established its fundamental laws. Further, he explained the rights and duties of the international authority
charged with promoting the international common good and

with drawing up and then promulgating "the code of international law of the nations." He clearly attacks the problem of the reduction of armaments, as well as that of an international armed force at the service of an international court.

Doctrine of Pius XII.

1. Principle. The human community has the right and the duty of defending itself against unjust aggression: "This right of being on the defensive cannot be denied even at present to any state." So Pius XII declared in an allocution to the members of the Sixth International Congress of Penal Law, October 3, 1953.

Note the Pope's words: ". . . even at present." In view of the terrible ravages of modern war, the following theory began to gain ground: It is no longer possible to have a just war, hence even a defensive war, because the remedy would be worse than the evil. The Pope, however, said: Even today a defensive war must be considered legitimate for a nation and for the community of nations.

2. Circumstances in which a war of defense is legitimate. Pius XII defined the two cases in which this war of defense is legitimate:

First, in the defense of a national territory which is unjustly invaded. This is the case of legitimate self-defense, valid for the individual victim of aggression and thence extended to the nation. This is a natural right. "A nation that is threatened or already victim of an unjust aggression, if it wants to think and act in a Christian manner, cannot remain indifferently passive" (Christmas Message, 1948). Hence, self-defense constitutes a duty for that nation.

Second, in the defense of higher and necessary goods which the Creator has intended for the life of the human community. Such defense is obligatory not only for the country victimized by unjust aggression, said the Pope, but also "for the solidarity of nations, which has the duty of not abandoning the nation which is the victim of an aggression."

This legitimate self-defense exists also in the case of the "cold war"; here, too, we may speak not only of a right but of a duty.

When there is question of the cold war, the offensive must be condemned without reserve from the moral standpoint. If it nevertheless comes about, those who are attacked have not only the right but also the duty of defending themselves. No state and no group of states can quietly accept political slavery and economic ruin. For the common good of their peoples they must assure their defense. This tends to stop up the attack and to bring it about that political measures be honestly and completely adapted to the state of peace which exists in a purely juridical sense between the attacker and the object of his attack (Allocution to the pilgrims of Pax Christi, September 13, 1952).

3. Moral reasons of legitimate self-defense by war. In the second chapter we saw that the purpose of the precept of peace was the protection of the goods of humanity as well as the goods of the Creator.

Now, said Pius XII, "among these goods there are some of such importance for the human community that their defense against unjust aggression is, without any doubt, entirely justified" (Christmas Message, 1948). The same reasons of a moral order that condemn war of aggression justify defensive war.

God's plan demands the defense not only of higher goods and higher values; there is also "the very existence of nations." Speaking of those who are attacked and of total war, which criminals without conscience might unleash to realize their ambitious plans, Pius XII declared that "if the other nations wish to protect their existence and their most precious goods, the only course that remains for them is to prepare themselves for the day when they must defend themselves."

We have just read the very severe terms used by Pius XII to designate those guilty of war of aggression: ". . . criminals without conscience." In the same discourse he again referred to them as "international malefactors." Besides, he declared that the Church must take into account the dark powers that have always been at work in history. None of these must be allowed "free rein." To prevent the triumph of injustice, of brutal violence and of conscienceless activity in the world is a compelling duty. By the same token the menace of war is obviated or it is shortened. The assurance that a duty of this kind will not remain unfulfilled will serve to discourage the aggressor and consequently to avoid war, or at least, should the worst come to the worst, ameliorate its sufferings.

Absolute pacificism lacks realism. It forgets or is ignorant of the fact that evil men always threaten to make evil use of their liberty; for this reason, defensive war is legitimate:

> Since human liberty is capable of unleashing an unjust conflict to the detriment of a nation, it is certain that, in given circumstances, this nation may arm and defend itself. . . . Those who direct the fate of nations may today—just as yesterday—become the victims of blind and senseless passions and again—which God forbid!—unleash tremendous conflicts (Allocution for the spiritual assistance of the Italian armed forces, October 19, 1958).

The passage of Pius XII's discourse to the members of Pax Christi (September 13, 1952) on the subject of the cold war cited above sets in relief another reason for the State's right and duty of defending itself against aggression. "For the common good of their peoples they must assure their defense. . . . No state and no group of states may quietly accept political slavery or economic ruin." The state or the states would be acting treasonably toward the common good of their peoples if they would not seek to defend the nation's right to liberty, independence and life.

The nature of the repulse—defense—specifies its meaning and its extent. Negatively it tends to repel the attack; positively it seeks "to bring it about that political and economic measures be honestly and completely adapted to the state of peace which exists in a purely juridical sense between the attacker and the object of his attack." So, again, peace must be the objective to be pursued. The Church believes in peace and is convinced that political and economic complications can be amicably settled, provided there is good will on both sides.

4. Conditions for a just war. Pius XII's teaching repeated the traditional doctrine on the just war, stressing the required conditions: ". . . the absolute necessity of self-defense against a very grave injustice affecting the community (hence a just cause and necessity); . . . when it cannot be prevented by other means and when it nevertheless has to be done, under penalty of granting free rein to brutal violence and conscienceless activ-

ity in international relations" (Allocution to the members of the Sixteenth Congress of Military Medicine, October 19, 1953).

Besides these three conditions (necessity of self-defense, a just cause over against a grave injustice, absence of other means), Pius XII had, on a previous occasion, mentioned a fourth condition, which had been stressed by writers since Vitoria: ". . . provided there exists a well-founded probability of success" (Christmas Message, 1948). Vitoria had insisted on the idea that the means must correspond to the purpose. For him, a war which might be just as far as its cause is concerned (reparation of an injustice), could be, if taken in its totality, unjust, if one foresaw that it would have harmful repercussions on the common good of the state, or on the more general common good of Christianity, or on the still more general common good of the world.[8]

Furthermore, close attention must be given to the condition which Pope Pius XII added, in view of the violent methods of present-day war; it attests to the wisdom and prudence of the Holy Father in solemnly affirming the duty of safeguarding, by a vigorous defense, superior values that are threatened.

> It does not suffice, in order to exercise self-defense against any kind of injustice, to employ the violent method of war. When the harm it entails is not comparable to that of the "tolerated injustice," one may have the obligation of "suffering the injustice" (Allocution to the Sixteenth Congress of Military Medicine, October 19, 1953).

In his great message of 1956, Pius XII returned to the conditions required for a war of self-defense. He spoke of the threats which a totalitarian country may exercise on another state by sending out its tanks "to sow death beyond the frontiers, in order to force civilized peoples to embrace a form of life which they definitely abhor." Here indeed is a case of legitimate self-defense, unjust attack! The Pope then went on to point out the conditions which justify defense:

> When, as it were, the doors to possible discussion and mediation have been closed, when there are threats of employing atomic weapons to obtain certain demands, be these justified or not, it is clear that in such circumstances the case may be verified in a

8. Msgr. de Solages, *op. cit.*, p. 60.

nation, where, all efforts to avoid it having proved abortive, war as a means of defending itself effectively and with hope of success against unjust attacks could not be considered illicit.

Patently, the Pope is referring to the invasion of Hungary by Russian tanks.

5. A national army for defense. Two results flow logically from the Church's position on defensive war. The first is the right and the duty of a nation to have an army.

In an allocution of May, 1958, Pius XII showed how war could spread to become a conflict between peoples and could affect the entire nation because of weapons of unimaginable power. Then the Pope added:

> The problem of the national defense hence takes on an ever greater importance, equal in complexity and difficulty to its solution. For this reason no nation, which wants to provide for the security of its frontiers as is its imprescriptible right, can forego an army proportioned to its needs, an army possessing the necessary means for courageous, prompt and vigorous action to defend the fatherland if it is unjustly threatened or attacked (Allocution for the spiritual assistance of the Italian armed forces, May 20, 1958).

We have had occasion in chapter four to point out that Benedict XV, in his vigorous action to forestall the dangers of war, had envisaged—not in an official document, but in a personal letter by his Cardinal Secretary of State to Lloyd George—not the suppression of armies, but of compulsory military service. Circumstances have changed. Threats continue in a world divided into two blocs. Without ceasing, Pius XII pursued his work of peace, his energetic struggle against the arms race. But by placing himself on the side of defense for all the reasons mentioned above, the Pope affirmed the right and the duty of a nation to possess and maintain a national army.

A second result of this position on defensive war is the duty of obedience on the part of subjects. In his Christmas message of 1956, Pius XII examined the case of a true democracy (with popular representation and a government elected by free ballot) which finds itself in extreme necessity and threatened in its life and independence. It takes measures of defense by the legitimate

means of internal and external politics. The Pope then pronounced judgment on those who would refuse obedience on the
score of conscience:

> A Catholic citizen cannot appeal to his conscience in order to re-
> fuse the services and not to fulfill the duties imposed by law.

The Pope added that on this point he was in full accord with
the thought of his predecessors, Leo XIII and Benedict XV, "who
never denied this obligation, but who deeply deplored the unlimited armament race and the moral dangers of life in the
barracks."

They pointed to general disarmament as an effective remedy,
with which opinion Pius XII concurred.

In the passage cited, the Pope did not intend to treat of the
grave problem of conscientious objection in all circumstances.
He wanted to instruct the consciences of young men, particularly
in Germany, who had taken up a position opposed to compulsory
military service and in favor of conscientious objection.

The principle enunciated by the Pope has possible application
in other countries, too. What the Holy Father condemns in a
Catholic citizen of a true democracy is "the appeal to his own
conscience to refuse services and not to fulfill duties imposed
by law."

It is well to note the distinction which the Sovereign Pontiff
makes between states that are truly democratic and those that
are not. He makes the illegitimacy of complete conscientious
objection depend on the structure of the state. In a state that
has popular representation and a government elected by free
ballot, conscientious objection is illegitimate. On the other hand,
in states that are only caricatures of democracies, where there is
neither a free ballot nor popular representation nor an elected
government, Catholics may consider themselves freed from the
obligation. Why this difference? Because in totalitarian states,
which tend to suppress individual moral responsibility, in order
to make of the consciences of their subjects docile instruments
of their will to power, of their thirst for expansion, to draw them
into the execution of their dictatorial designs for conquest, the
only means of protecting peace is to appeal to the consciences
of the subjects, to their "individual moral responsibility." In

states of this kind the citizens cannot delegate to their rulers the care of safeguarding the peace and of interpreting the common good.

Finally, no matter how difficult may be the direction of conscience as outlined by the Pope for the Catholic citizens of totalitarian states, it may be well to recall the rule given above with regard to penal sanctions about the partial objection of conscience, namely, the case where an act immoral in itself is commanded. "No higher superior is empowered to command an immoral act."

CONDUCT OF WAR

Principle. After denouncing war of aggression and praising every effort to outlaw it, the Church now enters the picture to recall the demands of the moral law even in the conduct of operations, once war has been declared. Pius XII set up the general principle:

> Even in a just and necessary war, effective procedures are not all defensible in the eyes of a man who possesses an exact and reasonable sense of justice (Allocution to the members of the Sixth International Congress of Penal Law, October 3, 1953).

Even while war was raging, Pius XII protested:

> It is no less painful and regrettable to note that often in the course of this war, the moral judgment concerning certain actions that run counter to the rights and law of humanity is made to depend on the fact that the one responsible belongs to one or the other of the parties in conflict, without regard to the conformity or non-conformity of these actions with the norms established by the Eternal Judge (Allocution to the Sacred College, June 2, 1943).

Modern weapons—ABC war: On various occasions Pius XII, in order to show the hideousness and immorality of modern war, described its effect in gripping words. We shall here report the remarks in which the Holy Father gave the most precise description, in scientific terms, of the destruction which the new weapons are capable of producing on the surface of the earth, on the life of plants and animals, on man, with biological effects lasting for generations.

Weapons capable—as We already had occasion to express Our fears in February 1943—of producing "a terrible catastrophe over the entire extent of our planet," of sowing total extermination of animal and vegetable life, of all human endeavor over ever-extending regions; arms capable henceforth—thanks to artificial radioactive isotopes of long average life—of infecting in a lasting manner the atmosphere, the soil, the oceans themselves, even at great distances from the areas struck and contaminated by nuclear explosions. Thus before the eyes of a terrified world arises the vision of colossal destruction, of entire regions made uninhabitable and useless for man, without speaking of the biological effects which may be produced, both by reason of the mutations provoked in germs and microörganisms, as well as by the fact of the uncertain effects which a prolonged radioactive exposure may have on the larger organisms, man included, and on their progeny. While on this subject, We cannot help making reference to the danger which future generations run from the mutations of genes which can be obtained and perhaps have already been obtained by means, tending to change the patrimony of man's hereditary factors from their natural development. For this reason, too, in all likelihood there will not be wanting among such changes pathogenetic deviations which are the cause of hereditary diseases and of monsters (Easter Message, April 18, 1954).

After this terrifying description, the Pope cried out in the same discourse:

We shall not cease making every effort so that, by means of international agreements—saving always the principle of legitimate defense—atomic, biological and chemical war may be effectively proscribed and outlawed.

ABC war presents some very serious moral and human problems, and Pius XII attacked them courageously. Above all, its suppression! "Is it not possible, through international agreements, to proscribe and outlaw ABC war?" (Allocution to Military Physicians, October 19, 1950).

Let us note the recourse to international agreements whose necessity the Pope showed in 1953 as the only means of proscribing war of this kind. But we have also seen above (in treating of disarmament) that in 1956 the Sovereign Pontiff expressed his thought on the matter with new force and new precision. The cessation of production and employment of certain weapons ought to be brought about not only by international agreements, but within "the framework of the Organization of the United Nations and with the engagements of the states transformed into strict obligations of international law . . ." (Christmas Message, 1956).

This would mark considerable progress in the organization of peace and the suppression of war. In the absence of a true community of nations, war has been long considered as the only means a state could use to obtain justice in a conflict and, in its eyes, to safeguard its rights. A great step forward is taken when it is recognized that war, for reasons which call for the organization of a community of nations and also because this means appears ever more and more dangerous, inhuman and inadequate, belongs to the international community. Certain theologians do not hesitate to assert that war, which has been after all a "procedure of replacement" in the absence of an international organization, a "functional enterprise," is destined to disappear as soon as the community of nations is truly organized and endowed with power. The use of force will then change its nature; war understood in the modern sense will no longer exist, but it will be replaced by the operation of an international police force.

But thus far we have not reached that stage. Nevertheless, Pope Pius XII, in his Christmas message of 1956, while regretting the defects of the UN, pointed out the steps that would have to be taken in its organization and the concept of its mission.

It ought also to have the right and the power to prevent any military intervention of one state in another, no matter what the pretext alleged, as well as to assure, by means of adequate police forces, the protection of order in the threatened state.

Thus the Holy Father foresaw that the UN would have at its disposition "police forces," whose duty it is to prevent all aggression, all military intervention, and to substitute in place of the violence exercised by one state against another a police action of the organized international community, possessing effective authority and powerful means of action to assure the efficacy of law and to protect peace.

A second question was put by Pius XII: Is "total" modern war —and ABC war in particular—permitted in principle?

The Pope replied: Apart from the case of legitimate self-defense and without the observance of very strict conditions, such a war is forbidden and constitutes a grave crime.

> There remains no doubt, especially because of the horrors and the immense sufferings produced by modern war, that to unleash it without a just reason (that is to say, unless it becomes imperative because of an evident and extremely grave injustice not otherwise reparable) constitutes a "crime," calling for the most severe national and international sanctions (Allocution to the Congress of World Medicine, September 30, 1954).

The conditions fixed by the Church's teaching regarding just war have also been applied to ABC war: an evident injustice, extremely grave, the absence of other means of avoiding it. The Holy Father added:

> It is impossible in principle to put the question about the liceity of ABC war, except in the case where it were judged indispensable for self-defense in the conditions indicated.

A third question was also raised by Pius: Let us suppose the case where a country attacked by an ABC war is forced to defend itself in the conditions indicated. Can nothing be done to avoid recourse to this horrible means of defense? The Holy Father replied:

> Even then all means must be employed to avoid it, with the help of international agreements or by demanding for such a war strict and clearly defined limits, so that its effect be kept within the bounds of strict demands of self-defense.

Thus the Pope, while recognizing the case of necessary and legitimate self-defense, makes an appeal to the means capable of protecting the peace and avoiding war, even at such a time: international agreements and strict limits imposed on the use of modern weapons. Certainly international morality has a word to say about the manner of carrying out aerial bombardments with atomic weapons, in order to restrain the liberties which flyers think they are authorized to take. For example, it cannot be admitted that those who have at their disposition such destructive weapons find it less dangerous for themselves to release them at an altitude where they know they will escape enemy fire, but do not hesitate to annihilate an entire city with its civilian population, as, unfortunately, was the practice so widespread during the last war. How many cities, or at least how many entire sections, were thus "sprinkled" by bombs with a cruelty and harshness which multiplied ruins and victims, whereas if the flyers had courageously descended over their objective and run their risk, as was their duty, such disasters could frequently have been avoided. Non-observance of the moral law was so general that many merely shrugged their shoulders and said: "That's war!" Such a specious and lamentable explanation must henceforth be rejected. Not everything is permitted in war. Especially in modern war, limits must be set to restrain the effects within the strict demands of self-defense.

Entering more profoundly still into the examination, from the moral viewpoint, of the use of weapons of ABC war in the case of legitimate defense and in accord with the conditions stated, the Pope raised a final question: "But if the use of these weapons produces consequences and such an extension of harm as to escape entirely from man's control, what is to be done?" The Holy Father replied:

> Every time the employment of a means entails such an extension of harm that it entirely escapes man's control, its use must be rejected as immoral. Here there would no longer be a question of "defense" against injustice and of the necessary "safeguarding" of legitimate possessions, but of the pure and simple annihilation of all human life within the radius of the action. This is not permitted on any score (Directives to the members of the Eighth Assembly of the World Medical Association, September 30, 1954.)

Respect for international agreements regarding conduct of war. At the beginning of the war in 1939, Pope Pius XII recalled to the belligerent powers the obligation they had undertaken of observing international conventions.

> We are pleased to recall certain declarations by which the belligerent powers, at the beginning of the conflict, publicly affirmed their intention to observe the laws of humanity and to conform themselves to the stipulations of international agreements in the conduct of the war.

This offered the Pope an occasion to mention some applications of these agreements.

> We should like to express in a special manner the hope that the civilian populations will be kept immune from all direct military operations; that, in the occupied territories, the life, property, honor and religious feelings of the inhabitants will be respected; that prisoners of war will be treated humanely and will be able without hindrance to receive the consolations of their religion; that the use of asphyxiating and poisonous gases will be banned (Address to the Belgian ambassador, September 14, 1939).

From the very first months of the war the Sovereign Pontiff stood out as the defender and guardian of the laws of humanity in hostilities that promised to become frightful. From that time, too, he called the attention of the responsible authorities to the international agreements they had signed. With his eminent authority he supported the force and the moral obligations of the agreements of the international community.

Several months later the Pope had to note with sorrow the systematic violation of the precepts of positive international law and of the natural law. He cited explicitly

> the atrocities (by whichever side they were committed) and the illicit use of means of destruction, even against noncombatants and refugees, against the old, women and children; contempt for human dignity, liberty and life, from which result acts that cry to God for vengeance; . . . anti-Christian and even atheistic propaganda, ever growing and very methodical, especially among the young (Allocution to the Sacred College, December 24, 1939).

The following year, March, 1940, the Pope raised his voice anew in protest against the violation of laws.

> Not rarely We witness with the greatest sadness violations of the laws that regulate the relations among civilized peoples. It happens that open cities, agricultural villages and hamlets are terrorized, set on fire and devastated by bombardments; citizens without defense, the sick, even helpless old people and innocent children, are deprived of their homes and often killed (Easter homily *Exultat*, March 24, 1940).

Once again in 1942, the Pope came forth as the defender of international agreements. He recalled their purpose and deplored their rejection and violation.

International agreements, whose object was to render war less inhumane by limiting it to combatants, to lay down laws regarding occupation and captivity of the vanquished, have, in many respects, remained dead letters. And who can foresee an end of this progressive deterioration? (Christmas Message, 1942).

The following year the Holy Father protested against the inhumane means employed in modern warfare, which makes no distinction between military objectives and others.

The pitiless progress of technology of war and the increasingly violent means of combat, which make no distinction between the so-called military and non-military "objectives," of themselves set before us the dangers which are necessarily included in the sad and inexorable concurrence between actions and reprisals, to the great harm of nations in particular as well as of the community of nations in general (Allocution to the Sacred College, June 2, 1943).

Pius XII again exhorted the belligerents to respect the laws of humanity in air warfare.

From the beginning We have done everything possible to urge the belligerents to respect the laws of humanity in air warfare; We now consider it Our duty, in the common interest, to exhort them again to their observance.

He then uttered the gravest warnings:

At the moment when the specter of the most terrifying engines of destruction and of death begins to haunt the spirit of men, it is not superfluous to warn the civilized world that it is approaching the brink of an abyss of unspeakable calamities.

Together with these general norms destined to make war less inhumane, Pope Pius XII gave some rules based on the same principles of humanity regarding particular problems: the problem of prisoners, of occupied territories, of the killing of hostages.

Prisoners of war. In this place we shall not speak at length of the charitable activity undertaken by Pope Pius XII, as was true also of his predecessor, Benedict XV, during the First World War, in supplying material aid and moral comfort to prisoners. We shall merely indicate the teaching of moral principles which the Pope enunciated on this point, in order to support or to complement international agreements.

Pius XII was very much concerned with the return of prisoners to their homes as soon as possible after the cessation of hostilities. He proclaimed that superior rights—those of the individual and of the family—took precedence over the rigidity of juridical texts.

> We are not ignorant of the fact that the rigid text of international law obliges the victor to release prisoners only after the conclusion of peace. But the spiritual and moral needs of the prisoners themselves and of their parents, the sacred rights of marriage and of the family, cry to heaven with a higher and stronger voice than all the juridical texts and demand that an end be made of prisoner compounds and concentration camps (Allocution to the Sacred College, June 1, 1946).

The Pope then replied to the arguments advanced by certain states to justify delay in freeing prisoners: the economic need of manpower, lack of means of transport. He calls on them to show human sympathy and even political wisdom, Christian charity, while at the same time suggesting solutions of a practical order.

Occupied territories. In the consistory of June, 1940, Pius XII expressed his sorrow at learning "how often, in more than one region, the treatment accorded non-combatants was far from conformable to the rules of humanity." He then mentions the demands of humanity, of equity, of justice, and the duty on the part of the occupying power "to bring the juridical order which they wish to establish there [in the occupied territories] into harmony with the dispositions of international law and above all with the demands of humanity and equity. They must not forget that, together with the safety precautions justified by the true needs of the war, the welfare of the inhabitants of the occupied territories remains an obligatory rule for those who exercise power. Justice and equity require that they be treated as the occupying power in a similar situation would want its own citizens to be treated" (Consistorial allocution, June 2, 1940).

Addressing himself directly to the occupying powers in 1941, Pope Pius XII told them:

> Let your conscience and your honor guide you in the manner of treating the inhabitants of the occupied countries with justice, humanity and wisdom. Do not impose burdens which you, in similar circumstances, would have resented or would resent as

unjust. A prudent and helpful humanity is the praise and honor of wise leaders.

The Pope thereupon enunciated as a solemn warning the following rule as a means of measuring the degree of civilization of a state in the two problems of prisoners and of occupied territories:

> The treatment of prisoners and of the inhabitants of occupied places is the surest measure and indication of the civilization of men and of nations (Easter homily, April 13, 1941).

Killing of hostages and other crimes. Before the members of the International Congress of Penal Law, the Pope enumerated the crimes "which international penal law ought to make impossible or of which it ought to free the community of states. Thus even in a just and necessary war, effective procedures are not all defensible in the eyes of a man who possesses an exact and reasonable sense of justice" (Allocution to the International Congress of Penal Law, August 3, 1953).

In particular the Pope pronounced himself on the killing of hostages:

> The slaughter en masse of innocent victims as a reprisal for the fault of an individual is not an act of justice, but a sanctioned injustice; killing innocent hostages cannot be justified because it is made a necessity of war.

Finally the Sovereign Pontiff inveighed against the crimes which had mushroomed in the twelve preceding years: massacres inspired by hatred of a race, the horrors and cruelties of concentration camps, the slaughter of hundreds of thousands "of beings unsuited for life," pitiless mass deportations, violence exercised on women and girls deprived of defense, organized manhunts among the civilian population to enroll laborers or more exactly labor slaves, unlimited arbitrariness in the administration of justice, reprisals on families.

The teaching of Pope Pius XII has thrown much precious light on the delicate problems regarding war. In this field, too, and in accord with the mission assigned to him, the Holy Father brought about the education of consciences, often troubled and perplexed, concerning the attitude to be taken on this complicated subject.

Three principal doctrinal points may be drawn from his teaching concerning war:

1. "War against war." To the fatalists who consider war inevitable, necessary, a harsh law of history; to the apologists of war, who extol it as a school of virtue and civilization; to the pretended realists, who see in war the only means of resolving a conflict between two nations—the Sovereign Pontiff opposed an energetic resistance and a solid refutation. He showed the reasons of a superior nature for which war must be condemned. He appealed to the conscience of nations and invoked their deep aversion for war. With the cry, "War against war," he launched a universal crusade to banish and proscribe forever war of aggression in the relations among nations.

2. The lasting duty of defending absolute values. On the other hand, to the absolute pacifists and to those who think that because of the ravages produced by modern warfare a just cause for war could no longer be found nowadays, the Pope declares that there still exists and will always exist an imperious duty of defending absolute values. Defensive war, given the conditions he has well defined, always remains legitimate, under penalty of permitting injustice to triumph and international criminals to gain the upper hand.

3. An evolution of war. Even here an evolution is taking place. Also defensive war can no longer be regarded simply as a settling of accounts between two nations. Henceforth all are interested in the least tension that appears between two neighboring nations, in any corner of the globe. The community of nations does not have the right to remain indifferent, passive, inert in the face of a violation of justice and of international law. The Pope calls for recourse to international agreements and their sanctions, to the authority and to the decisions of the UN, to its international police force. The intervention of all these new elements will certainly produce an essential modification in the concept of war. The threat of war which, in times past and till the present day, formed a fundamental obstacle to the union of nations, in the future will put into action the law of solidarity existing in the community of nations, in order to prevent, through police action, the eruption of a conflict, or to quench it in its beginnings.

6

THE CHURCH AND THE COMMUNITY OF NATIONS

*We who hold from God the mandate of
promoting the welfare of all nations . . .*
—PIUS XII, Appeal, November 10, 1956

To THIS day very many Christians still have not become sufficiently conscious of the social, collective and universal character
of the religion of Jesus Christ. They have retained an individu-
alist concept of morality and religion. The mystery of the catholicity of the Church has escaped them.

These Christians should meditate on the dimensions given to
his Church by our Lord: "Go . . . and make disciples of all
nations." In chapter two we cited the text of Benedict XV,
teaching that the law of charity applied to nations as well as to
individuals. Pope Pius XII employed very powerful expressions
to show the universality of the Church and her mission, not only
with regard to individuals, but also with regard to nations and
peoples: "The Church is Mother—*Sancta Mater Ecclesia,* a true
Mother, the Mother of all nations and of all peoples, no less than
of individuals" (Christmas Message, 1945).

From this universal maternity of the Church, the Pope will
draw its supranational character. Because the Church is a
mother, she must give herself to all peoples, and yet may not
belong to any. Because she is a mother, she must live among all
peoples, and she is not and cannot be a stranger anywhere.

Again, citing the prayer of Psalm 85: "Lord, all the nations
thou hast made must needs come and worship thee," Pius XII

191

declared: "All, peoples as well as individuals, are called to enter the Church" (Allocution to the Sacred College, February 20, 1946). In the same discourse the Pope spoke of the Church as "the educator of the nations."

Is it not her mission "to lead all nations to their eternal salvation" (Christmas Message, 1946)?

Then there is a text that speaks of the mission the Pope fulfills regarding the nations by bringing them the message, by helping them to discover the truth, to recognize its demands as well as those of morality, by teaching them their rights and their duties as well as God's design for them and for the community of nations:

> We have received from Christ the mission of announcing the truth to the world, of helping the nations to know it, to love it, to put it into practice, to insure its peaceful penetration to the very ends of the earth, beyond every national frontier (Discourse to the International Congress of Philosophy, November 21, 1946).

Those would signally enervate the text of the Holy Father and falsify its meaning who would interpret it as follows: "The message of truth must be brought to all men of all nations . . . It is directed to individuals within the various nations." That is true, of course; every human person, whatever his nation, must be affected by this message. But the word of the Pope goes much farther. The truth must be brought to the nations, to the nations as such. As nations they have certain rights and duties. They are destined to enter the organization of the "United Nations," even though, as a matter of fact, for the time being it is states that are united. The community to be established is not to be envisaged as a world-wide organization of men poured into one immense agglomeration of individuals, abstracting entirely from all the characteristics proper to their nation. This community of the peoples must be constructed while always safeguarding the unity and the respect for their particular physiognomy and the wealth of their diversity.

In the first section we shall study the nature of the relations of the Church with the community of nations and its organization. In the second section we shall consider the contributions which the Church makes to the community of nations.

NATURE OF THE RELATIONS OF THE CHURCH WITH THE
COMMUNITY OF NATIONS AND ITS ORGANIZATION

1. *Some false concepts:* It is necessary, first of all, to get rid of the false concepts of those who do not know the Church, her divine origin, her mission, her purpose. For them the Church is a human society, taking its place along with other earthly societies and, like them, pursuing interested ends to satisfy its appetite for political domination and conquest.

Pius XII took pains to combat this error:

> It is not the role of the Church to envelop and in some manner to embrace all of human society after the fashion of a gigantic worldly empire. This concept of the Church as an earthly empire seeking world domination is fundamentally false (Allocution to the Sacred College, February 20, 1946).

The Pope offers several arguments to prove the falsity of this theory.

First, the Church "is not an empire, especially not in the imperialist meaning ordinarily given to this word nowadays." Certainly, she has received from her divine Founder the mandate to spread throughout the earth and to conquer every creature for the Gospel (Mk 16:15). But, "in her advance and in her expansion, she follows a path just the opposite of modern imperialism."

In *The Social Doctrine of the Church* we had occasion to deal with this penetrating analysis of the Holy Father. "The Church progresses first of all in depth, then in length and breadth. Primarily she seeks man himself." In the second section we shall see the contributions the Church makes to society by her educative action regarding man, his conscience and finally all his activities.

Modern imperialism, on the contrary, follows an exactly opposite road. "It proceeds in length and breadth." It has an exaggerated tendency toward expansion. It does not seek man as such, but "the things and the powers to which it subjects him" —for example, a regime of prestige for the state; an economy of production, to which men are sacrificed; a propaganda which respects neither the truth nor the dignity of man.

Furthermore, the Church and imperialism do not move on the same plane. Ignoring or contemning the spiritual and moral domain, imperialism extends its action to temporal and technical affairs; it is completely preoccupied with material goods, earthly satisfaction and pleasures.

The Church, on the contrary, knows how to remain faithful to her spiritual, supernatural and social mission of leading man to eternal life through their temporal existence and through the duties of their state of personal life: their life as married people, parents, workers and citizens.

Frequently, through the mouth of the Popes, the Church has stated her position, namely, that she refuses to intervene in the conflicts of temporal interests, the problems of political technique.

Thus the Church does not enter into all the concrete questions regarding the forms of organization which the community of nations may take: its structure, its services, its institutions, its programs of action, its methods of procedure, its projects. This constitutes the proper sphere of the states and their international society.

> The Church does not intend to come out in favor of one or the other of the particular and concrete forms by which the various nations or states tend to resolve the gigantic problems of their internal organization as well as their international collaboration, as long as these solutions respect the divine law (Christmas Message, 1942).

Her proper domain is that of the divine and moral law, of which she is the guardian and interpreter. She speaks when this law is threatened or violated. It is her mission to teach it, to defend it, to protect it against false interpretations or errors. Every page of this book has shown the Church and the Papacy engaged in the exercise of this mission on the level of international life.

The same holds true of the different political systems which the nations adopt and their practical application.

> Among the different systems connected with the times on which they depend, the Church cannot be called upon to adopt one rather than another. Within the limits of the divine law, which is valid for all and whose authority binds not only individuals

but nations as well, there is a large field and a liberty of movement for the most varied forms of political concepts. The practical application of a political system depends in a manner that is often decisive on circumstances and causes which, considered in themselves, are foreign to the purpose and the action of the Church . . . (Christmas Message, 1940).

Finally, the Church does not judge according to exclusively political standards, according to purely earthly purposes, but solely according to morality and the divine law.

> The Church cannot agree to judge according to exclusively political criteria; she cannot bind the interests of religion to directions determined by purely earthly goals; she cannot run the risk of having her religious character called into doubt; she cannot forget even for a moment that her quality as representative of God on earth does not allow her to remain indifferent, even for an instant, regarding the "good" and "evil" in human affairs. If she were asked, she would have to refuse, and the faithful, belonging to one or the other party, would have to understand and to respect such an attitude on her part, by virtue of their faith and their supernatural hope (Christmas Message, 1951).

This is the doctrine of the Church on her independence regarding the concrete forms states may assume, regarding political regimes and systems, and attitudes concerning technical problems with a purely earthly purpose.

Pope Pius XI applied this doctrine when, in Article 24 of the Lateran Pact signed in 1929 by the Vatican and Italy, he defined the position of the Holy See in the field of international relations:

> The Holy See, regarding the sovereignty which belongs to it in the international sphere, declares that it wishes to remain and will remain foreign to temporal competitions between other states and to international gatherings called for this purpose, at least as long as the parties in conflict do not make a unanimous appeal to its mission of peace, in each case, however, reserving to itself the right to exert its moral and spiritual power.

This text defines and exactly delimits the mission of the Church in international problems. On the one hand, Pius affirmed her will to remain foreign to temporal competitions between the other states and within the League of Nations. On the other hand, he proclaimed the sovereignty which belongs to her in the international sphere and her disposition to enter into the picture as a mediator of peace, but under two conditions: a) the unanimous appeal of the parties in conflict; b) while reserving to herself the right to exercise her moral and spiritual power.

This attitude of the Papacy, always careful to safeguard its moral and spiritual mission and its non-intervention in temporal conflicts on the international plane, is the decisive refutation of the unjust accusation of political ambition and temporal domination imputed to the Church. It is very clearly defined in this text of Pius XII:

> The Church in no manner has the intention of dominating the nations or of extending her power to purely temporal affairs. Her sole desire is to bring the light of the faith to all nations, to foster the development of human culture, as well as fraternal concord among the peoples (Letter of Pius XII to the International Missionary Congress, August 9, 1950).

2. *The true concept:* In the Encyclical *Summi Pontificatus,* Pius XII gave a formula which goes directly contrary to the accusation raised against the Church, and places in the right perspective the nature of the relations of the Church with the community of nations. The Church

> . . . extends her maternal arms toward the world, not to dominate, but to serve. She has no intention of substituting herself in place of other legitimate authorities within the field proper to them, but she offers them her help after the example and in the spirit of her divine Founder, who "went about doing good" (Acts 10:38).

Here the nature of the relations of the Church with nations and states is well defined: not domination, but service, by the simple accomplishment of her spiritual and social mission.

But in order to understand better the kind of services which the Church can render to nations, it is necessary above all to grasp her fundamental character: she is supranational.

The supranational Church: The Catholic Church, of which Rome is the center, is supranational by her very essence.

In his great allocution to the College of Cardinals of December 24, 1945, Pius XII treated this subject very amply. He announced that in the forthcoming consistory he would name cardinals of various nationalities.

We have decided that the greatest possible number of races and peoples should be represented, and that the Sacred College, in consequence, should be a living image of the universality of the Church.

Have all Catholics sufficiently reflected on this great decision which the Church took at that time to realize her catholicity, her supranational character?

How is this supranational character to be understood? Pius XII expresses it in a twofold sense: the unity of the Church and her universality. "The Church is supranational inasfar as she is an indivisible whole and universal."

The Church is an indivisible whole, because Christ with His Church is undivided and indivisible. Together with His Church, Christ makes *totus Christus*—"the whole Christ," to use the profound thought of St. Augustine. This integrity of Christ, according to the holy Doctor, signifies the indivisible unity of Head and body *in plenitudine Ecclesiae*, "in this fullness of life of the Church" which unites all lands and all times of redeemed humanity, without any exception.

We have here the doctrine of the mystical body, which St. Paul constantly meditated upon and dealt with profoundly in his Letters. Christ, who loved his Church even to the point of sacrificing his life for her, united her to himself in the profoundest and most intimate manner in order to make her his mystical and social body. He, the God-man, is the principle of her unity and her integrity. He and she make but one in the work of the redemption. In her and through her Christ, the Head of this body, continues to accomplish his redemptive mission throughout the world. He and she form the whole Christ, as a single person. And all of us, the members of Christ, together with her form the whole Christ, who must grow in the unity of charity until the end of times and extend into the space of the universe in order to bring together all peoples.

Anything that might be done to make the Church the captive or the slave of this or that particular people, of this or that nation, would be "a sacrilegious attack upon the whole Christ and simultaneously a criminal assault on the unity of the human race." For all of mankind is destined to enter into the supernatural unity of the mystical body.

Such is the first aspect of the supranationality of the Church: she groups together all men of all nations, of all peoples, into the unity of one body, one family, of which she is the mother, embracing all peoples in the same love and bringing to bear, without ceasing, her powers of unity in this humanity torn and divided by sin: "the unifying powers of divine grace; the powers of the unifying Spirit, for which the world is hungering; truths which always and everywhere retain their value; ideals which inspire always and everywhere."

This spirit of supranationality must penetrate and impregnate "her visible head, the Sacred College, every activity of the Holy See." All Christians must be concerned, today more than ever, "to safeguard this supranationality and this indivisible unity of the Church."

The Church is supranational in another sense: she is universal in the sense that she is a stranger nowhere on earth and that she "lives and develops in all the countries of the world and all the countries of the world contribute to her life and her development."

It is important to grasp well this character, which Pius set in relief in a striking historical comparison: "Formerly the life of the Church, under its visible form, displayed its vigor by preference in the countries of old Europe, from which it spread, like a majestic stream, to what one might call the periphery of the world. Today, on the contrary, she appears as an exchange of life and energy among all the members of the mystical body of Christ." Exchange of services, of prayers, of spiritual goods, of charity, even of material help, of human values. Thus the former mission lands which did little more than receive from the Church, today are governed by their own hierarchies and contribute to all the Church goods both spiritual and material.

One might be tempted to regard the supranationality of the Church as putting her so far above the nations as to lose contact with the life of the peoples and human realities. But precisely the contrary is true, and Pius XII refuted the false idea in this very trenchant passage:

Thus supranationality does not keep her suspended, as it were, in inaccessible and intangible outer space, far above the nations;

on the contrary, just as Christ was in the midst of men, so the
Church in which He continues to live likewise exists in the midst
of peoples. Just as Christ assumed a true human nature, so the
Church, in like manner, assumes into herself all that is authentically human and makes of it a source of supernatural strength,
no matter where or under what form she finds it.

Note these words: ". . . all that is authentically human"; the
Church respects it, takes it up, confers an eternal value upon it.
Thus with the human values of civilizations, of creations of art,
of thought, of culture, of science, of technology in all the nations
of the world. The Church considers nothing as strange or indifferent. The Church loves all these human values as matter
she is called upon to inform, to purify, to transform. The Apostle
Paul gave a universalist perspective to her goal: ". . . to restore
all things in Christ." All things! Sin alone must be rejected as
the great and, in the final analysis, the only obstacle. By becoming incarnate, the Word took upon himself the entire human
nature, everything except sin, which, incidentally, as St. Thomas
acutely remarks, does not prove the reality of human nature.

In the Christmas message of 1956, Pius XII spoke of the work
of Christ the Redeemer. The redemptive Incarnation came to
free the human race from sin, to cure this wound, to restore in
man the dignity of a child of God, to triumph—if not always exteriorly, at least interiorly—over the general disorder caused by
original sin and aggravated by personal faults. This interior triumph of the Christian is assured by the divine grace of Jesus
Christ; he gives it in the Church and through her. Thus the
Church carries on the redemptive mission of the Savior in the
world. We shall see how thereby she exercises her beneficent,
purifying, illuminating, elevating and unifying influence on the
community of nations.

What are the relations of the Church with states in the community of nations?

Let us begin by quoting a very important text of Pius XII:

The Church is not a political but a religious society. This does
not, however, hinder her from having not only exterior but also
interior and vital relations with states. Indeed, the Church was
founded by Christ as a visible society, and as such, she meets
with states on the same plane; in her solicitude she embraces the

same human beings and in many forms and under various aspects she uses the same goods and the same institutions. To these exterior relations, in the sphere of nature, because of the fact that men live in common, there are added other interior and vital relations, which have their principle and origin in the person of Jesus Christ, as Head of the Church. For the Son of God by becoming man, and true man, by that very fact contracted a new relationship, truly vital, with the social body of mankind, with the human race, in its unity, which implies the equal personal dignity of all men, and in the many particular societies, those especially which, existing in the bosom of this unity, are necessary to assure exterior order and good organization, or which at least give them a greater natural perfection (Christmas Message, 1951).

Two kinds of relations are indicated by the Pope: exterior and interior.

The Church is a visible—not a secret—society. She lives in the open in every country with all her organization, her dioceses, her parishes, her churches, her religious congregations, her movements of Catholic Action, her various works. Her existence and her activity enter into the life of the nation. She comes into contact with states. The same individuals are simultaneously her children and citizens of the state. Hence the Church regards the juridical regime of separation of Church and State as contrary to the best interests of the citizens, who are members of both societies, and to the common good of the state itself. "The Church uses the same goods and the same institutions" as the state. Let us briefly explain this remark.

Even where, as in France, a regime of separation officially exists, the demands of the national life are stronger than the texts of law imposed by a majority at a time that was convulsed by religious struggles and partisan passions. In the first place, the Church as a moral personality must take into account the laws of the state for its societies of ecclesiastical goods, its associations, its diocesan organizations, its schools, its works of all kinds, its rectories, its buildings, its religious edifices. Hence inevitably arise relations with the representatives of the state for the application of legal regulations to these various institutions.

Furthermore, on the occasion of the great anniversaries of the native land, movements of beneficence, of solidarity, of efforts to organize aid in favor of all the various categories of victims of national trials (veterans, those displaced, orphans, the blind, etc.), the public authorities are wont to solicit the cooperation of the ecclesiastical authorities.

Finally, on the national level, representatives of the Church are necessarily in contact with the various ministries of the Interior, of Foreign Affairs, of National Education, of the Army, of Health, etc.

The Holy See desires to establish diplomatic relations with the greatest possible number of states, either by nunciatures (in the same category as embassies), or by internunciatures (with the standing of plenipotentiary ministers), or by chargés d'affaires and regents. On the other hand, at the present time there are forty-seven foreign diplomatic representations at the Holy See; of these, thirty-three are embassies and fourteen are legations.

With the states which maintain relations with it, the Holy See seeks to establish a modus vivendi, which varies according to the countries; this is done principally by concordats.

In order to understand this beautiful and meaningful doctrine better, we shall comment on each part of this text, in which the Holy Father shows how the Church has interior and vital relations with states.

Christ, Head of the Church—First of all, let us consider the Church in the person of her Head, Jesus Christ. By reason of his redemptive incarnation, by his sacrifice, his death and resurrection, the Son of God has established a new vital relationship with the entire human race. He is its Savior. He liberated it from sin, which was the obstacle to intimate relations with God. He brought it life, divine life, eternal life. He established it in a new relationship of family life with the heavenly Father. He gave to men the power of becoming children of God by a participation of his divine filiation.

This same redemptive mission Jesus Christ continues today and throughout all generations. He continues it in and through the Church, which he illumines, inspires and governs, invisibly by his Spirit, visibly by his hierarchy.

The Church—The Church is not a new intermediary between Christ and men. The Church's mediation does not overlap with that of Christ; she does not join herself to the mediation of Jesus Christ, her Head. He is and always will be "the only Mediator." But he employs the Church as his body, in order to accomplish the work of salvation of the human race. He is the source of truth and the source of graces for mankind, hence also for the Church.[1] She continues his mission of truth, by transmitting his message, by defending and teaching his truth. In particular, she teaches men and nations that there exists an order established by God, an order of beings and of ends.

Then, too, she communicates the supernatural powers of Christ's grace, which assists men in discovering, in their intellect enlightened by faith, the entire order established by God and to realize it through the powers of their will, fortified by the grace and the charity of Christ.

Unity of the human race—Christ as living in his Church and as its Head has established new relations, interior and vital, with the human race, forming a unity with the social body of humanity.

This unity of the human race, as we already saw in chapter one, was an essential reality in the design of God, the Author of nature, Creator and Father. Here Pius XII considers it first in each of the human beings who compose the one humanity, in the equal personal dignity which unites them in their inmost beings, rising above their differences and idiosyncrasies. In the interior of his mystical body, Jesus Christ has vital relations with every member. With regard to those who are outside, Christ, the Head of his Church, sends his graces to all, so that they may be ordered to his mystical body and drawn to it; they, too, are called by a common vocation to the supernatural life of the children of God.

This unity of the human race also plays its part in the many particular societies in which men live by reason of their social nature and where they find the help they need. In the first place

1. "If the future belongs to democracy, a role of the first order in its realization must come from the religion of Christ and of the Church, as the messenger of the word of the Redeemer and the continuator of His mission of salvation. Indeed, it is she who teaches and defends the truth; it is she who communicates the supernatural powers of grace, in order to realize the order of beings and of ends established by God, as the solid foundation and the directive norm of every democracy" (Christmas Message, 1941).

comes the family, a natural society, the source and school of life; then especially the state and the community of states, which guarantee exterior order, the good organization of society, each one indeed pursuing his own common good, which, however, must be brought into intrinsic relation with the unity of the human race, as was explained in chapter one. The state and the community of states are therefore "the forms of unity and of order among men, necessary for human life and cooperating for its perfection" (Pius XII).

Manner of action of Christ and of the Church in their vital relations with states—We are speaking of an entirely interior action, in the realm of conscience, as we shall show in the second half of this chapter.

If the Church can accomplish this educative work in man for the welfare of society, the reason must be sought in "the most profound and the most effective union that is conceivable," Pius declared in defining it in this striking formula: "The Church living in the heart of man, and man living in the bosom of the Church."

In the course of the Christmas message of 1951, Pius XII portrayed this vital union in action and in its effects on man's interior —on the intellect and will of citizens and their rulers:

> And how is all this brought about if not by means of the continuing, illuminating and strengthening influence of the grace of Christ on the intellect and will of citizens and their rulers, so that these may recognize and pursue the goals assigned by the Creator to all the fields of men's lives in common, so that they may labor to direct the collaboration of individuals and of peoples toward these goals, and so that they may exercise social justice and charity within the States and among them?

This new and intimate relationship between the Church and states is one of vital elevation and confirmation. But how is this intimate relationship between the Church and states and the community of states to be described? Pius XII answers: "With them, as an organization of peace, Jesus Christ, the Prince of peace—and with Him the Church, in which He continues to live —has entered a new and intimate relationship of vital elevation and confirmation."

These two terms must be well understood:

An intimate relationship of *elevation.* For "by this union, the

Church elevates man to the perfection of his being and of his vitality" (Pius XII). Men—both citizens and rulers—thus enlightened by the grace of Christ in their intellect discover the plan of God, the higher purposes assigned by God to the social life, the very noble values they have to respect and to preserve, which elevate them above the tendencies of selfish nature when left to itself. Fortified by the grace of Christ in their will, they are more resolute in cooperating for the realization of God's great design for the community of nations, and for the advancement of humanity by the fraternal collaboration of men and nations; by grace they are inclined to practice the social virtues of justice and charity.

A relation of vital *confirmation,* in the sense that society is the first beneficiary of the educative work accomplished by the Church in the hearts and consciences of men. By that very fact society finds itself established on a solid foundation, whence it receives cohesion, equilibrium and security in its natural social order. Thus every natural order is sustained, "confined," by the supernatural action of divine grace. The temporal receives solidity by this vital contact with the eternal.

THE CHURCH'S CONTRIBUTION TO THE COMMUNITY OF NATIONS

We distinguish: the community of nations in itself, abstracting from its concrete organization; and the concrete organization of the community of nations.

To the community of nations as such the Church contributes a twofold benefit: 1) A message of truth and unity; 2) Education of conscience.

1. *A message of unity and truth.* The Church's primary mission is to announce the message of Christ. Now this message serves in a very concrete manner the cause of the reconciliation of nations, since it is essentially a message of unity and of peace.

> Substantially it is nothing else than the divine call to reconciliation, first between men and God, and then among men themselves —in a word it is the message of the most exalted peace (Discourse to the Italian Center of Studies for International Reconciliation, October 13, 1955).

The Pope then explains how the message of the word and the doctrine of Christ is calculated to reunite men and nations:

This message is in effect the announcement of the one origin and the one last end of all men and of all nations; of the one God and Father of all; of the one and unifying precept of the love of God and of neighbor; of the one Redeemer and of the Church established by Him for all nations, so that there may be but one Shepherd and one flock. This message, which in its origin, in its means and in its goal is inspired by the concept of the unity of creatures in a single God evidently tends toward peace and unity.

Christians still have not become sufficiently aware of the originality and the internal power of Christ's message as a means of bringing men and nations together and thus contributing to the organization of the community of nations. At the present time when, in the midst of formidable convulsions and constant threats to the world's peace, the process of the unification of humanity proceeds with great difficulty, the message of unity brought by Christ two thousand years ago takes on an astonishing and marvelous character of actuality. It is based on the great truth of the unity of the human race: unity of origin, unity of nature, unity of final goal. To this truth he gives unshakable foundations.

First, the fatherhood of God. "One God and Father of all." Other theories—human inventions—will also seek to speak of a universal brotherhood. But they will wallow in a vague sentimentality, powerless to give solid and profound reasons for this duty of brotherhood, since they do not recognize the foundation, which is the fatherhood of the one God. For Christians the duty is clear and imperious; all men are brethren and must be treated as brethren, because they all have the same Father in heaven. This is the great message Jesus Christ revealed to the world!

This message rests on a second foundation: in order that this truth may pass into the lives of men, who are always subject to the law of sin which divides, notably the sin of egotism which is so characteristic of human nature injured by original sin, the message of Christ teaches "the one and unifying precept of the love of God and of neighbor." "One," because the same precept imposes on Christians the obligation of loving God and their brethren. The second precept of love of neighbor is "like" the precept of the love of God. Hence by the same virtue of charity the Christian can satisfy this great precept, which is the "whole" law of the Lord, his new commandment, his supreme testament, the sign by which his disciples are known. Love of neighbor is the tangible proof, the undoubted mark, the most evident manifestation and most sincere expression of the love of God. He who pretends to love God whom he does not see, while he does not love his neighbor whom he sees, is a liar (1 Jn 4:20).

Then, too, a precept which tends to bring men together, to unite them by the same love with which they love God their Father by obeying his commandment of love, indeed has a "unifying" tendency.

Finally, the third foundation: the redemptive incarnation and the Church, "the one Redeemer," "the Church founded by him for all nations."

The Son of God became man and gave his life so "that he might gather into one the children of God who were scattered abroad" (Jn 11:52). He founded his Church to unite all of them supernaturally under his guidance into "one flock" (Jn 10:16), one body, one family, one community of salvation, with the same faith, the same hope, the same baptism, the same Eucharist, the source and permanent hearth of charity, the center and bond of unity.

We have already quoted above the text in which Pius XII proclaimed his mission, received from Christ, of announcing the truth to the world, of helping nations to know it, to love it, to put it into practice and to spread it throughout the entire universe, above and beyond all national frontiers.

In fact, it is not only by the message of unity in the strict sense that the Church brings an immense benefit to the nations, but also and quite simply by the constant exercise of her mission of teaching the truth.

Which truth? First, the divinely revealed truth, that which touches the mystery of God, his internal and trinitarian life, that which is contained in the great dogmas of the Blessed Trinity, the Incarnation, the Redemption, the Church, the eternal truths of salvation. Let no one say that these supernatural truths, if they can serve as a light and life for private individuals who study them, have no direct relation to the life of nations, that they exercise no influence over the community of nations!

One fact will suffice to give an idea of what, on the contrary, the union of the nations can expect from the knowledge and the illumination of these higher truths. Every year, beginning with 1939, Pope Pius XII, bowing down before the crêche of the infant Savior at Christmas, invited all men to recall the lessons of the mystery of the redemptive Incarnation. In his Christmas messages the head of the Church drew thence a powerful synthesis, which he applied to the actual problems of international life. Without ceasing he stressed the fact that, in order to restore peace and to organize the community of nations in the truth, it was necessary to return to these fundamental truths regarding God, Jesus Christ, the order established by God, the absolute order of beings and of ends: ". . . to return to the order fixed by God, also in the relations between states and nations" (Christmas Message, 1945).

But the Church by her message not only teaches supernatural truths inaccessible to reason; there are also the truths which man can attain by his reason—the natural law written by the Creator in the reasonable nature of man.

Now, here is one of the great benefits which the Church brings to the community of nations. In the first chapter we recalled that the natural law had been abandoned by modern philosophers and had been rejected by the theories of juridical positivism. We pointed out the tremendous harm thereby produced in the minds of men and in the life of nations. Pius XII did not hesitate to affirm that

> . . . the deep and final root of the evils We deplore in modern society is the negation and the rejection of a rule of universal morality, whether in individual life or in social life and international relations; that is to say, the contempt and the forgetfulness, so widespread nowadays, of the natural law itself (Encyclical *Summi Pontificatus*).

In teaching the necessity of the natural law, in defending it against the attacks to which it is subjected, this pope rendered the nations an incalculable service. He stopped a devastating flood. Even now, certain jurists are trying to rediscover the natural law, and the hope may be expressed that in the light of the teaching of Pius XII, as well as in consideration of the harm done by the abandonment of the natural law as the foundation of law and institutions, progress will be made in the law of the nations, progress in the direction of an authentic humanism.

For, in working to bring about a rediscovery of the natural law, Pius supported the promotion of a true humanism. Thereby he affirmed the power and the nobility of human reason, he testified to his confidence in man. True, he mentioned the limits of human nature, but also its grandeur. He asked, on this basis of the natural law, for loyal and complete collaboration of all men of good will, of all those who believe in man and desire to defend and preserve the dignity of the human person, the integrity of his liberty, the inviolability of all his essential rights and those of the family, of all those who, whatever be their philosophical or social beliefs and opinions, are resolved to protect the order of nature as the Creator has established it.

The Holy Father declared as much to a group of Catholic intellectuals from various countries:

> There exists a vast field in which men, freed of prejudices and passions, can come to agreement and assist one another mutually in favor of a real and valuable common good, since reason suffices to establish the bases of international law, to recognize the inviolable character of the person, the dignity of the family, the prerogatives and the limits of public authority.[2]

Is it not remarakble that the Pope, setting himself against the false doctrines professed by men, should make himself the defender of human nature, of the natural law, of the natural order, as the Vatican Council in the nineteenth century had made itself the defender of reason and of its power to arrive at a knowledge of the existence of God against the fideists and traditionalists?

Considering the purposes of every organization of the world, Pius XII emphasized the necessity of respecting the natural order established by God:

2. Discourse to the participants of the Eleventh Plenary Assembly of Pax Romana (Easter, 1957), on "the intellectual Catholic at the service of the world community in formation."

As a matter of fact, no organization of the world can be viable, unless it harmonizes with the totality of natural relations, with the normal and organic order that governs the particular relations of men and of different nations. If these things are missing, it will not stand and endure, whatever be its structure (Allocution to the Congress of the Universal Movement for a World Federation, April 6, 1951).

Why and how did men arrive at the point of denying and rejecting the natural law? Because, in Europe, they abandoned "the doctrine of Christ, of which the chair of Peter is the depositary and the mistress." So true is the teaching of the same Vatican Council, which reclaimed the powers of reason, but which also declared that supernatural revelation—that which the Savior brought to mankind and of which the Church is the depositary and interpreter—is morally necessary for the human race. The Church, said Pius XII, is "the guardian, by the will of God and by the mandate of Christ, of the natural and supernatural order" (Christmas Message, 1942), or, again, she is "the guardian of the supernatural Christian order in which nature and grace are united" (Pentecost Message, 1941). Consequently, she is competent "to judge whether the foundations of a social organization are conformable to the immutable order of things which God has manifested through the natural law and through revelation" (*ibid.*).

When the authority of the Church was rejected by the Protestants, the divinity of Jesus Christ was first doubted, then denied, and little by little even the truths of the natural order were questioned. Thus came about the laicization of society, "withdrawing man, the family and the state from the beneficent and regenerating influence of the idea of God and of the teaching of the Church" (Encyclical *Summi Pontificatus*).

Here again it is truly the welfare of the nations that the Pope desires and pursues, by helping them to recover this idea of God, "the almighty Creator and Father of all, supreme and absolute Legislator, and just Judge of human actions." Pius XII constantly showed forth how, by the denial of God, the entire moral order was shaken. This is especially true in *Summi Pontificatus:*

When God is denied, the entire basis of morality is shattered at the same time, and the voice of nature, which teaches even the ignorant and the tribes that have not yet been civilized what is good and evil, licit and illicit, and makes everyone conscious of the responsibility for his actions before the supreme Judge, is quenched or at least seriously weakened.

By the same token, the divine law gives moral authority to human law itself:

Where the dependence of human law with regard to the divine law is denied, where appeal is made solely to a vague and uncertain idea of purely earthly authority, where an autonomy founded only on a utilitarian morality is asserted, human law itself logically loses in its most serious applications the moral authority required as an essential condition in order to be recognized and to be able to demand sacrifices.

The Holy Father has described, under the most varied forms and in all fields, the consequences of an abandonment of the idea of God, already of the rational plane and of faith in God. We shall close with a quotation which shows more particularly on the international level the repercussions of the disappearance of faith in God, the Father of all men, and of a sense of a community of nations as willed by God:

When faith in God, the Father of all men, begins to disappear, the spirit of brotherhood likewise loses its moral base and its power of cohesion; and when the sense of a community willed by God, which includes reciprocal rights and duties regulated by determined laws, starts to vanish, their place is taken by a sickly hypersensibility which tends to divide, an instinctive inclination to an exaggerated affirmation of rights, real or imaginary, a neglect often unconscious, but no less harmful for that reason, of the vital needs of others. The way is then open for the struggle against all, a struggle in which only might makes right Christmas Message, 1947).

2. *Education of conscience:* How will this message of truth and unity and this teaching of the moral law and of the natural law exercise their influence on the organization of society and on the community of nations? Through the intermediary of consciences, through the mediation of all consciences—and first of all those of the Christian laity, who live at the heart of the human community.

Therefore the Church's second mission is the formation of

consciences. She regards this mission as "essential" for herself.

> The Church cannot remain inactive in the recesses of her temples and thus relinquish her divinely providential mission of forming the complete man, and consequently collaborating unceasingly in the construction of a solid foundation of society. This mission is essential for her. Considered from this point of view, one may say that the Church is the society of those who, under the supernatural influence of grace, in the perfection of their personal dignity as children of God and in the harmonious development of all their human inclinations and energies, build up the powerful bastion of the human community (Allocution to the Sacred College, February 20, 1946).

How does the Church go about fulfilling this mission of the education of consciences for the greatest good of society? The important discourse, from which the preceding paragraph was excerpted, provides a long explanation. The Church seeks above all to reach man in the heart of society; she tries to form him, to perfect the divine image in him.

This labor of education takes place in man's interior, in the recesses of his conscience. But it has its repercussion on his whole family life, his professional, social and civic life, his various activities. Society then gathers the fruits. It can count on men thus formed with a sense of their dignity as children of God, of their well-balanced liberty, of their personal responsibilities, as men capable of taking the initiative, of accepting positions in the service of the common good, of assuming social responsibilities, conscious of the bonds of solidarity and equality with their likes in matters pertaining to their human dignity, attached to their traditions.

Pius XII describes these men whom the Church gives to human society under the four following characteristics:

> . . . men established in their inviolable integrity as images of God; men proud of their personal dignity and of their well-balanced liberty; men justly jealous of their equality with their likes in matters pertaining to the deepest basis of their human dignity; men attached in a stable manner to their country and their traditions; in a word, men characterized by these four qualities contribute to human society a solid foundation and procure for it security, balance, equality and normal development in space and in time.

Perhaps it may cause surprise to see Pius XII stressing as one of the four qualities that of stability of attachment to a country and its traditions, at a time when men are in perpetual movement, very frequently changing their residence, especially in the popular quarters, and when, thanks to modern means of communication, change is the order of the day. Precisely in the same passage where Pius speaks of this stability, he also describes the contemporary and sad phenomena of emigration, of expatriation, of deportations by which entire populations are torn from their lands and from their hearths. Besides, this pope's special solicitude for those who have known suffering and his requests to the nations to resolve the problems of emigration and immigration are well known. If he asked for the preservation of family customs, the reason is that, in the maelstrom of contemporary life, its events should not cause the abandonment of age-old traditions, of venerable customs; special attention should be given to those who, for various reasons (emigration, military service), are far distant from their native land.

As far as the other three elements are concerned, Pius XII frequently showed himself the defender of the dignity of the human person, of personal responsibility, of the conscience of citizens in a true democracy, of the liberty of man. The Christmas message of 1956 particularly merits re-reading. Pius XII there insists on the positive value of the concepts of conscience and responsibility, on the importance of free will in human life. He portrays the grandeur of liberty, by taking a position against those who want to see in man only a mechanized being and in his acts "the result of natural processes."

Man dominates these developments and these complexes, because he is above all a spiritual substance, a person free to act or not to act, and not merely the result of an evolution of natural processes. In this consists his dignity, but it also determines his limits! For this reason he is capable of doing good, but also evil.

Nowadays it is fashionable to criticize the defects of institutions. No doubt, they have their failings. But Pius XII forcefully stressed in the first place the moral value of citizens, their individual moral responsibility, the capital role of the power and the weakness of men, of sin and of grace.

"In fact, the state itself and its form depend on the moral value of the citizens . . ." Pius then called attention to the tendency of the modern state to withdraw from the individual the care and the responsibility for his own life in order to transfer them to public institutions. He adds: "A modern democracy thus constituted has to fail in the measure that it no longer addresses itself or no longer can address itself to the individual responsibility of its citizens."

This, then, is the education of consciences that must be accomplished! The states that enclose themselves in a strict laicism in order to refuse the collaboration of religion in this moral undertaking of the greatest urgency seriously harm themselves and bring misfortune on their people.

> The reform of institutions is not as urgent as that of morals. . . . In the life of states themselves the power and the weakness of men, sin and grace, play a capital role. Politics of the twentieth century cannot ignore this fact nor can they persist in the error of wanting to separate the state from religion in the name of a laicism which the facts cannot justify.

For this reason Pius XII could speak in his first encyclical of a "reëducation of humanity" and declare that "if it is to have any effect, [it] must be above all spiritual and religious. Consequently it must proceed from Christ as from its indispensable foundation, be realized in justice and crowned by charity."

In order to accomplish this work of the reëducation of consciences, the Church of Jesus Christ possesses means that are singularly effective: the teaching of the moral law, the natural law and the Gospel, the commandments of God and of the Church. Then there is the practice of the virtues, charity above all, cleansing of the heart, control of the passions, mastery of the instincts and of the tendencies of nature to egotism, examination of conscience and confession. There is the sacramental and liturgical life of the Church, notably the life of the Eucharist and of the redeeming Sacrifice, to help toward an interior transformation under the action of a vital assimilation through Christ and a participation in the Paschal mystery.

With regard to the international community: In a still more direct manner the community of nations benefits from the action and the influence exercised by the Church in her mission as educator of consciences, under three principal aspects.

First, Pius XII as head of the Church made it a duty for every Christian to labor for the achievement of the community of nations now in formation. Thus the consciences of Christians have been enlightened on a problem regarding which many of them had been hesitant and doubting. The duty is clearly laid down and it is founded on the example and the order of Christ.

> A Christian cannot remain indifferent in the face of the evolution of the world. If, under the pressure of events, he sees a more compact community of nations coming to the fore, he knows that this unification, desired by the Creator, must lead to a union of minds and hearts in the same faith and the same love. Not only may he, but he must, labor for the achievement of this community still in formation, for the example and the order of the divine Master constitute for him incomparable light and power (Pius XII, Allocution to the Eleventh Plenary Assembly of Pax Romana, April 25, 1957).

Here is a duty of conscience which must be fulfilled out of respect for God's design for the community of nations. Thus is clearly presented the duty of Christians to obey the definitely expressed will of God, which is then fortified by the formal declaration of the Sovereign Pontiff, which we cited in chapter one: "According to the divine will, the nations together form a community having one goal and common duties." But there is more to this design of God; the Christian, taught by the Church and its visible head, knows that a great work of unification must be accomplished. "He knows that this unification willed by the Creator must lead to a union of minds and hearts in the same faith and in the same love."

For him who loves his God and his brethren, what other motive could have so powerful an influence on his conscience and engage him in such effective cooperation for the construction of this world-wide community? If we still stood in need of conviction, we ought to listen to the voice of a very moving witness, a female political figure, an apostle of international institutions.[3]

3. Dr. Marga A. M. Klompe, member of the Dutch delegation to the General Assembly of the UN from 1947 to 1952; deputy to the second

After showing the grandeur of the task and of the grace which rests on the Christian to work for the unity of the human race, a unity reëstablished on new bases through the redemptive work of Christ, Dr. Klompe writes:

> The Christian is conscious that he will never acquit himself perfectly of this task. He knows that without ceasing he brings obstacles to the realization of this unity and of this community by the limitation of his means, by his weakness, by the contempt, the hatred, envy, jealousy, national egotism and by an opportunist policy based on pure economics. But he may not and he must never weaken; he must apply himself with all his powers to attain this objective, with the consciousness that thus he is doing the will of the divine Creator. Precisely when the Christian is penetrated by the thought of this human unity founded by Christ, he searches for new means and new methods to establish this unity as a visible reality in the world, in order to concretize it in the forms of community which are possible for us. Then there will result from the multiple attempts and trials in the field of international collaboration something more that the exterior technical forms of organization; an interior, deeper evolution will take place, which will lead toward an elevated goal and thence into the plan of God.[4]

Then, in calling the Christian to the duty of laboring at the construction of the community of nations, the Church forms his conscience for this marvelous work, both by preserving it from the deviations and errors of thought and action in this matter and by tracing for it in a positive manner the way to follow.

The Church has protected the consciences of Christians and of all men of good will by denouncing the cult of force, of race, of nation, the divinization of the state, the totalitarianism of means and of ends, all the errors which have poisoned the atmosphere of the relations between nations and have brought the world to a frightful war, as they will not fail to do again, if they should grow and continue to spread.

Positively, by her living magisterium, the Church has traced

---

chamber of the General Estates from 1948 to 1956; meanwhile, member of the consultative assembly of the Council of Europe from 1949 to 1956 and member of the assembly of the Community of Coal and Steel from 1952 to 1956; minister of social assistance in the Dutch government.

4. *Le monde attend l'Eglise* (Editions Fleurus, 1957), p. 44.

the road to be followed if men sincerely desire to preserve peace and to organize it: the community of nations will become a living reality, if it rests on the order of truth, of liberty, of security, on the order of justice and charity, and if the order of peace to be established has for its foundation the primacy of the universal moral law, the natural and divine law.

Lastly, if it is animated by a spirit, all this international order will avoid being dominated by the supremacy of techniques, which will become more and more necessary as the unification of the world proceeds. Now, the Church supplies it with that spirit by penetrating the consciences she forms by her educative mission: a spirit of common brotherhood, a spirit of universalism, transcending everything that divides men and nations and sets them at odds, the sense of the international and world-wide community.

> Humanity cannot rise above the present crises and desolation to take the road to a more harmonious future, unless it represses and dominates the forces of division and of discord, thanks to a sincere spirit of brotherhood, which unites in the one same love all classes, all races and all nations (Christmas Message, 1947).

They would deceive themselves egregiously who saw in this disposition of universal brotherhood only a vague and weak sentimentalism. On the contrary, there is question of a virtue, which must manifest itself by positive acts of generosity, of the gift of self, of sacrifices for the constitution of a true community of nations, with all the exigencies of a charity as wide as the world, of a charity that finds no rest until it has done everything possible to relieve all the misery of humanity and to remedy effectively all the distress and all the trials of people throughout the world.

THE CHURCH'S CONTRIBUTION TO THE CONCRETE ORGANIZATION OF THE COMMUNITY OF NATIONS

We have made the distinction between the community of nations and its concrete organization at various times. During this second half of the twentieth century, the UN is the form that tends to represent the world community: an organization of states. Between the two wars it was the League of Nations. Whatever form the organization takes or will take, the Church preserves intact and teaches a complete concept of the community of nations. The UN did not yet exist when Pius XII presented an entire body of doctrine regarding the rights and duties of nations, regarding the principles that would have to govern the future organization of the world community.

At the present time it is this concrete organization we are considering. What contribution does the Church make to it, besides the benefits it assures to every international organization?

In particular, the Church supplies a threefold assistance: 1) the beneficent support of the Papacy; 2) the active collaboration of international Catholic organizations and of Christians engaged in international action; 3) the climate which the existence of the universal Church creates in the world and which favors the action of the UN.

1. *The beneficent support of the Papacy.* It is a constant fact in the history of the Papacy that all the Sovereign Pontiffs have desired, encouraged and sustained the efforts undertaken since the beginning of the nineteenth century for the constitution of an international organization.

Already in 1899, at the moment when the Conference of The Hague was being held, Leo XIII noted a grave lacuna in the relations among states: "There is wanting in the international consortium of states a system of legal and moral means capable of determining and of actuating the rights of each. Hence nothing remains except recourse to force, to the competition of states in the development of their military might.[5]

It should be noted that the vision of the Papacy at that hour discovered a woeful deficiency in the international "consortium" of states: the absence of a juridical and moral organization capable of dominating force by law. At that moment the Pope put the finger on the plague which continued to spread—the armament race. But he also indicated a positive solution—the institution of mediation and arbitration. He went farther than the facultative arbitration envisaged at that time by Count

5. Second diplomatic note of Cardinal Rampolla in reply to the second circular of Count Mouraviev (February 10, 1899).

Mouraviev. "An institution of mediation, invested with authority, surrounded with all the necessary moral prestige, endowed with indispensable guarantees of competence and impartiality, not binding the liberty of the parties in conflict, would be less exposed to meeting with obstacles."

While war was raging, on April 1, 1917, six months before President Wilson made his proposals, Pope Benedict XV called for "the institution of arbitration, with its exalted function of keeping the peace according to norms to be drawn up and sanctions to be determined against the state which would refuse either to submit international questions to arbitration or to accept its decisions."

Here again the Papacy first proposes sanctions as guarantees.

In the Encyclical *Pacem* of May 25, 1920, Benedict XV clearly expressed the desire that "the ensemble of states, discarding all mutual suspicions, should unite to form but one society, or better, one family."

The Pope defined the mission of this "Society of Nations": to stop military spending in the armament race; to suppress war by making it impossible in the future; to assure to every nation, with the limits of its legitimate frontiers, its independence as well as the integrity of its territory.

To this society of nations Benedict XV from that hour gave the impressive support of the Church. "To the nations united in a league founded on the Christian law, the Church will furnish its active and earnest cooperation for all their undertakings inspired by justice and charity."

Pius XI interested himself in the work of the League of Nations. He approved of it in principle and acknowledged its necessity. But he also pointed out a defect. Peace is stressed in the official documents, but it is not established in minds and hearts. "Would it not be possible to impose on all the nations a kind of international code, adapted to our age, analagous to that which in the Middle Ages governed this veritable League of Nations which we call Christianity? True, it also witnessed very many injustices. But at least the sacred value of law remained uncontested, a certain rule according to which the nations would have to render an account."

The Pope then showed how the Church of Christ was an

institution capable of guaranteeing the inviolability of the law of nations.

Four years before any project of an international reorganization of nations and when war had broken out, Pius XII spoke of "a stable and fruitful international organization such as all men of good will desire." He elaborated on its function and spirit: "An organization which, because it will respect the rights of God, can assure the mutual independence of nations great and small, impose fidelity to agreements loyally consented to and safeguard, in the effort of each for the prosperity of all, the healthy liberty and the dignity of the human person."[6]

In his first Christmas message (1939), while enumerating the five fundamental points for a just and lasting peace, the Pope mentioned in the third point the creation or the reconstruction of international institutions for the loyal and faithful application of agreements or, in case of recognized need, their revision. Concerning these international institutions the Pope declared that they have "an exalted mission, which is at the same time difficult and full of serious responsibilities."

In the Christmas message of 1941, Pope Pius XII returned to the necessity and the function of these institutions, "so that mutual confidence may be reborn."

The end of the war was approaching. Statesmen were preparing a new organization. In a radio message to the world on September 1, 1944, the Pope expressed his satisfaction at the efforts undertaken and his wishes for their complete success:

> Today, when in the light of so many harrowing experiences, the desire of such a universal institution of peace forces itself more and more on the attention and the solicitude of statesmen and nations, We express with pleasure Our satisfaction and We formulate the wish that the concrete realization correspond truly in great measure to the grandeur of the purpose, which is the maintenance, for the advantage of all, of tranquility and security in the world.

Four months later, in his Christmas message of 1944, the Pope pronounced words of considerable weight on this subject. He

6. Reply to the new minister of the Republic of Haiti, November 10, 1939.

spoke again of the absolute order of beings and of ends as a moral requisite for the unity of the family of nations. In connection with this moral requisite he showed the capital importance of a community of nations.

> The absolute order of beings and of ends . . . includes, as a moral requisite and as the capstone of a social development, the unity of the human race and of the family of nations. . . . If this moral requisite were realized in a society of nations which would avoid the structural defects and the deficiencies of previous solutions, then the majesty of absolute order would reign and dominate equally the deliberations of this society and the application of these sanctions.

In September, 1948, on the eve of the opening of the third session of the Assembly of the United Nations, the Pope received some American pilgrims. He referred to the work of the Assembly, where "men of knowledge and experience, of great character and noble ideals, fully conscious of their serious responsibilities toward civilization and culture, will set to work, will employ all their efforts to bring about a rebirth of confidence in the bosom of the family of nations. . . ."

The Pope added: "If ever an assembly of men, united at a critical turning point of history, had need of the help of prayer, it is indeed the Assembly of the United Nations. And therefore We ask you to pray."

In the same year (1948), in his Christmas message, recalling the duty on the part of states to show a united front in defense of peace, the Pope cried out:

> May the Organization of the United Nations become the complete and pure expression of this international solidarity of peace, expunging from its institutions and its statutes every vestige of its origin, which was necessarily a solidarity of war!

Besides, in this same message the Pope showed how solidarity among the various nations "imposed on each multiple duties toward the great family of nations."

Finally, as we had occasion to remark in the chapter on disarmament, in the Christmas message of 1956, Pius XII dedicated some important passages to the authority of the UN.

He paid respect to the very noble program which forms the

foundation of the UN: ". . . to guarantee the absolute values in the common life of nations."

But the Pope also noted with sadness that this program had been forgotten by certain members of the UN. "The recent past has shown that false realism succeeds in gaining the upper hand with a goodly number of its members, even when there is question of reëstablishing respect for these same values of human nature which are brazenly trodden under foot."

This or that case is no longer judged in the light of these absolute values; instead there are "unilateral views which tend to be put into practice according to circumstances merely to serve the function of interest or of power." As a result, "charges of disturbing the peace are treated in very different ways, so much so that the respective importance they have in the light of these absolute values is purely and simply reversed."

Pius XII's verdict is severe. The aggression committed against Hungary by Soviet troops in snuffing out the spontaneous uprising of the intellectual elite and of the workers called forth, in all the countries of the world where the onesided propaganda of Soviet Russia did not reign, a general indignation and reaction such as, doubtless, was rarely seen till that time.

Pius did not dream of diminishing in the least the authority of the UN. Indeed, he desired to see its authority bolstered. He declared this expressly: "We desire to see the authority of the United Nations strengthened." He even indicated the practical means to be used for this purpose: the sending of observers "to the places where man's essential values are endangered"; sanctions against the states which would refuse to admit such a mission, namely, "they ought not to be allowed to exercise their rights as members of the organization," since they showed by their refusal "that they have a concept of the state's sovereignty that undermines the very foundations of the United Nations"; "the right and power to prevent any intervention of one state in another under any pretext whatsoever, as well as the assurance, through sufficient police forces, of protecting order in the threatened state."

Finally, we have already quoted (in the chapter on disarmament) the proposal of the Pope regarding the commitment of states to renounce the production of certain weapons; as far as Pius XII was concerned, this commitment could only be made by common agreement, transformed into a strict obligation of international law and effectively controlled within the framework of the United Nations.

Patently the Papacy has, in the words of Benedict XV, contributed "active and impressive cooperation" to the organization of the community of nations.

At a time when no such organization yet existed, the Popes called for it. They portrayed the great and noble mission it was to fulfill. In the eyes of all Christians and of the entire world they stressed its urgent and imperious need. They described the spirit that must animate it. They protected it and put it on guard against errors and deviations that might compromise it. They demanded a strengthening of its authority.

2. *Active collaboration of Catholics in international action.*
To the construction of the community of nations the Church contributes the active cooperation of Catholics engaged in international organizations. Some of these are of a public nature—intergovernmental organizations and international institutions; others are private—non-governmental organizations, and—particularly for our purposes—the International Catholic Organizations (I.C.O.).

Organizations of a public nature: About the only thing very many people know about the UN is the existence of the Security Council and the General Assembly, because of the coverage given their meetings by press and radio. They are aware, too, that there is a Secretary General of the UN, who carries out missions of observation in various parts of the world. But it is sad to note the general ignorance surrounding the intense and fruitful work accomplished by the organisms attached to the United Nations.

We shall mention first the Economic and Social Council (ECOSOC). It concerns itself particularly with cultural, economic, social and humanitarian problems. The Council has played an important part in giving technical assistance to underdeveloped countries. It has regional economic commissions (Europe, Asia,

Far East, etc.), a social commission (social aspects are more and more taking a place alongside the examination of the world's economic situation, which was the principal object of discussion during the first years), special commissions for problems pertaining to population, the rights of man, the condition of women, assistance to children, etc. The competence of the Council is consultative; the veto plays no part in it.[7]

There are, besides, great specialized institutions. We have given a number of extracts of allocutions of the Holy Father to their representatives assembled in Rome: the Organization for Food and Agriculture, the World Health Organization, the International Labor Office. The last-named concerns itself with the bettering of the conditions of labor and with raising the living standards of laborers throughout the world. It has been in existence since 1919. The International Labor Office possesses more than a merely consultative function. In its activity it brings together representatives of professional organizations of workmen and employers, either for the elaboration of international agreements or even for its administrative council.

Finally, we may mention UNESCO, which has as its goal the promotion of education, science and culture in the world and thus intends to contribute to a better understanding among the nations.

What is the attitude of the Church with regard to these neutral organisms of a public nature? In his discourse to the Eleventh Assembly of Pax Romana, April 27, 1957, Pius XII gave some very precise directions on this matter. First, he enunciated the principle that the Christian cannot remain indifferent in the face of the evolution of the world; he may and must labor at the construction of the international community.

After pointing out the social and universal responsibility of Catholic intellectuals in matters pertaining to the spread of Christian truth and its concrete application in all sectors of activity,

7. The Economic and Social Council meets twice a year in ordinary session. In each of these sessions numerous questions—fifty or sixty—are discussed. It has eighteen members elected for a period of three years by the General Assembly of the United Nations. Decisions are made by simple majority vote.

Pius XII put this question: "Is it true to say that one may not work for the world community in institutions where God is not expressly recognized as the Author and Legislator of the universe?"

Two levels of cooperation must be distinguished in this connection.

First of all, there is question of cooperation in all the enterprises striving directly for the betterment of the condition of the poor and disinherited. The Christian must be ready to lend his assistance in such undertakings, because, without forgetting that his ultimate goal is to contribute to the eternal salvation of his brethren, he "will recall that the coming of the kingdom of God in hearts and social institutions very often requires a minimum of human effort, a simple demand of reason, to which every man submits normally, even if he does not possess the grace of faith."

There follows a beautiful text, calling upon Christians to collaborate in all the great international undertakings of social charity:

> The Christian will then be ready to labor at the assuagement of all material miseries, at the universal development of basic education, in a word, at all the enterprises tending directly to the betterment of the lot of the poor and the disinherited, certain that thus he is fulfilling a duty of collective charity, that he is preparing a greater number of men for a personal life worthy of the name, that in this manner he is fostering their spontaneous entry into the great assembly of efforts which directs them toward a better condition, permits them to perceive the light and to embrace the only truth that will make them truly happy.

Then, the problem of cooperation takes on a very different color for those Catholics who are charged with a more weighty task, who enjoy a certain public standing and thereby can exert more influence on the public mind. Their participation in uncertain undertakings may appear to include approval of an inadmissible political or social system. In itself, of course, the truth tolerates neither mixture nor impurity.

The Holy Father here recalls a rule of conduct on which we commented in *The Social Doctrine of the Church:* the possibility of cooperation on the part of Catholics with men of good will who are unbelievers, provided they want to work for the common good in accord with the demands of the natural law; we have likewise cited his directive to Catholic intellectuals (Pax Romana).

It is impossible to stress sufficiently the following text of Pope Pius XII addressed to this same group; he traces a line of conduct for Catholics called to exercise their action in neutral organizations. This text confirms his intention of seeing the establishment of cooperation among all those who are resolved to base their action on the natural law and the law of nations, which human reason can attain by its unassisted powers. Catholics will have a role to play in these organizations, in order to keep them correct in thought and action and to animate them from within like a leaven.

> For that reason the cooperation of Catholics is desirable in all the institutions which, in theory and practice, respect the dictates of the natural law. They will seek to keep them on the right road and by their active presence to play a beneficent part, which the divine Master compares to that of the salt and of the wheat. In these organizations which propose to themselves a universal humanitarian goal they will find generous souls and superior minds who are capable of rising above material preoccupations, of understanding that a truly collective destiny of mankind presupposes the absolute value of every person that composes it and the establishment beyond the limits of time of that true society whose earthly community is but the reflection and the foreshadowing.

At the end of his great discourse to the Second World Congress of the Apostolate of the Laity, (October 5-13, 1957), Pius XII, speaking of the function of laymen in the missions of Asia and Africa, gave the following two directives:

> First, to collaborate with the neutral and non-Catholic movements and organizations, if and to the degree you thereby serve the common good and the cause of God. In the second place, to participate more in international organizations. While this recommendation is addressed to all, it concerns specifically the agricultural technicians.

These words showed his deep interest in international organizations, his wide concept of the cooperation of Catholics with neutral and non-Catholic organisms, provided it rests on a solid foundation, and finally, his deep desire to see Catholics respond in large numbers to his appeal for their participation in and their active dedication to all the efforts tending toward the establishment of a true community of nations.

Organizations of a private nature: Besides the organizations of a public nature, there is a considerable number of non-governmental organizations, hence of a private nature. About a thousand of these exist, and their number is growing. We shall speak here only of the International Catholic Organizations (I.C.O.). There are about forty of these under various forms: organizations of Catholic Action, organizations comprising professional or social categories (intellectuals, Pax Romana, teachers, employers, nurses, journalists), organizations pursuing determined objectives (protection of young women, fight against alcoholism, techniques of information for the spread of the Christian message).

Some of these organizations represent mass movements; they exercise an influence over a considerable number of members. We may mention in particular the World Union of Organizations of Catholic Women, with thirty-six million members in seventy countries and territories; the I.O.C. International, with its two million members, which held a congress with 32,000 delegates of young workers from eighty-five countries and territories in Rome in August, 1957; the International Confederation of Christian Syndicates, with its three million members belonging to twenty-one countries, but which does not form part of the International Catholic Organizations, because it admits also Protestants and other non-Catholics; the International Federation of Christian Worker Movements, with three million members.

What is the role of the International Catholic Organizations? First to assure the presence and the active cooperation of Catholics in international life. Problems of life today present themselves on a world-wide scale. The UN is in reality an organization of states; they are capable of facing these international problems with financial means and powerful techniques. But it is very important that the aspirations of the peoples be able to make themselves heard and the collaboration of private initiatives be exercised there. Here we have the role of the non-governmental organizations. In the organizations of a private character Catholics must be present as a body, with their numerical force, the multiplicity and the variety of their apostolates, the wealth of their experience; it is necessary that they be *au courant* with everything that is thought, studied, realized on the international level.

Next to represent, defend and spread Christian thought regarding the problems of international life. Besides their technical aspect and also under this aspect, all the problems affecting man and the human community present a human, moral, spiritual and religious aspect. The Church, guardian of the natural and the supernatural order, teaches truths, exposes principles and safeguards values in the name of the natural law and of revelation.

If one may rejoice at the fact that the fundamental documents of the UN proclaim the dignity of the human person, the role of the family as the foundation of the community and other principles of the human, social and international order which meet the demands of Christian doctrine on not a few points, at the same time it cannot be denied that a real danger exists of having materialistic tendencies creep into the organizations of the UN. On numerous occasions Pius XII called attention to the peril of the invasion of an irresponsible technocracy, a growing depersonalization in modern society. On the international level there is the risk of having experts, technicians and commissions— whose cooperation is certainly necessary and may be very helpful —determine in a very systematic manner, which does not take into account sufficiently the movement of life and the needs of man, technical solutions which are apparently quite satisfactory, but which may involve the sacrifice of fundamental principles of morality and essential values. The example cited in chapter three with regard to birth control and contraceptive practices, proposed as the solution of the world's population problem, furnishes a sadly eloquent example.

Hence the International Catholic Organizations have a very necessary mission to fulfill in protecting values and in defending the principles of the natural law and of Christian doctrine; in this manner they assist in assuring the rectitude of international action. Their part is all the more important, since the positions taken on the international level will have their repercussions on the national legislation of the various countries.

Then, to form competent apostles and specialists in the study of international problems. In questions as complex as international problems there is no room for improvisation. Isolated men and women find it difficult to acquire the requisite knowledge and practice. The International Catholic Organizations in the first place give their members an international sense, make them acquire an international conscience according to the spirit of the pontifical documents; they help them to escape from a narrow nationalism and to have a world view. They teach them to discover, to know, to understand, to embrace sympathetically and to esteem civilizations the most diverse, the most distant. For action of this kind it is necessary to have specialized technicians, delegates or consultants capable of taking part in meetings, preparing cases and presenting memoranda.

It is also to insure Catholic representation at the United Nations. Though it is true that private organizations have only a consultative voice, real progress over the League of Nations can be seen in the fact that they can make known their aspirations, their labors and researches on all questions under study in the UN. They do so by the "consultative status" accorded them by the UN.

Two hundred and fifty-three non-governmental organizations have obtained the consultative status with one or the other international institutions. Of this number only nine of the International Catholic Organizations are represented with UNESCO and nine with the Economic and Social Council. But we have mentioned their influence, the number of their members, as a result of which they represent important sectors of Catholic world opinion.[8]

Lastly, to labor at bringing the nations together, to cause misunderstandings, ignorance and rivalries which form an obstacle to a true community to disappear. Here Catholics are called

---

8. We must add to the aforementioned other cases in which international Catholic organizations have obtained consultative status: four with UNICEF (International Fund of the United Nations for Assistance to Children); two with F.A.O. (Food and Agriculture Organization); one with the World Health Organization.

upon to play a very effective role in creating "that atmosphere of understanding and mutual respect," of which Pope Pius XII spoke, "without which no international action can have any deep and lasting effect."

Coordination of the international activities of Catholics: Very many Christians still do not know the power, the variety and the fruitful action of the organisms which coordinate the international activities of Catholics. We shall mention the principal ones:

The Conference of the International Catholic Organizations. This forms a permanent bond between the organizations. It assures uniformity of action among Catholics, by acting as a point of contact for the different organizations. It respects their autonomy and does not direct their activities. The Secretariate of State closely follows its action with great interest, and the Holy See is regularly represented there.

The Conference, comprising thirty-three members of the International Catholic Organizations, meets once a year in general assembly. Others assist as observers. The assembly studies a current international problem, and listens to reports of the work accomplished by various commissions.

Between the ordinary sessions, the Conference has a "Permanent Committee," composed of nine elected organizations; this committee carries out the decisions of the assembly, prepares the agenda for the next meeting and counsels the International Catholic Organizations. A permanent secretariate of the Conference exists at Fribourg; it has charge of the internal life of the Conference.

The International Catholic Organizations have three centers of information and liaison.

1) The information center of the International Catholic Organization is at Geneva, beside the Palace of the Nations. Its function is to establish contacts with the UN and to supply information regarding the international activities of the UN.

2) The International Catholic Center of Civilization with UNESCO at Paris. The Holy See has a permanent observer at UNESCO. The Paris Center informs and documents the Conference of the International Catholic Organizations regarding the

activities of UNESCO in the entire educational and cultural field. On the other hand, it brings to the attention of UNESCO the activities of the International Catholic Organizations and the results of their work.

3) A center of liaison between the International Catholic Organizations and the missions at Rome. This center has as its aim, on the one hand, to inform and to document the missions and every qualified person on the activities of international organizations and of the International Catholic Organizations, and, conversely, to inform and document the International Catholic Organizations and every qualified person on missionary problems.

This simple enumeration of international Catholic organisms bears witness by itself to the presence of Catholics, their active participation, their loyal cooperation in the great undertakings of the international community to combat the dangers that threaten any part of humanity, to organize a more just, more peaceful, more fraternal international society, to work at raising the standards of nations and civilizations.

3. *The atmosphere which the universal Church creates is one which favors the life of an international community:*

No one more than the Catholic Church disposes of powers of reconciliation, of understanding, of unity, capable of influencing the deepest and most intimate convictions, those which dominate life. It is the duty of the Church's children to set these powers in motion.[9]

These words of Pius XII to Catholic students clearly set in relief the fruitful role of the Church in bringing about a rapprochement of nations. She disposes of interior powers, which act on the deepest recesses of the heart, in order to create a climate favorable to a community of nations.

First, powers of reconciliation, in urging men and nations to forgive one another, to forget past hatreds and offenses, to put into practice the Our Father, which, coming from the heart of Christ the Redeemer, reconciles men among themselves by re-

9. Pius XII to the students of the Cercle Richelieu, April 9, 1953. Cf. the discourse to Pax Christi, September 13, 1952.

conciling them with God. The Church alone can dare, while war is raging, to remind Christians that legitimate love of one's native land must exclude hatred of the enemy, as well as the lust for vengeance, insatiable pride, incurable rancor,[10] and recall the evangelical law regarding the mutual pardon of offenses.

Then, forces of understanding. There can be no sincere effort of understanding without a vigorous asceticism of abnegation, of denial of self to open oneself to others, in order to understand that one has need of them and that men are mutually complementary, all members of the same body, rising above the divisions of frontiers and continents. The Church causes this purifying asceticism to penetrate to the depth of consciences of various peoples in order to teach them to discipline national pride, the sentiment of race superiority, self-sufficiency of a civilization which needs nothing from any outside source, self-complacency in a culture which shuts itself up hermetically against all others. The Church "seeks to facilitate respect for and deep understanding of the most varied civilizations," as Pius XII said in the Encyclical *Summi Pontificatus.* She identifies herself with no form of civilization, with no culture. She is receptive to all, ready to make alliances with all, to receive the spiritual values they contain in order to vivify them and make them submissive to Christ.

Finally, powers of unity, for if, as we are going to see, she brings about a *rapprochement* of man and nations exteriorly by the unity of her government, her doctrine, her worship, she affects the very depths of souls by her message of unity, as analyzed at the beginning of the second half of this chapter, by the unifying powers of grace, of charity and most especially of the Holy Spirit, the principle of unity, because he is numerically one, the same in all and in the entire Church.

10. "At the present time there is danger that in many souls the noble and legitimate sentiment of love of the fatherland may degenerate into the passion of vengeance, into insatiable pride on the one side, into incurable rancor on the other. A Christian, while faithfully and courageously defending the fatherland, must nevertheless abstain from hating those whom he is obliged to fight" (Pius XII, Allocution on the pardon of offenses, July 10, 1940).

COMPARISON BETWEEN THE JURIDICAL UNITY OF THE COMMUNITY OF NATIONS AND THE JURIDICAL UNITY OF THE CHURCH

A new and very important text of Pius XII will permit us to deepen the idea of the unity of the Church, by comparing it with the juridical unity of the community of nations on the temporal plane of international institutions.

> The institution of a community of nations, such as has now been partially realized, but which is to grow and be strengthened to a more elevated and more perfect degree, represents an upward movement, that is to say, from a plurality of sovereign States to a higher unity.
>
> By virtue of the mandate of her divine Founder, the Church of Christ has a uniform universal mission. She must receive into herself and gather into a religious unity the men of all nations and of all times. But in a certain sense her manner of proceeding is reversed. In the first case, the higher juridical unity had to be created. In the case of the Church, however, the juridical unity with its universal purpose, its constitution, its powers and those who exercise them were established from the beginning by the will and the institution of Christ himself (Discourse to the Fifth Assembly of the Union of Italian Catholic Jurists, December 6, 1953).

This is a very enlightening comparison, since it shows us the points in which the two communities resemble one another and in which they are distinguished from the point of view of their juridical unity.

They agree in the universal character of their mission; both extend or ought to extend to all men, all nations—embrace them all. They are distinguished by the character of their juridical unity.

In the temporal community of nations, a higher juridical unity still must be created. Pius XII stresses the point that this institution of the community of nations has only been partially realized in the UN and that it must perfect itself. It portrays an upward movement, toward a higher unity still to be attained. The three terms by which he defines it contain precisely all the obstacles opposed to unity: a plurality of sovereign states.

A "plurality": Eighty states, with different languages, mores, customs, civilizations, in very varying degrees of evolution, with interests that are opposed to one another. . . . The goal to be attained is the realization of a true unity among these opposite elements. There is a long way to go!

"Of states": This is true at present of the UN, where only states have authority, where only the representatives of the states have an active voice. Concretely the aspirations toward unity manifest themselves on the level of states, in the relations between states. This is not yet a true community of nations.

"Of sovereign states": The UN still rests on the basis of sovereign states. Now, we are aware what real obstacles the principle of the sovereignty of states creates for unity. Great efforts still have to be made to bring about a true unity!

Pius XII did not stress the difficulties in order to reduce the authority of the UN. As we have seen, he wanted this authority strengthened. He desired to show forth the grandeur and the extent of the task undertaken in the construction of an international society and, as he did on several occasions, to point out the exceptional qualities of the men who are accomplishing this task: qualities of intellect, of the spirit of initiative and invention, of foresight, of genial intuition, of prudence, of courage, of energy and of tenacity.

THE JURIDICAL UNITY OF THE CATHOLIC CHURCH

In the Catholic Church, on the contrary, a higher juridical unity exists since her establishment by Christ himself. Her unity consists in the first place of "her universal goal," assigned to her by the Incarnate Word: "Go, make disciples of all nations . . ." In a passage of the discourse we have cited Pius XII declared: "The function of this universal community is, from the beginning, to incorporate as soon as possible all men and all nations, and thereby to gain them entirely to the truth and to the grace of Jesus Christ." Here we have the essential mission of the Church; this is her calling. The Church is herself only by being universal, Catholic and one. She is in a state of development; she is a living being that grows, a body that expands. It is a marvelous sign of her divine origin that, while spreading in space and developing her life through time, she must constantly run the risk of seeing her unity threatened by the accretion of new peoples, having their own traditions, customs, beliefs and rites; yet all the time this unity manifests itself in a most striking manner and the principle of unity that animates her comes more powerfully to the fore.

Unity also shows itself in "her constitution, her powers and in those who exercise them." Christ himself gave to Peter and to the Apostles the constitution of his Church; he established it on the authority and the powers of the Pope, the successor of Peter, and of the bishops, the successors of the Apostles in communion with the Sovereign Pontiff.

The Pope is the guardian and the center of unity; for he has the complete and supreme authority to govern the Church visibly as Vicar of Jesus Christ, acting in the name of Christ himself, the true invisible Head of his body; the Pope is the depositary of the powers which Christ confided to Peter, so that he and his successors might exercise them in his name, in his stead, and thus bring his people into unity, so that there might be "but one flock and one Shepherd."

All these powers of teaching, of government, of sanctification —powers of orders or of jurisdiction—are given to the Pope with a view to unity: to maintain, to defend, to affirm the unity of doctrine, the unity of discipline, the unity of charity and of the sacramental and liturgical order with regard to the Eucharist, which causes the unity of the body, because in reality it contains Christ himself, in whom the Church is one.

Does not the existence of particular churches, entrusted to bishops, the successors of the Apostles, seem to threaten the unity of the universal Church? Not at all. Because, first of all, even before having charge of his particular diocese on a personal title, the bishop, together with the Pope and the other bishops under the Pope's authority, is a pastor of the universal Church. This shows forth the admirable unity inscribed into the divine constitution of the Church, which manifests itself in the extraordinary circumstances of Ecumenical Councils or habitually in the ordinary and universal magisterium of the Church, that is to say, in the unanimous preaching of the same truth by the body of the bishops spread throughout all the dioceses of the world, in communion with the Pope.

Further, if Christ decreed to multiply the heads of particular churches, he did it to insert the Church deeply in the life of the various nations, with their own characteristics, their history, their race, their mentality, so that everything human might be elevated to a higher plane. But if Christ has given his people fathers and heads, this was not to cause them to become isolated, but rather to make them participate in a more real and total manner in the collective life of the entire Church. Here we see the deep meaning of the bishop's paternity over his people. He has the duty of having this people go over from the particularities of one region to the Catholic communion, to beget in them the life of the one, universal and Catholic Church, to nourish them with the teachings of the Head of the Church in all fields, to associate them actively with all the happenings in the universal Church, with her sufferings, her hopes, her missions in the world.

UNITY OF THE CHURCH—EXEMPLAR OF HUMAN SOCIETIES

The Church can present her unity to the community of the nations as a living exemplar. She has existed for twenty centuries, while about her a great number of political societies have disappeared. She has had to grow and to face historical circumstances which brought great disruption in the lives of nations.

Pius XII himself called attention to this model which the existence of the Church furnishes to human societies: "Why should not the institution divinely founded by Our Lord Jesus Christ be regarded as an incomparable examplar, from which societies of the human order could only draw profit?" (Letter to the president of the Social Weeks of France, July 10, 1946).

To those who ask what the Church's role is in seeking the welfare of human society, in establishing a lasting peace, Pius XII replied that several answers might be given. But he immediately adds: "In any case, the great and definitive reply, which embraces all the others, always remains the unity and integrity of the Church resting on God and on Christ" (Allocution to the Sacred College, February 20, 1946).

An official text of the Holy See supplies an excellent conclusion to this last chapter. It demonstrates that the Church "of all ages has labored exceedingly in favor of an international community conceived under one form or another." Then it enumerates the characteristics proper to the Catholic Church, which give it a privileged position in cooperating in the construction of a true international community.

> The sublime doctrine of Christ, the divine Founder of the Church; her catholicism in law and in fact; the universal expansion of Religious Orders and the organizations of the apostolate, likewise international in scope; the special position of the Papacy, placed above the interests of every country—all these put the Church in a privileged and indisputable position to labor effectively for a true international order.[11]

---

11. Letter of Msgr. Dell'Acqua, substitute of the Secretariate of State, on "the international community," for the Seventeenth Social Week of Spain (June 5, 1957).

Résumé

As a conclusion to this work, we shall draw from the papal teaching certain leading ideas, which sum up the Church's doctrine on the community of nations.

1. *True foundation of the community of nations:* The true foundation of the community of nations, a foundation which will supply its juridical unity, consists in the unity of origin, of nature and of purpose of all members of the human family.

In human nature, substantially one and identical in all men everywhere, there exists an immanent law of development, which brings men and nations to discover their solidarity, their interdependence, the fact that they complement one another. This tendency was inscribed in human nature by its Creator to draw men and nations to unity, mutually to communicate their particular resources, all together to form a community of nations with a view to the universal common good. Hence the constitution of a community of nations has been willed by God in his loving design for men. Sent by the Father, Christ Jesus came to save humanity divided by sin through his redeeming Sacrifice, to lead it to a higher unity in supernatural charity, to embrace it completely in the unity of the mystical body according to his supreme desire: ". . . that all may be one."

2. *Necessity of a rule of universal morality in the relations among states:* The denial and the rejection of a rule of universal morality in international relations, as in individual and social life, lie at the root of the evils of modern society; they have been the cause of numerous conflicts and wars between nations. Neither

237

the supremacy of force, nor national egotism, nor self-interest, nor the ambition of a nation can ever be the supreme norm of action or a normal rule of international relations.

These relations must be dominated and inspired by the sovereignty of "the moral law, manifested by the Creator by means of the natural order and inscribed by Him in the hearts of men in indelible characters" (Christmas Message, 1941).

International natural law or the law of nations dictated by nature contains the principles on which the positive law, intended to define more exactly the demands on nature and to adapt them to concrete circumstances, must be founded.

Thus, in the community of nations, "every state is then inserted into the organization of international law, and thereby in the order of the natural law, which sustains and crowns everything" (Discourse to Catholic Jurists, December 6, 1953).

3. *Construction of an international order:* All the nations must collaborate in the construction of an international order, as guarantor of the absolute values of the superior moral law and of the natural law in the common life of nations.

This international order must have as its constant objective the maintenance, the protection, the defense and the organization of peace among the nations.

So that it may fulfill this mission, it must be above all an order of truth and veracity with regard to the understanding and the creation of habits of loyalty and confidence among the nations. It must likewise be an order of liberty in order to obtain the common support of citizens who are responsible and capable of taking an active part, without being paralyzed by an extremely centralized or a police state. It must finally also be an order of security, for the protection of persons, of their lives, of their rights and of the property which the Creator has put at their disposition for their development.

Since it is essentially an order of justice and equity in the respect, the protection and the application of international law and of agreements among the nations, it must safeguard the rights of nations and facilitate the accomplishment of their duties by means of a strictly maintained, active and generous solidarity.

Last of all, the international order will find its perfection and crown in the primacy of the law of charity, which develops mutual respect, understanding and collaboration in a common task among the nations.

4. *International order is also an economic order:* The international order, which is a juridical and political order, also presents aspects of an economic order.

It must continue its share to suppress the disproportions and evident differences in the living standard of nations, investments, the degree of productivity. It must seek to promote a more equitable distribution of goods and a participation on the part of all nations in the raw materials and the resources of the earth. It must organize, with respect to persons and the common good, a policy of emigration and exchange of populations in order to bring about a more rational distribution of men on the face of the earth. By protecting peace and working for a progressive and simultaneous limitation of armaments, it will succeed in freeing great financial resources to develop the works of peace and to intensify aid to underdeveloped countries.

5. *Doctrinal and ideological obstacles to the community of nations.* The great doctrinal and ideological obstacle against which the Papacy has struggled with constant firmness is the doctrine of the absolute sovereignty of the state. If every state wants to remain absolutely sovereign and not recognize above itself either a superior and universal rule of morality or an international law or the authority of an organization of nations, then it is useless and impossible to make any progress toward a true community of nations. If the state is the absolute sovereign, it and it alone will claim the right to judge situations according to its own interests or its plans of expansion.

In the same sense, Pius XII condemned "the idolatry of absolute nationalisms," just as Pius XI had condemned National Socialism.

Patriotism is a virtue; love of the fatherland, a duty. The national life is "the glory and right of a people." All the citizens are bound to work for the development of the nation's life. On the other hand, nationalism presents a danger when it drives a state to deny solidarity among the nations, to withdraw itself into an egocentric mentality, to use the nation as a base for its totalitarian and expansionist policy, in a word, when it begets a nationalist state.

6. *Obstacle of armaments:* With striking continuity and energy, all the popes since the time of Leo XIII have denounced the armament race as a constant danger to the peace of the world as well as a crushing burden to the economy of the various countries. They have besought the heads of states to work out together practical means for putting an end to this infernal cycle. They have proposed concrete solutions to bring about a mutually agreed, organic and progressive disarmament, both in the material and in the spiritual order.

If the popes intervene in this technical field of military art, their sole purpose is the fulfillment of their spiritual mission— to promote brotherhood among men in the name of a God of peace and of love, in the name of his design for the community of nations.

For the same reason they have unceasingly presented themselves as defenders of the right and they have multiplied their appeals and their efforts in order to substitute the moral force of law for the material force of arms.

7. *War, a disruption of God's design:* The totalitarian states exalted war. They inculcated a mystique of war, glorified its effects on civilization and the virtues which it calls forth in man. They attached to war "the value of a bloody and decisive explanation regarding the meaning of human life and of civilization."[1]

Without embracing such gross errors, others have considered war as an inescapable and natural fact of history, a normal and adequate means of settling conflicts, an event outside the field of the moral law and the responsibility of statesmen.

Pius XII swept aside all these disastrous theories, which have contributed so much to spread war or to cause it to be accepted

1. Joseph Leclerc, "Pie XII devant la guerre," in *Etudes*, January, 1945.

with powerless resignation. War of aggression he condemned as a crime. He demanded that it be banned forever and proscribed. For those guilty of unleashing it he demanded penal sanctions on the part of human tribunals, since they were already judged by God's tribunal. He uttered the slogan: "War against war!" Instead of the inhuman means of war, without significance for the reëstablishment of right in a conflict, he proposed the use of police forces within the framework of the international community, in order to defend a country unjustly attacked and to restrain violators of right. In this situation, defensive war alone is legitimate; the sinfulness of men and abuse of liberty on their part must always be reckoned with.

8. *The Church and the temporal international community:* The natural and the supernatural order are distinct. They must not be separated, but united. The temporal, specifically here the temporal international society, has nothing to fear from contact with the eternal, as far as its autonomy is concerned. On the contrary, not only does the Church, a spiritual and supernatural society—living indeed in time and in the world, but not of the world nor of time—respect the autonomy of the temporal in its own sphere, the autonomy of the temporal international community in its organization and action which she supports; there is more (and we have here an idea which Pius XII greatly illuminated, by bringing great clarity anew to the traditional problem of the relations of nature and supernature): under the influence of and by contact with the eternal, the temporal receives a greater consistency; through the supernatural and the action of grace, nature recovers the balance and the stability it had lost by sin.

For that reason Pius regarded that as true realism which takes into account the eternal realities, for "the means which lead to the eternal realities are the same as those which give to temporal realities their internal vigor and their stability" (*Sertum Laetitiae,* 1939). A realism that does not want to consider the reality of sin and of grace is false.

The Church, a supranational spiritual community, offers the temporal community of nations, in order to aid it in progressively forming its juridical unity, invaluable support and assistance through the enlightenment of its own unity established since its foundation, through its educative action on consciences, through the unique position and the universal mission of the Papacy far above all particular interests, without any earthly ambition, completely independent.

By her doctrine of truth, the Church, the guardian of the natural and of the supernatural order, the Church which teaches and interprets the natural law, can aid the temporal international society effectively in discovering and respecting the fundamental laws of the natural order, in safeguarding the absolute values on which rests the common life of the nations, in maintaining the temporal institutions of the community of nations in rectitude and in their internal purpose.

9. *Spiritual character of the problems of peace and of the international order:* The Church, which has the mission to defend and maintain spiritual and moral values in a world that seeks to reject them, through the voice of the Sovereign Pontiff proclaimed that above the technical, juridical, political and economic aspects of the problems which the establishment of the community of nations entails, there exists a spiritual and moral problem of peace and of the international order.

At the root of the drama that has bloodied mankind, it is necessary to see the very grave crisis of a spiritual order which prepared and unleashed it. The rejection of a rule of universal and divine morality unchained the appetites of nationalism, the egotisms of individuals and of nations. Moral values were abandoned. The law of self-interest gained the upper hand. The passions were given free rein.

Pius XII showed that the problem of peace is essentially of the spiritual order. The Church makes her contribution to peace "by stirring up and stimulating the practical understanding of the spiritual crux of the problem." Constituting an international order implies recognition, respect and defense of absolute values of the spiritual and moral order: justice, charity, liberty, truth, unity, respect for the order of beings and of ends established by God.

Considered from this point of view, the Church fulfills a function of paramount importance. "She teaches and defends the truth; she communicates the supernatural powers of grace in order to realize the order of beings and of ends established by God. . . . The Church by her very existence stands before the world as a luminous beacon that unceasingly recalls this divine order" (Christmas Message, 1944).

Those states that set obstacles to this mission of the Church or that persecute her gravely injure the common good of their peoples. If the Church vindicates her liberty in the world in order to fulfill her spiritual mission, she does so solely in the name of her divine origin, in the name of the welfare of nations which she has a mandate to promote.

The Church demands that she be left in peace, "so that, free and without hindrance, she may place her supernatural energies at the service of understanding among the nations and of peace" (Christmas Message, 1941).

> Peace cannot be assured unless God reigns in the order of the universe He has established, first, in the society of states duly organized, where each one realizes within itself the organization of peace among free men and their families, and then, exteriorly, that of nations, of which the Church, in her field of action and according to her function, makes herself the guarantor (Christmas Message, 1951).

10. *Return to God and to Jesus Christ, a condition of peace and of the international order:* After calling attention to and analyzing the root cause of the evils from which the international society suffers, Pius XII insistently pointed out the remedy in solemn pronouncements and with a prophet's voice, which dominated his time and penetrated into the future as well. And what is the remedy? Return to God, to Jesus Christ, the only Savior and Redeemer of mankind, to the moral law in all spheres of life, to the fundamental truths of Christianity, to the civilizing work of the Church, to the Christian order.

With sadness he stated that one of the great obstacles to the Church's mission of peace consists in the fact that "a deep Christian sense is wanting in too many in the world nowadays; true and perfect Christians are too rare. As a result, men themselves place an obstacle to the realization of the order willed by God" (Christmas Message, 1951).

Without doubt, the Christians interested in international problems perceived the obstacles standing in the way of the relations among nations, hindering the establishment of a true community. Were they sufficiently conscious of their personal responsibility for the delay in the fulfillment of God's design because of their lack of faith, of solid convictions, of confidence in their Church, of the meaning of true liberty? Pius XII characterized as superficial those individuals who are incapable of seeing "the value and the creative power of Christianity in all its truth and all its extent" (*ibid.*). He summoned all true Christians to courageous, austere, positive action, in order to cooperate in the establishment of order and harmony in the world in union with all men of good will (Christmas Message, 1957).

THE POPE'S MISSION IN A DIVIDED HUMANITY

At the present time the world is divided into two power blocs, whose concept of man, of liberty, of democracy are diametrically different and whose political, economic and social systems are opposed to one another on essential matters. True, both employ the same terms, but with greatly varying significations.

Here we have the most crucial problem impeding the constitution of a true community of nations!

To rebuild the bridge between the two blocs, a common principle is needed—a positive ideal of human and moral civilization, with common values. It can only be of a spiritual order, because only the spiritual is capable of really and truly bringing men together, outside of material interests, which tend to divide and clash, if they are left to themselves and not subjected to a moral law.

Now, the sole point on which the two blocs come together is in the material order—on the basis of materialism. We are witnessing two materialisms of different kinds: the one integrally applied in the name of a doctrine, the other often unconscious, diffuse or veiled; the one going to the limit of absolute atheism, the other respecting beliefs or, in certain countries, even officially affirming faith in God.

Both of these blocs are dominated by the fascination which the prodigious developments of technique and economy exercise over them.[2] Now, not only can this not be a principle of unity, at least inasfar as this concept of technique and of economy is not guided by a higher moral principle of fraternal collaboration among nations to ameliorate the needs of all of mankind, but contrariwise the competition between the two blocs, the striving after prestige and superiority, the preoccupation with gaining the victory over the other party in the field of technique necessarily entail opposition, rivalries, conflicts. To convince oneself, it is only necessary to consider the competition and the struggle in which the two sides engage with regard to sputniks, missiles, atomic bombs, nuclear experiments, the most murderous weapons of future warfare. We are well aware that at the end of the road we shall not find peace, but the danger of war.

Pius XII exposed the essence of materialism in the following words:

> Materialism is a progressive depreciation and finally the abandonment of supraterrestrial and supernatural, spiritual and religious realities, which can go to the limit of absolute atheism; it admits only the realities which are a matter of sense experience, which can be measured and numbered. . . . Materialism concerns itself with the worship of matter, of the body and strength, of money, of power (Letter to the Congress of German Catholics, August 16, 1950).

This materialism has penetrated everywhere, even into those countries which profess attachment to the values of a human and Christian civilization. France is not free of it. Pius made mention of it in his encyclical on Lourdes:

> The world, which offers so many just reasons of pride and hope in our day, is likewise subject to a powerful temptation to ma-

2. "Without any doubt, one cannot help admiring the economy for all that it has produced and promises to produce. At the same time, with its apparently unlimited ability to produce goods without number and by reason of the multiplicity of its relations, it exercises over many men of the present time a fascination which goes beyond its possibilities and goes over into fields that are strange to it. In the error of such confidence accorded to modern economy the two parties between whom the modern world is divided again come into contact" (Pius XII, Christmas Message, 1954, on coexistence).

terialism, often denounced by Our predecessors and by Ourselves. This materialism is found not only in the condemned philosophy which dominates the politics and the economy of one part of humanity.[3]

He then pointed out the forms of this materialism: the love of money, with its results on the lives of people; worship of the body, excessive seeking after pleasure and avoidance of all self-denial; contempt of human life destroyed even before birth; unlimited pursuit of pleasure, forgetfulness of one's brother, egotism, injustice—"in a word, a concept of life that regulates everything exclusively with a view to material prosperity and earthly satisfactions."[4]

This materialism, unless combatted, inevitably and quickly leads to the abandonment of every precept of a moral law above individuals and nations, to the thirst for material goods, to jealousy and cupidity with regard to other nations, to ambition and conquest, to national egotism, to a nationalism that denies the existence and the bonds of the international community—in a word, it leads straight to war.

In the other bloc, that of Communism, materialism defines and dominates everything: both the concept of man, of life, of society (there is neither God nor soul nor a hereafter), and the economic, political, social system which sacrifices the rights and liberties of the human person for the prestige of the state, its propaganda, its domination, its imperialist and colonial expansion throughout the world.

3. Encyclical of July 2, 1957, addressed to the French episcopacy for the centenary of the apparitions at Lourdes, in which Pius XII called all the faithful of the world to the observance of a Marian Year.

4. In the Encyclical *Sertum Laetitiae*, addressed to the bishops of the United States under date of November 1, 1939, Pius XII, after praising the work accomplished by Catholicism in the United States, described the consequences of the abandonment of the moral law: ". . . boundless and blind egotism, the thirst for pleasure, the vice of drunkenness, immodest and costly styles in dress, the prevalence of crime even among minors, the lust for power, neglect of the poor, base craving for ill-gotten wealth, the flight from the land, levity in entering into marriage, divorce, the break-up of the family, the cooling of mutual affection between parents and children, birth control, the enfeeblement of the race, the weakening of respect for authority or servility or rebellion, neglect of duty toward one's country and toward mankind."

Bringing about a *rapprochement* and establishing peace cannot be realized by leaning on regimes or social systems. Rather this is the work of the individuals who live in one or the other of the blocs. Pius XII once remarked that there are millions in the two camps who "have preserved, in a more or less live manner, the imprint of Christ; they must work together on the same score as faithful and fervent believers, they must be called to renew the basis of the unity of the human family" (Christmas Message, 1954, on coexistence).

The forces of peace in the world are far from negligible. They are the nations themselves to whose aversion to war and passionate attachment to peace the popes have called attention; there are the great international institutions, the UN and its services; there are all the men who, whatever be their religion or their civilization, believe in the primacy of the spiritual and are resolved to save human values.

Entirely apart from the blocs, with complete independence regarding their politics, in the face of the materialisms that threaten the peace of the world, with a deep personal concern for the life of mankind, the mission of the head of the Church appears in all its grandeur and necessity to save the peace and to assist the nations in making it just and lasting. Pius XII has set in clear relief the principle capable of bringing the nations together and of establishing a community of nations, namely, international natural law, a complete concept of human community—and illuminating everything by its trancendent quality, the Good News of salvation brought to mankind, the message of truth, which frees and unites men, defends and safeguards the moral and spiritual values of true human civilization.

INDEX